Folklore and Society

Series Editors

Roger Abrahams

Bruce Jackson

Marta Weigle

A list of books in the series appears
at the back of the book.

The World Observed

The World Observed

REFLECTIONS ON THE FIELDWORK PROCESS

Edited by Bruce Jackson and Edward D. Ives

University of Illinois Press   *Urbana and Chicago*

© 1996 by the Board of Trustees of the University of Illinois
Manufactured in the United States of America
1   2   3   4   5   C   P   5   4   3   2   1
This book is printed on acid-free paper.
All editors' and contributors' royalties from this volume
have been contributed to Amnesty International.
Library of Congress Cataloging-in-Publication Data
The world observed: reflections on the fieldwork process /
edited by
    Bruce Jackson and Edward D. Ives.
        p.   cm. — (Folklore and society)
    Includes bibliographical references.
    ISBN 0-252-02229-7 (acid-free paper). —
    ISBN 0-252-06533-6 (pbk. : acid-free paper)
        1. Ethnology—Field work. 2. Folklore—Field work.
    3. Sociology—Field work. I. Jackson, Bruce. II. Ives,
    Edward D. III. Series.
    GN346.W67   1996
    306'.072—dc20   95-50152
                                                    CIP

Contents

Introduction: Ideas of Order
Bruce Jackson and Edward D. Ives

Published works grounded in fieldwork are almost always logical and purposive.[1] That's because they're all retrospective documents: the end justifies the middle and beginning, it makes them rational. The retrospective universe is *always* ineluctable. It's the future that's blank and the present that's ambiguous. In real time, a depressing number of apparently wonderful ideas are duds, and a blessed number of blind alleys lead to grand spaces we never suspected were there.

What is the source of sense, order, logic, coherence, and meaning? It wasn't there before we started out; had it been, we could have stayed safe and warm at home. We begin with curiosity, we develop and ask questions, we develop notions of which questions do and do not matter, and later we develop notions of which answers do and do not satisfy. The experience of doing the work continually refines our notions of the work we're doing, how we see and hear, our sense of what matters and what doesn't.

Usually fieldworkers tell you about conclusions, about how things turned out. Our articles and books and films gloss over the long periods of ambiguity and discontinuity; they're rich in detail about where we wound up after resolving or sidestepping ambiguity and cutting away what prevented us from making or seeing the connections. We may write about how we spent our days, how we got this or that information, but rarely do we document the despair of the fieldworker confronting an undifferentiated infinitude of possible data. We offer instead the reasoned conclusions of the researcher who has intelligently organized and interpreted a clearly delimited and fixed body of information.

Nearly everyone we know who's ever done much fieldwork has at least one story he or she tells about the way or the moment things started making sense. The insights the stories are about inform the rest of the research in those projects and the documents coming out of them, but rarely do the stories find their way into print. These stories are about us rather than the subjects of our inquiry. We rarely publish them because we assume that our thinking process is far less significant than what our thinking discovered, and that our research experience is of far less importance than the experience of the people we study. It is almost as if writing about our own continuing education is unseemly.[2] In the acknowledgments pages of our books we thank our teachers, the foundations and agencies that gave us money, the librarians who lent us books, the companions who forgave us for whatever. In ever more creative ways, we always say the same thing: these people and these institutions made our work possible.

Imagination also makes our work possible. Leaps of the imagination and connections made by our imagination are the lifeblood of our work. This book is about how the imagination talks to us.

As has been our habit in our occasional visits in Buffalo and Orono these past thirty years, the two of us spent an evening not long ago catching up on gossip about friends and scoundrels, listing for each other books essential to read or safely to be avoided, talking about great passages in *Let Us Now Praise Famous Men,* and telling stories.

Once again, many of the stories had to do with fieldwork experiences. Fieldwork experiences are a common topic for us, not just because we have both published books on the subject (Ives 1980, Jackson 1987), but because we've both done a great deal of it and we both enjoy it.

That evening, Ives told the story that is the basis of his article in this book. Jackson recounted a conversation in a Texas prison in which he learned that intentions, actions, and attitudes may have only coincidental relationships with one another. One of us said that we'd both written about how you do fieldwork but neither of us, nor anyone else we could think of, had written about how you understand what happens when you do it. Another hour into the night and we resolved to assemble a book of essays about how the chaos of fieldwork comes into focus, how things make sense.

We asked colleagues and friends whose work we respected to write about how fieldwork matters came to make sense for them. They were men and women who had done fieldwork in folklore, anthropology, sociology, and history. Some of them have been at it nearly forty years; some are reporting on projects they did recently as graduate students. Initially, we asked them to tell about epiphanies, moments when things suddenly came into focus in ways that had not been planned or foretold. The contributors extended our subject. Some wanted a larger view (as Portelli, who discusses how a generation made itself accessible to fieldworkers) or a narrower one (as Becker, who discusses how his attempt to understand a single word led to a fundamental understanding about medical education.)

The essays gathered here are about how these individuals learned what they had learned. Some of the essays deal with epiphanies; others detail a more laborious path to understanding. All are about fieldwork as a vital process, an interaction between subject and researcher, sometimes over long periods of time. The papers are about learning how to make connections and coming to understand how things work, what things mean, and what was really going on out there.

Several recent studies have attempted to demystify the fieldwork process and deconstruct the presentation of field-gathered data. In *People Studying People: The Human Element in Fieldwork* (1980), for example, Robert A. Georges and Michael O. Jones help us see how the gathering of field materials involves bilateral complex human interactions. Many of the contributors to James Clifford's and George E. Marcus's anthology, *Writing Culture: The Poetics and Politics of Ethnography* (1986) suggest that publications based on field research are not so much scientific facts as personal and social constructions. Those works and others like them look at the doing and publishing of fieldwork.

The essays gathered here are about *thought*. They are about fieldwork insight, not what got collected in the field or what books or films got made. That is to say, the personal narratives in this book serve exactly the opposite function of the personal statement common in most recent ethnological, folkloric, and sociological studies, statements wherein process is described only to provide a locus or rationale for the material, the "real" substance (see Tedlock 1991).

Two-thirds of the essays in this collection represent fieldwork done in groups that are enclaves within the general area of the investigator's own culture, yet only Portelli can be said to have looked at a culture of which he was a part, and he is the one who speaks of the problems arising from the lack of "the sense of otherness." Otherness in the rest range from the "not very" of Lynwood Montell's gospel singers to the "almost completely" of Nancy Kalow's street children, Barre Toelken's Navajo, Carol Silverman's *Roma*, and Dwight Reynolds's Egyptian epic singers. On this evidence, then, if fieldwork is a sine qua non for folklorists, anthropologists, and sociologists, this fieldwork is almost always pursued in a group somewhat different from the investigator's own. And since the difference frequently involves matters one takes for granted or doesn't even think about in the home culture, it is small wonder the learning process is full of false starts and wrong turns. Paradoxically, there may be less danger of self-deception working in a truly exotic culture, where one knows the old ground rules don't apply, than in an environment near at hand, where one is apt to make the assumption that they do. Candace Slater and Reynolds are examples of the former; save for their academic training, in no way could their experience as North Americans have prepared them for what they found. Ellen Stekert, Neil Rosenberg, Jackson, and even to some extent Toelken are examples of the latter; assumptions of similarity proved variously misleading for all four.

Toelken reveals that even in the simple act of how we learn a language we may be culture-bound. He was after the names of things, nouns, in a culture focused on movement, verbs. His focus on what for the Navajo were the less important parts of language "led them to assume that [he] was only playing around."[3]

Indeed, several of these pieces point to the difficulty and necessity of understanding one's own locus and seeing oneself as part of the condition being documented. We're not simply there gathering up someone's data in some innocent and neutral fashion. We shape the product and we influence the event.

Alessandro Portelli helps us understand the difficulty of seeing one's own world. He writes about a political movement of which he was a part and how he realized that the contemporary documentation missed the point of what was going on and the subsequent documentation reflected as much the personal history of the informants as the events of those critical days in 1968. The history an oral historian discovers is not just of an event but of what happens to memory itself.

Dan Rose knew there were two Americas, but he didn't experience that knowledge until he occupied the same space in two radically different modes. From that horizontal perception he extrapolates a vertical one, a difference in status not just of degree but of radical kind that influenced his subsequent work.

Slater writes about feeling in and out of place, of learning who and what you are when you're out there, of fitting in in the field and feeling out of place out of it: "Looking back over my own descriptions, I find myself returning time and again to the intensely visceral quality of fieldwork as well as to the psychic dislocations and, often, real discomfort it implies." She writes of the link "between the field experience and that of artistic creation. Both processes are at once tedious and exhilarating. Both flirt regularly with failure. Both are extended struggles."

Silverman raises important questions about the ethics and legitimacy of representation: what is the difference in what ethnologists like herself do and what commercial filmmakers or any other cultural packagers do? When is the outsider a critical translator or mediator, and when a parasite or betrayer? "Was I an actor or ethnographer, or some of both?" Silverman asks. A good and difficult question, one that is perhaps never answered finally.

If false starts and wrong turns are part of the common fieldwork experience, so is the ability to recoup and learn from them, and frequently such discovery comes on us all of a sudden. There it is, and we wonder why we never saw it before. Carol Burke came to see the sweet American farmhouse world as generating its polar opposite in the prisons for women, not as two separate entities but two interdependent and opposing communities. Rosenberg learned that the micropolitics of who talks to whom about what can be dizzyingly complex. As he made his way deeper into specific networks of individuals he came against harder and harder resistance from other particular interests, none of which any of the players would admit to. He thought he was engaging in a simple inquiry and learned that he was a player in a field of games that preexisted him by far. "So where I saw a continuum," he writes, "they looked from the perspective of their own experiences and saw discontinuities."

The perception can range all the way from the shattering and capitalized "Eureka!" that reduces the past to rubble to the almost inconsequential and lowercase "oh" that nudges your foot gently back onto the path. For Rose it seems to have come quite suddenly while he was being driven around in a friend's Ferrari; for Toelken it seems to have been a series of discoveries and reconsiderations, the coming of wisdom with time, more than any single enlightenment; for Jackson it came twice, first in the course of a telephone call from a friend while his study was still in progress, and second while he was writing the essay which closes this volume. All of them share a certain irony that is also the stuff of humor. The frame of reference shifts and the fieldworker stands exposed, the victim of a self-created joke. So long as it doesn't lead to the delusion that *now* one has the truth for sure (in which case we recommend a careful rereading of Toelken's article), it can be a healthy corrective.

Sometimes this corrective comes while one is still in the field. Slater discovered herself "moving to the beat" along an odoriferous side street in Recife, and eventually that helped her understand the critical nature of the physical aspect of the fieldwork experience. Anthony Barrand was able to make sense of one dance tradition when he remembered information about another he had put aside fifteen years earlier. We find it especially interesting to see how often such enlightenment came about not in the field but later during a review of notes, tapes, photographs, or other documentation back home. "At home," says Kalow, "I started seriously reviewing, for the first time, all the footage I had shot, and was taken aback to realize what I had missed." For some the delayed reaction may take longer: Jackson needed six years, Ives a decade, and Stekert and Toelken took nearly thirty years. Toelken's came in a series of revelations over that time, Stekert's came at the very end.

"We can teach ourselves a good deal by looking back at ourselves participating in fieldwork situations," says Stekert, and to that end we would point up the tremendous importance of complete and careful documentation. Memory itself is useful, but memory tends to play the past to suit present needs. Frequently it is what we *don't* remember but what turns up starkly in the record that gives us the frame-tilting jolt. Keeping complete journals and carefully documenting all tapes and photographs seems so much clerkish fussbudgetry in the press and excitement of the field, but we neglect such activities at the peril of future wisdom.

Sometimes our sense of what matters or our insight into the meaning of things occurs in imperceptible steps; the thing just grows. More often, there are moments when we experience quantum leaps, moments when we are capable of seeing or hearing or understanding something for the first time or in an entirely new way. In the course of transcribing a tape for a new audience, Stekert realized that what she had long thought was a story-telling session was really a test and initiation session—of her. Montell went out to document a singing tradition, learned that the singers had reasons very much their own for wanting him to do that documentation, and found himself incorporated in a community that altered and enriched his life. Michael Buonanno, studying the Palermitan puppet theater, realized that the language and behaviors of street people held the key to the language and behaviors of characters in the *Rolando* epic, and that the epic puppet theater in turn reflected the life of the streets.

Epiphanies are understandings that catch us by surprise; they're leaps of the imagination that make sense only when we're on the other side. The essays in this collection focusing on fieldwork epiphanies indicate that luck may be involved in getting the necessary pieces in place, but it isn't luck that makes insight happen: you have to be ready for it. The comfort all the essays provide is this: The time we spend seeming to wander in darkness may not be wasted time after all; we are often traveling the right road, but it takes the pain of travel to teach us where we were really going.

Notes

1   One rare exception is Dan Rose's *Black American Street Life* (1987) in which the decaying character of the prose and the typography match what is happening in Rose's personal life at that point in the narrative.

2   See Tedlock (1991) for a lengthy discussion of this pattern, and of autobiographical statements in ethnographic studies.

3   Toelken's essay also raises one of the critical ethical questions of fieldwork: just because we have questions doesn't mean we have a right to the answers. Some answers don't belong to us, and ownership of certain information by one person may harm another. The notion of scientific purity, of free inquiry in which knowledge is its own justification and reward, is an academic luxury or conceit. Fieldwork is done among real people in the real world, and their interactions with us, at whatever level, change the conditions of their world. And they change us as well.

References Cited

Clifford, James, and George E. Marcus, eds. 1986. *Writing Culture: The Poetics and Politics of Ethnography.* Berkeley: University of California Press.

Georges, Robert A., and Michael O. Jones. 1980. *People Studying People: The Human Element in Fieldwork.* Berkeley: University of California Press.

Ives, Edward D. 1980. *The Tape-Recorded Interview: A Manual for Field Workers in Folklore and Oral History.* Knoxville: University of Tennessee Press. 2d ed., 1995.

Jackson, Bruce. 1987. *Fieldwork.* Urbana: University of Illinois Press.

Rose, Dan. 1987. *Black American Street Life: South Philadelphia, 1969–1971.* Philadelphia: University of Pennsylvania Press.

Tedlock, Barbara. 1991. "From Participant Observation to the Observation of Participation: The Emergence of Narrative Ethnography." *Journal of Anthropological Research* 47, no. 1:69–94.

From Entertainment to Realization
in Navajo Fieldwork
Barre Toelken

The process of fieldwork enlightenment I shall describe in these pages was not a particularly pleasant one; and it was anything but the rapid flash one always hopes for under ideal conditions. It played itself out over a period of thirty years from 1954 to 1984 in dramatic moments which seemed in and of themselves coherent, definable, and developmental, but which in retrospect appear today as nothing but suddenly recognizable pinpoints of dim light through a blanket of ignorance. Thus, this essay is not so much about how I discovered something as it is an account of the bothersome realization that the substance of my fieldwork has brought me to things beyond my capacity to understand or control. That it took me thirty years to learn enough to know I was over my head should stand as a precautionary example for anyone engaged in fieldwork outside his own culture; that my flawed preliminary findings are still quoted approvingly by colleagues who have not followed the later developments prompts this essay and should stand as a lesson to me as well as a sobering comment for all of us on our shared scholarly disinclination to rethink.

During the years from 1954 to 1956, I lived off and on with an extended Navajo family: most of that time, I was in Montezuma Creek Canyon in southeastern Utah with the family of Yellowman (which included not only his wife and several children but his in-laws as well); sometimes I stayed with Yellowman's younger brother, "Mike," in Dinnehotso, Arizona, sometimes with his sister Mabel in Kayenta, sometimes with his sister Bonnie, his brother Herbie, and his mother—"Grandma Johnson" to local whites—just west of Blanding, Utah, where Navajo "squatters" lived on land "owned" by white ranchers. Although at first I knew only a few phrases of Navajo learned from some forestry school chums at Utah State University, and although I had almost no cultural knowledge of the Navajos (I would not have been able to define or spell "Athabascan," for starters), I had blithely married a niece of Yellowman and was happily fulfilling the easterner's dream of "living among the Indians." By turns I prospected for uranium; herded sheep; guided white people around Monument Valley as if I knew all about the place; buried Navajo friends who died of starvation, exposure, and chronic diarrhea; complained (to anyone who would listen) about the ignorant and insensitive government; and generally began to see myself as an insider who knew about the Navajos and their situation from personal experience. Lastly, too slowly, I began to learn the Navajo language.

To be sure, the Navajos did not make my linguistic efforts easy, for their favorite sport lay in teaching me either the wrong words or the phrases most likely to be mispronounced by whites. Later on, I discovered that their nonchalance about my language acquisition stemmed from their clear recognition that I understood little about language and its power: I always asked for the nouns (What do you call this? What do you call that?), while the Navajo language itself is based on movement and therefore "prefers" highly conjugated verbs (Gary Witherspoon estimates about 356,200 conjugations for "to go," the most commonly used verb). My rather primitive insistence on learning the least important words led them to assume that I was only playing around, and this unfortunate fact in turn established the real context for my interactions with the Navajo and thus for whatever "discoveries" I might have made: I was surrounded with richly articulated data, but I was in no position to recognize or understand most of it.

Of course, even with minimal language competence, I could not help but notice that during the winter months parents told hilarious stories about a coyote to their children. On a typical evening, we would hear two or three such stories, and always the narration was accompanied by a lively discussion about meaning and application. Under the impression that these were only "children's stories," I was struck by how "adult" they sounded. The Navajo apparently brought up their children on meatier narratives than those I heard when I was young (Coyote is described as selfish, oversexed, gluttonous, foolish, self-destructive, as well as unpredictable and potentially dangerous to others). What eventually captured my intense interest, and what led to my later study of these stories, was the slowly dawning realization that they were more complex than "mere" children's stories, that they were told to and for everyone present, and that they could only be told in the winter without serious complications. Not only were the Navajos careful to tell the stories only in winter but they believed the stories *must* be told, else their children would grow up in a meaningless world. They believed the stories were true, but they almost never saw the etiological ending of a story (e.g., that's how the bobcat got pointed ears) as being at all explanatory of anything. The meaning they believed in was that which was dramatized in the story, not disclosed explicitly in the narrative itself. I would see that there were two levels of meaning in the Coyote stories: one surface level of funny narration which was entertaining and articulated with such artistic wording that it evoked complicated responses which indicated another— perhaps more important—level of moral or cultural reality.

The Navajos, who seldom punish children physically or correct their behavior with direct criticism, often use laughter as a corrective. I noticed early on that in the Coyote stories, the very actions which brought the most laughter from the audience were those which were clearly morally reprehensible, those which—if performed by living persons—would provoke the greatest disapproval and anxiety among family and friends. For this reason, the big "key" for me was not the "text" of the Coyote story but the live performance of it in a Navajo context where both the style of live narration and the lively responses of the audience combined in such a way as to create meanings which were not explicit in the story. To the extent that this "discovery" led me in the direction of contextual and performance analysis (and thus eventually put me into the intellectual company of some of the best folklorists of our times—at least in my reading), I could claim it as my decisive professional "moment" and let it go at that. But in fact, the realization had sat lazily in the back room of my mind for several years while I went ahead with my doctoral work in medieval literature: Old English and *Beowulf*, Middle English and Chaucer, the Old Icelandic sagas—in other words, texts, texts, and more texts. My major professor, Arthur G. Brodeur (who had taken his doctorate at Harvard with Kittredge), admitted that Albert Lord had developed some interesting ideas about oral formula and did not doubt that the *Beowulf* might have been sung during its development, but insisted that, gentlemen, in this course we were not dealing with Yugoslav singers but an Anglo-Saxon writer. If there were formulas in *Beowulf*, it showed simply that the writer was familiar with formulas. So forget about the Yugoslav coffee shop until after class and get down to business. I argued with Brodeur no more willingly than he had with Kittredge, so the idea of creating my own dynamic model for culture-based performance remained unformed until some years after my graduate work was completed and I had begun to think again.

I took advantage of a small travel grant from the University of Oregon; and with the help of Jan Brunvand and John Wilson Foster, I reestablished contact with the Yellowman family and began in earnest to record their stories on tape, catching each narrative event as fully as possible and then later trying to account for everything that had happened. In order to cope with the complexity of what I was finding, I decided to focus on a single story, a favorite of Navajos of all ages, in which Coyote causes rain in order to drown some prairie dogs who have been insulting him. With the aid of his stooge, Skunk, Coyote kills a number of prairie dogs and other small animals, and puts them down into a fire pit to cook while he hatches a plan to cheat Skunk out of most of the food. The plan backfires, of course—as do most self-serving plans, according to Navajo belief—and Coyote only gets a few bones to gnaw on. The Navajo assumption, clear to anyone over three years old, is that this story actually dramatizes the personal loss which will normally be experienced by anyone who tries to gain something for himself at the expense of others or without regard to others' needs. That a scholar can spend almost thirty years "decoding" such a clear story without noting its application to his own efforts is only one of several ironic embarrassments to be dealt with in this essay.

In any case, I presented a paper on Yellowman's storytelling at the Toronto AFS meeting in 1967 and was later invited to enlarge the piece for inclusion in a special issue on folklore genre for *Genre* quarterly to be edited by Dan Ben-Amos. That essay, "The 'Pretty Languages' of Yellowman: Genre, Mode, and Texture in Navajo Coyote Narrative" (Toelken 1969), was well received and has been reprinted a number of times. Indeed, the piece is still being quoted by scholars who are as innocent today as I was in 1969 of the weaknesses in it. On my part, I continued to collect and study other stories told by Yellowman, and I tried to keep abreast of others' efforts to deal with the performance aspects of narration. As I studied Dennis Tedlock's work with the Zuni and Dell Hymes's work on the Kathlamet Chinook, I began to feel uneasy about the format with which I had been presenting the Navajo stories; partly because of real conceptual difficulties in the translation of Navajo into English, I had found rational paragraphs to be the most convenient for maintaining the narrative flow, for the paragraph allows the translator to "fudge" on some difficult phrases in the interests of overall clarity. But obviously, if one presumes to deal with style and presentation as elements of meaning, then disguising these features or burying them with well-intentioned convenience hardly leads to acceptable results.

So it was that I decided to retranslate everything more exactly, using the phrases (like Hymes's lines and scenes) actually indicated by the way Yellowman narrated—pauses, "false starts," interruptions, breaths, laughter, and everything. By this time, however (1979), my Navajo language, which had never been in prime condition, had really rusted away; I enlisted the help of a Navajo graduate student, Orville Scott, who was at the time working on his Ph.D. in biology at the University of Oregon. He had a fine command of his language, enjoyed the stories immensely, and was blessed with a father who had been a medicine man and who was available to us by phone when we had difficulties. We worked with the story of Coyote making rain, and we listened through it time after time, coping with the translation and the meaning of each line—something which did not allow for convenient rationalization. I am sure that no serious student of folklore or of language will be surprised to hear that we discovered a number of important elements of phrasing, style, and meaning which had not been mentioned in the comments on my first prose translation. Somewhat more embarrassing, however, was the discovery of a few features which I had not even heard on the tape previously, as well as a few others which I had already asserted were not there. In the process, I felt I had learned more about the Navajo language and about Navajo stories than I could have bargained for. Scott became involved anew with his culture to the extent that he started using his Navajo clan name, and within a few weeks went from Orville, to O. Tacheeni, to Tacheeni Scott while we were deciding how to put our names to the resultant article, "Poetic Retranslation and the 'Pretty Languages' of Yellowman," in Karl Kroeber's *Traditional Literatures of the American Indian: Texts and Interpretations* (Toelken and Scott 1981). Later, using his Navajo language perceptions, Tacheeni Scott was able to make some new discoveries with the electron microscope and went on to be an active biologist; I continued to work with the cultural meanings in the Coyote stories.

Not long after the appearance of "Poetic Retranslation," I was invited by a group of reservation Navajos and their local schoolteachers to participate as the only non-Navajo speaker in a series of lectures on Navajo culture. Speaking before a Navajo public, each lecturer would be followed by a panel of Navajo elders consisting of local tribal judges and medicine men; I was to give a non-Navajo assessment of Navajo worldview, including the function of Coyote stories in the expression and perception of cultural values among the Navajos themselves. I was flattered to be asked and traveled to Sweetwater, Arizona, to make my presentation, which was warmly received, especially because it was winter and I was thus able to play a few tapes of Yellowman's narrations and then engage my audience in a discussion of their meanings. We had a hilarious and entertaining discussion, and I waited confidently for the responses of the panel of elders, which reconvened after a lunch of grilled mutton, frybread, and coffee.

As I had hoped, they found my comments valid and interesting—surprisingly so, one of them admitted, given my limited capacity to speak the Navajo language. The last commentator, a medicine man (the Navajo term *hataɫi*, "a singer," does not distinguish gender, although indeed most *hataɫi* are male) in his sixties, waited several long minutes before he began his comments, a rhetorical signal that what he was about to say was of some importance. He started by pointing out how different my approach was from that of white teachers in earlier eras: "Now the whites are admitting that our stories are important and that we ought to listen to them. This is a significant change. If the whites are going to know about our stories, then it's even more important for you young people here to listen to them, too. We should never forget our stories, because they are central to our lives; they are alive with our breath." I thought back to a meeting a few years earlier in which an angry Navajo woman had stood up and told a roomful of whites who were discussing, as usual, how to help the Navajos survive: "Don't try to save us physically unless you are willing to see that we keep our culture; we Navajos will live as long as the stories are wet with our breath!" The singer went on with his comments:

"Since our friend here has worked so hard to understand the stories, and since everyone here is interested in talking about it, maybe it would be a good opportunity to share with him—and with some of our younger folks who may not know much about it yet—what the Coyote stories are *really* about." He then gave an impromptu two-hour lecture in which he used each of the stories I had mentioned as an example of how the narratives are used selectively in the process of Navajo healing ceremonies.

In order for me to make this particular moment of enlightenment clear, I need to make a brief linguistic and ritual discursion. First, the Navajo tend to believe that language, rather than simply describing reality, actually creates it and controls it. We create the world in which we live by speaking about it; we create the system of harmony in which our rituals are used to retain or regain health by singing and narrating sacred stories; we create the moral atmosphere in which we live by telling stories which dramatize the moralities we live by. Speech events are not merely informative or entertaining, then, though of course they may also have these functions; oral articulations are the means by which our spirit (the inner-dwelling silent wind: *niłch'i bii' sizínii*) interacts with and shapes the outer wind which animates the entire world. Gary Witherspoon has written on this eloquently, and anyone who wants an expert view of the matter should consult his *Language and Art in the Navajo Universe* (1977). This shaping and interaction is nowhere so intensely focused as in the long and complicated myth-songs which are performed by *hatałi* in the course of healing ceremonies, which form the center of Navajo ceremonialism.

Health—either its maintenance or its reestablishment—is the main reason for performing any Navajo ritual; in fact, it can be fairly said that most rituals (or "sings") do not take place unless there is a patient with an illness (or potential illness) which can be defined so well that a particular ceremony is found to be appropriate and potentially efficacious. That witchcraft is considered an illness with important symptoms and treatments—both for the victim and for the perpetrator—is a fact that needs to be borne in mind in the following discussion.

The healing ceremony, once chosen (or determined by a diagnostician who may use anything from star-gazing to hand-trembling as methodology), can last a few hours or a few days; it may involve nighttime rituals both indoor and outdoor; in most cases it entails the creation and dismantling of sand paintings on the floor of the home in which the ceremony takes place; there might be related ritual dancing, shock rituals, body painting, burning of incense, distribution and application of medicines; throughout, there would be the singing-recitation of the myth which animates the particular ceremony, relieved now and then by pauses for normal conversation and even jokes. The singer will often light up a cigarette, relax for a while, and then explain the next part of the ceremony—perhaps going over some of the phrases which accompanying singers will repeat in chorus. Either in these conversational breaks or in the myth recitations themselves, participants will hear and make allusions to Coyote's various and well-known adventures. I had heard it done hundreds of times without wondering why it was happening; indeed, if anything, I assumed that the humorous references were made for the purpose of relieving the strain and stress of a long ceremony. Someone would say, "Just like the time Coyote gambled his skin away playing hoops with the beavers!" Everyone would chuckle, stretch out a leg or lean back, and then get ready for more of the ritual. Or right in the middle of a myth, Coyote would come running along, stop, look over the edge of a canyon and yell at the Spider People, "You're acting awkward and preposterous; you don't even know how to copulate right!" and then run on. The sing participants would laugh, and the singer would continue to narrate the myth with a twinkle in the eye.

Now, after all these years of empirical observation, Little John Benally was telling me (and, to be sure, he was telling local Navajos who might not have been fully aware of it after all *their* empirical observation) that these abridged references to Coyote stories in the healing ceremonies were not for comic relief or momentary distractive entertainment; they were part of the articulated ritual itself. It goes something like this: everything done during a ritual is an attempt to establish or reestablish order and harmony in the world. The symmetrical sand paintings, the continual four-way repetition of narrative lines (suggestive of the four directions and thus of circularity and centeredness), the circular sound of the "bull-roarer," the sunwise movement of ritual objects and human participants within the hoghan and the back-and-forth movements of dancers outside—these and other elements of the ritual represent articulations in sound, music, gesture, color, and wording of the desired condition known as *hózhó*, "beauty" (understood by Navajos to include harmony, balance, order, health, togetherness, cooperation, long life, family and clan stability, fertility, and psychological peacefulness). The oft-quoted phrase, "May there be beauty above you and below you, on all sides of you, before you and behind you," is not a superficial prayer for nice scenery on the way through life but an innocent English mistranslation of a passage found in many Navajo healing rituals that concludes, in effect, "Because of this ritual, you are now back in a proper harmonious relationship with nature and with humans [and, therefore, so are we: your family, neighbors, and friends]."

Where do the wiseacre one-liners about Coyote fit into this wonderful and ideal system? For one thing, the Navajos may be idealists about order and harmony, but they are also realists about the difficulty of maintaining it for very long: disease, psychological threats, personal egotism and selfishness, bodily delights and addictions, witchcraft, and inadvertent contact with dead enemies (for example, in wartime, or by visiting white cities with cemeteries) provide constant destabilizing elements in life which one can seldom avoid. The Coyote stories provide an embodied dramatization of these factors in the person of Coyote himself, who, although sacred in some respects, is simultaneously and enthusiastically defective like the rest of us. Lévi-Strauss notwithstanding, this is not a simple binary system in which something is either A or not-A; this is a complex analog system in which most things are A and not-A at one and the same time. In the midst of a healing ceremony, one may still be subject to the kinds of human impulses that lead inexorably to illness; thus, the reference to a Coyote story in which Coyote egotistically loses his skin by gambling it away playing a hoop game he knows nothing about, mentioned even elliptically in a ceremony for curing a skin disease, reminds us that behind the symptoms lie other psychological factors which must be recognized and dealt with before one is really cured. On the positive side, in the Coyote story itself, Coyote eventually grows his own skin back by being buried in the ground for a while and starting all over again: thus, patience and natural processes are invoked. Also, the hoops described in the story are the same hoops through which a patient crawls (or which are passed over his body) during several well-known healing ceremonies. So oral reference to the story actually promotes the healing process of the ritual. On the other hand, they are also the hoops which witches pass over their bodies when they change from human to animal form, thus we are simultaneously reminded of trouble. It is enough to realize that the mere mention of a Coyote tale can suggest (even create) a state of wholeness and healing while simultaneously bothering us with the dramatized recollection that we are actively engaged in bringing about the very imbalances we seek to cure. Parallel to this, many of the most powerful and successful singers are suspected of being witches, and thus one can never be totally sure if a ceremony has reestablished harmony or whether the seeds for more sickness have not been planted by a singer who wants more business.

This is complicated enough for Navajos to worry about, but it should now be quite apparent that for Little John Benally to have added this third level, a medical/ritual (shall we not say psychosomatic?) dimension to my study certainly provided me with more than enough puzzles of my own to solve. For one thing, I needed to check out his concepts with other Navajos, and I needed to go back through my recorded stories to see if I could relate each one to a ceremony in which it would be meaningfully employed. On the one hand, I was overwhelmed by the sudden complexity of a subject I thought I had become knowledgeable on; on the other hand, I was excited by the scholarly realization that I was on the verge of something well worth knowing more about: beyond stories as dramatizations of worldview, I was now also looking at stories as articulations of medical and psychological conditions. Exciting. Great stuff. Obviously, more fieldwork was required, and I made more trips to Navajo country.

I was now asking pointed questions about how Coyote stories, or particular motifs in them, fit into an apparent tripartite system of reference more or less like the following: (a) "surface" narrative, which coherently articulates or represents (b) a fabric of moral worldview assumptions, which in turn are so important as elements of harmony and health that they can be used as (c) cameos of ritual healing power.

Yellowman, after admitting that these connections were obvious, avoided talking much about them. He suggested that I needed to talk to a singer, and the sooner the better. Since the singers are the ones who really know about this system, I took his advice and began looking for someone who was willing to talk. There were not many; I began to suspect that this "obvious" knowledge was nonetheless under ritual control somehow and that people were not accustomed to just conversing about its phenomenology. Knowing the Navajo penchant for symmetry in fours, I should also have suspected that my system was not complete, but this simple idea—and its ramifications for my work—never popped into focus until Epiphany: the first week of January 1982. I had been attending a *yeibichei* dance during the previous couple of days, and after its conclusion, I had the chance to stay overnight with an affable elderly singer who was full of marvelous conversation. We sat in his hoghan until late at night, drinking coffee and swapping Coyote stories to the delight of his grandchildren. Then, as the others dropped off to sleep, and after what I thought was a properly respectful pause, I started putting questions to him. To my relief, he answered cheerfully and with nice detail, and even volunteered other related stories and cultural footnotes (naturally, since I had not wanted to imply I had anticipated that he would share his views with me, I had not brought along a tape recorder, so I took notes as I could on the few scraps of paper I could find on me).

Then, after a long silence, he began asking me a few questions; he started with, "Are you ready to lose someone in your family?" I wondered what could have given him that idea, and I wondered if I had somehow not understood him, so I asked him to explain. "Well, when you take up witchcraft, you know, you have to pay for it with the life of someone in your family." I assured him I had no interest in taking up witchcraft and asked why he had brought it up. It turned out that *I* had brought it up, by asking the kinds of questions I had concerning the Coyote tales. For, just as the tales themselves in their narration are normally used to create a harmonious world in which to live, and just as elliptical references to the tales can be used within rituals to clarify and enhance the healing processes, so the tales can be dismembered and used outside the proper ritual arena by witches to promote disharmony and to thwart the healing processes. In discussing parts and motifs separately, by dealing with them as interesting ideas which might lead me to some discoveries of my own, I had been doing something like taking all the powerful medicines to be found in all the doctors' offices in the land and dumping them by the bucketload out of a low-flying chopper over downtown Los Angeles. My friendly host advised me not to ask any more questions of the sort I had been pursuing: "Of course, if you become a witch, those who help you along will need to take someone from your family. If you're not a witch, but people think you are, those who are afraid of you will try to kill someone in your family anyway. And if you keep talking on this subject, everyone will think you're trying to become a witch, and they won't talk to you about these things at all. My advice to you is: don't go deeper with this subject unless you're going to join the witches." There was a very long respectful silence indeed until we fell off to sleep.

What is Navajo witchcraft, and what has it to do with fieldwork and the pursuit of scholarly goals? The witchcraft itself is difficult to define, though there are entire books about it: those interested should read at least Clyde Kluckhohn's *Navajo Witchcraft* (1967), and Margaret Brady's *Some Kind of Power: Navajo Children's Skinwalker Narratives* (1984). Suffice it to say for the purposes of this essay that the symptoms of witchcraft are, among others: extreme acquisitiveness, competition, aggressive behavior, selfishness, and the tendency to separate and dismantle those things which are recognizably functional as constellations of harmony. Personal recognition, analytical perspicacity, fame, tenure, money, and acclaim obviously do not appear on a list of healthy virtues for the Navajo. The effects of witchcraft on others are death, separation, poor health for humans and livestock, insanity, poverty, isolation.

In an essay titled "Life and Death in the Navajo Coyote Tales," in Brian Swann and Arnold Krupat's *Recovering the Word: Essays on Native American Literature* (1987), I gave a brief account of all this research, plus an outline of how the "fourth level" of meaning—witchcraft—relates to the rest of the material which I had been accumulating over the years. I also used that occasion to make clear my intention to "back off" from this area of Navajo studies. Why, then, do I now put forward this self-indulgent account of the matter as an example—among a collection of others more positive in their content—of some kind of enlightenment? There are several reasons. One is that it has forced me to an ethical consideration about the "necessity" of scholarly inquiry: a topic may be interesting and "important," but there may always be a question about the propriety of following up on it. Just as a moment of enlightenment may lead a scholar to pursue a subject further, so enlightenment may clarify the need to call a halt. For me, the decisive factor would be the extent to which the fieldwork partners we work with are adversely affected by the work; these people whom we often call "informants," who usually settle for a footnote and a nice word or two, can be unwittingly belittled, even endangered, by their cooperation with the folklorist.

But where was this enlightenment when I needed it? Yellowman would only tell tales in the winter, so I collected them only during the winter; I even made it easy on him by assuring him that I would not so much as play the tapes back unless it was winter, and I made sure I taught my Native American courses only in the winter so that I could talk about the Navajo tales legitimately. And Yellowman had set about telling me everything, including the stories told before dawn during deer hunting; we had planned doing a book together, provisionally entitled "Going Through a Navajo Life." Meanwhile, I developed, I believe, a reputation for being a sensitive folklorist. The question is, did Yellowman benefit from all this activity, and was he upset/pleased/surprised—aware, even—of my decision to withdraw from deep-level Navajo folklore? Neither this question nor any potential answer for it came anywhere close to my mind until recently, when I visited, or tried to visit, the family in southern Utah, and was confronted with a cluster-bomb of recognition based on Navajo logic.

A few years ago, Yellowman began having trouble with his legs (one needs to recall not only the Navajo cultural stress on "going" but also to know that well into his seventies Yellowman could still run after a deer all day until it was exhausted). He began to seek out the singers who could help him with his ailment, and—just before I moved from Oregon to Utah, where I might have visited him more often—he had a heart attack coming out of the sweat lodge and died. One of his daughters—in fact, the one who gave me the title "The Pretty Languages"—was nearly killed in an automobile wreck that took the life of her own daughter. A son has had a "schizophrenic episode" and is maintaining his equilibrium chemically. Brother Mike died in a rockfall. Brother Herbie drowned in the Colorado River while picnicking with his family. Yellowman's sister suffered a heart attack. Yellowman's wife has had to give up grazing rights to the area in Montezuma Creek where we all used to live—in part due to the oil fields which now cover the area and have brought almost all customs about land use into question, while ostensibly bringing wealth to a few Navajos. The family is scattered, and to a large extent estranged from each other; as far as I can tell, no one is telling the Coyote stories in the family. A Navajo foster son of mine has committed suicide. In recent years, I have been asked to testify in two different criminal trials involving Navajo witchcraft, both of which were concluded without the apprehension of the putative witch.

Are all these facts "coincidental"? In terms of our own lineal and post hoc logic, no doubt they are. At least, I can see no clear way in which any one of these could have directly brought the others to pass. From the Navajo perspective—and it is obviously from this view that the Yellowman family is looking at the matter—these facts are related because the people involved are all related; there is no way to view this constellation of happenings as coincidental. I doubt if they see their father's narration of Coyote stories as having *caused* a series of family injuries, but it would be unavoidable for them to see their troubles and the possible misuse of the stories as intertwined somehow. There thus exists the distinct possibility, from their point of view, that the exciting discoveries which they have helped with over the past thirty years have been for them more endangering than entertaining.

We would all have been better off, perhaps, had we sought our enlightenment from the Coyote tales themselves: there we find one example after another of how disastrous it is to insist on seeing what one is not supposed to see, to obtain what one should not have, to seek for any kind of gain at another's expense, to play a game reserved for others. One of the reasons the stories are so eloquent, it seems to me now, is that—far from needing analysis and explication—they are in and of themselves dramatic analyses and enactments of the weaknesses and arrogances that cause trouble for all humans. Yellowman knew I was using the stories to better understand Navajo worldview, but was he employing the stories for a broader purpose in telling them to me? Is there a reason why his most often-told story, at least in my presence, is that one about Coyote making rain in order to drown the prairie dogs that are insulting him? This is the story I have spent more than thirty years trying to understand, and it not only features Coyote getting swept away by his own plans, it ends with a scene in which Coyote, deprived of the meat he has tried to get by manipulation, has to beg for a few morsels from Skunk, who has taken the food up to an overhanging ledge:

> Skunk dropped a bone and Coyote looked up, they say.
> It dropped at his feet.
> "Dear friend, share some with me again!" Coyote said.
> "Certainly not," he said to him they say.

He was begging, to no avail, it is said.
Skunk kept dropping bones down to him.
He chewed the bones, they say.
That's how it happened, they say.

That's indeed what they say, and they have been saying it for a long time.
When I recently mentioned this scene to Tom Yellowman and asked what
he thought of its application to my studies, he smiled and said, "Oh, it could
apply to all of us, you know. But don't forget that other part, just before the
end, where Coyote finds the four skinniest prairie dogs that Skunk left in
the fire pit with their tails sticking out. Remember? He pulls each one out
and holds it up and says (wrinkling his nose in contempt) 'Aah, there's not
enough here for me to eat; there's nothing in it for me,' and throws each
one away over his shoulder. I guess we've all done that, somehow."
    Tom might also have mentioned the continuation of that scene:

He thrust repeatedly in many places, it is said, and couldn't
        find any.
Nothing, it is said.
There weren't any, it is said.
He couldn't, he walked [frustrated] around in circles.
He went around and he picked up those little prairie dogs he
        had thrown away.
Then he picked up every little bit and ate it all.
Then he started to follow Skunk's tracks, it is said, but he
        couldn't pick up the trail.
He kept following the tracks, back and forth, to where the rock
        meets the sand.
(He didn't look up.)

The separated, meatless bones dropped by Skunk to a disappointed
Coyote so totally absorbed in his own search are perhaps better than none
at all; and the small sliver of Navajo worldview I have been able to acquaint
myself with has been certainly a reward in itself. But the enormity and complexity of the living whole have eluded the best efforts of long-range fieldwork, and that needs to be admitted and confronted. Not only were basic
ideas and concepts missed and misunderstood but the very fieldwork itself

stood a strong chance of being dangerous to the informants as well as to myself and my family (which is why I have given it up). Another, perhaps in part intellectual, danger is that the readers of my earlier articles may think they know something about Coyote stories and start discussing them with others. Already Tom Yellowman has heard a non-Navajo telling these stories in public and giving explanations from my works, and I am now expected by my Navajo family to be the patient in a series of Beauty-Way ceremonies to protect us all.

Foremost in my thoughts at the present time is William A. Wilson's long-standing admonition that we should start with our own people first: even there, we may risk embarrassing or endangering our informants, but since we ourselves are part of their picture, we may hope we can be more responsive to the ethical issues, more quick to recognize insiders' perspectives and values; less ready to play the romantic jungle explorer. In any case, fieldwork, which is often viewed as a means of coming up with more artifacts or texts for study, needs to be reexamined as a model for human interaction. We already have plenty of "things" to study; what we lack is a concerted effort to understand fieldwork itself as an interhuman dynamic event with its own meanings, texts, and contextual peculiarities. Otherwise, we run the risk, demonstrated by my reckless forty years of Navajo fieldwork, of believing ourselves to be the objective beneficiaries of other peoples' traditions which we are free to submit to our analysis. It is folly.

That's what they say.

References Cited

Brady, Margaret. 1984. *Some Kind of Power: Navajo Children's Skinwalker Narratives.* Salt Lake City: University of Utah Press.

Kluckhohn, Clyde. 1967. *Navajo Witchcraft.* Boston: Beacon Press.

Toelken, Barre. 1969. "The 'Pretty Languages' of Yellowman: Genre, Mode, and Texture in Navajo Coyote Narratives," *Genre* 2, no. 3:211–35.

———. 1987. "Life and Death in the Navajo Coyote Tales." In *Recovering the Word: Essays on Native American Literature,* ed. Brian Swann and Arnold Krupat, pp. 388–401. Berkeley: University of California Press.

Toelken, Barre, and Tacheeni Scott. 1981. "Poetic Retranslation and the 'Pretty Languages' of Yellowman." In *Traditional Literatures of the American Indian: Texts and Interpretations,* ed. Karl Kroeber, pp. 65–116. Lincoln: University of Nebraska Press.

Witherspoon, Gary. 1977. *Language and Art in the Navajo Universe.* Ann Arbor: University of Michigan Press.

2

Four Moments
Candace Slater

Stories on a String

The chapbooks known as *folhetos* or *literatura de cordel* were for much of this century the principal reading matter of poor and semiliterate subsistence farmers in the Brazilian northeast as well as of northeastern transplants to the urban south. When in 1977 I began my research on these "stories on a string" (the string refers to the cord on which the booklets were traditionally suspended for display), the great majority of *cordel* studies centered on historical description and, above all, textual analysis. But the authors of these verse narratives were often as much performers as writers, chanting aloud their stories in open-air fairs. Furthermore, although a growing number of the buyers were members of the middle classes—tourists, intellectuals, and students dutifully completing high school civics assignments—a good percentage were still subsistence farmers or urban laborers nostalgic for the country home they had left behind. I was therefore interested not only in the particular themes on which the poets had written and presently were writing but also in the effects that the relationship between them and these very different sorts of customers might have on their work.

I began interviewing *folheto* buyers as well as poets in Rio de Janeiro. The former tended to be members of the crowd of displaced northeasterners which formed every Sunday morning about a particularly popular poet-singer in the mammoth São Cristovão Fair. I also spoke with the generally younger *cordel* buyers who jammed the plaza called the Largo do Machado on weekend evenings. In both instances I sought to maximize the limited time available by talking to the greatest possible number of individuals, using as a basis a list of some twenty questions that I memorized so as not to have to consult a distracting piece of paper.

And yet, while this approach got good results in Rio, it proved considerably less satisfactory when I journeyed north to the Pernambucan capital and port city of Recife. The *cordel* poet's situation here was very different from what I had encountered in the south. Instead of trying to sell the maximum number of booklets within a limited number of hours the vendors worked long weekdays in the city's principal marketplace, the Mercado de São José. Furthermore, they made no attempt to advertise their wares through oral performance. Rather, in recent years they had come to rely exclusively on displays of *folhetos* to attract an intermittent trickle of potential customers. Uncomfortable with strangers and considerably less accustomed to the notion of an interview than their more media-oriented southern counterparts, these buyers were often put off by the direct approach that had previously worked so well.

In an attempt to speak with as many poets as possible, I traveled extensively through the backlands, where many still resided. Those days I was not on the road, however, I spent in the marketplace. Although after a week or so, I had exhausted my usual store of questions, but I nevertheless kept going back, in part because I could not think of a better way to spend my time. As one older poet, José de Souza Campos, had a wobbly chair on which I could perch beneath the umbrella shading his *folhetos,* I found myself listening to him talk for hours with customers and fellow poets in the plaza that was home not just to *cordel* authors but also to prostitutes and policemen, shoeshine boys and on-the-spot photographers, itinerant barbers and snake oil peddlers. sitting around

I had a lot of doubts about what I was—or, more precisely, wasn't—doing. My anxiety intensified whenever a team of researchers or reporters, laden down with tape recorders and cameras, appeared. Most of these individuals, usually Brazilians from Rio or São Paulo but also sometimes European academics, appeared not to notice my presence. To the few who did inquire what I was doing, I answered "Research," but I really wasn't sure. Was sitting around day after day listening to a seemingly unending stream of casual conversation "research"? And how was I ever going to gain the confidence of the buyers who, given that the great majority of women in the immediate vicinity were either prostitutes or the wives and daughters of vendors, eyed me with perplexity or outright suspicion?

A strong distaste for the market as a place fortified my doubts. I really didn't mind the poets' sunstruck plaza, but I heartily disliked the obligatory walk down the long street packed with makeshift stalls hung with slabs of meat and piled high with brains and kidneys beneath a milanese of flies. I found it hard to take the heat, the reddish dust that clung to everything, and, especially, the rancid smell that always made me gag.

Things went on like this for several months until one Saturday when, in deference to the growing heat of summer, I set out to buy an electric fan. Because the catch-as-catch-can market offered far better prices than the more elegant department stores, I found myself headed for the long street once again despite the fact that it was not one of my workdays.

It is still hard to explain exactly what happened. I was picking my way about the booths that crowd the avenue each morning when I suddenly noticed that I was in step with the crowd. The sides of beef dangling from heavy hooks smelled as bad as ever, the flies buzzed and circled, the shoppers pushed and shoved each other as always but, curiously, the street seemed to have acquired a marked rhythm. Yet more curiously, I too was moving to the beat.

One day not long afterward, José de Souza Campos left me in charge of his stand while he ran a pressing errand. To his surprise and mine, by the time he returned an hour later I had sold a half-dozen pamphlet stories. Amused and not unimpressed, he started to take advantage of my presence to see other business or to enjoy a cup of coffee with his friends. ("I'll split the profits with you," he would exclaim, "so be sure to sell at least a hundred!")

Since I did not look like a prostitute and seemed much too young to be the poet's wife, people concluded that I must be his daughter—foreign accent, blue eyes, and all. And so, they started talking to me as well as buying my *folhetos*—"after all, you know, we all have to make a living." At the same time, the once seemingly aimless conversations among *cordel* authors became increasingly interesting to me, probably because I had new questions based on my experiences as a sometime-vendor. In short, I started to believe that I was "doing research."

When I tried to tell my friend, the *cordel* poet, what had happened to me on the crowded street he just laughed. "You can," he observed, "lead a horse to music, but that doesn't mean that you can make him dance."

Trail of Miracles

One of the sites to which I traveled as part of my investigation of *cordel* literature was Juazeiro do Norte, the largest city in the arid backlands of the state of Ceará. At one time a major center of *folheto* production, Juazeiro is best known as the continuing focus of a massive pilgrimage to a local holy figure, Padre Cícero Romão Batista (1844–1934), and many of the publishers and poets whom I encountered had much to say about the priest. As a result, I found myself becoming increasingly interested in the pilgrimage and the vast web of oral as well as written stories that play a crucial role within it.

I later spent two periods of just over five months each in Juazeiro. During the first, I lived with a new friend in her small house on the Rua do Horto, the steep and winding road on the outskirts of the city where many former pilgrims had settled. Here, I spent my days taping stories recounted by her neighbors. During my second stay in Juazeiro, I collected tales from a number of the many visitors who come from all over the vast, dry northeast between late August and early February.

To encourage pilgrims to talk with me I volunteered for the dawn shift in the parish's visitor registration center. In the process of taking down information about each group, I was able to meet the organizers called *fretantes,* some of whom agreed to introduce me to known storytellers among their number. I would then appear after the evening mass in the *rancho* or rustic pilgrim hotel where the group was lodged. Because of the initial contact with the *fretante,* people were usually expecting me. While some were fearful of foreigners or distrustful of my motives, most were curious about "the girl straight from the United States of North America" who wanted to hear their stories.

Usually converted single-family homes lining the streets around the church of Our Lady of Sorrows, the *ranchos* are packed during the pilgrimage season with hammocks strung crosswise in every direction to accommodate a maximum of weary pilgrims. The women usually cook meals on a grate in the backyard. In many cases, a single shower may serve as many as a hundred people.

Unlike the residents with whom I could speak at length on multiple occasions, the pilgrims were eager to see the sights of Juazeiro and thus were normally available for conversation only in the brief hour following lunch or at night after the mass, which many attended. Because they were in transit there was no time to cultivate an ongoing relationship. Often, even storytellers who appeared disposed to talk suddenly would sometimes become tongue-tied in my presence. "Excuse me, but I've forgotten everything," the individual might murmur with a sheepish grin I quickly came to recognize but could not truly comprehend.

Two weeks went by and soon it was almost time for the vacation I had promised myself following the big pilgrimage in early November. One of my students back in the U.S. had arranged for me to spend a few days with relatives of his in the coastal capital of Fortaleza. There, he assured me enthusiastically, I would find a swimming pool, a garden full of palm trees, fountains, and bougainvillea, and, above all, a warm welcome. "You'll feel right at home with them, you'll feel as if you'd always known them," he assured me. Sometimes when the sun beat down on the roofs of the *ranchos* with particular violence, I would imagine myself luxuriating in the shadow of a palm tree beside the long blue pool.

During the three days of the pilgrimage I met a group from the state of Maranhão whose members were planning to go on from Juazeiro to the shrine city of Saint Francis of Canindé. Because Canindé is only about an hour and a half from Fortaleza, they invited me to accompany them. Thinking it would be interesting to see another, quite different pilgrimage site and curious about the dynamics of the journey, I accepted their invitation. Very early the next morning we sputtered out of Juazeiro.

In order to avoid tolls or a fine for carrying more than the legal number of passengers, the ancient bus in which we were traveling kept to unpaved back roads full of unmarked curves that forced the driver to slam on the brakes. These narrow escapes grew more dramatic as night fell. Time and again, parents would be jolted out of an uneasy slumber to retrieve even sleepier children from the tiny rocking chairs that had skidded to the front of the bus. Sometime after midnight, the bus had not one but two flat tires. Declaring the double mishap a warning sign from Padre Cícero, the driver parked along the highway and slung a hammock between two trees while the passengers tossed and turned in their hard seats. Well after noon the next day we lurched into Canindé.

Our group spent the next two days visiting the churches and numerous unofficial holy places in the city. When it came time for me to leave for Fortaleza, the pilgrims, almost none of whom had ever seen the ocean, piled into the bus. Around sunset, we arrived in the city and made straightway for the beach. Then, after the bedazzled children had finished splashing in the warm waves, the bus headed for the wealthy neighborhood where my hosts lived.

Because all of the houses on the wide and leafy avenue stood behind high walls with shards of glass cemented on top to discourage burglars, it was hard to distinguish the numbers in the dusk. When the driver finally located the correct address, a group of pilgrims accompanied me to the front gate. One man rang the bell. Dogs started barking madly and a pair of eyes appeared behind a crack in the grating. "I'm the friend of Daniel that you have been expecting. The American professor," I announced, embarrassed at the commotion I had caused.

The iron door opened slowly and a woman in a starched white apron surveyed the group. "Come in," she finally said to me, looking dubiously at the bus. After we had exchanged good-byes in the mounting darkness, the pilgrims roared off toward Canindé and Maranhão and I found myself within the confines of the gate.

The half-lit house and grounds were even bigger and more beautiful than I had imagined in those shadeless afternoons in Juazeiro. There were the swimming pool, the palm trees, and bougainvillea, even a cement lion with a large, open mouth from which water bubbled into an enormous marble seashell.

The maid went ahead of me into the house and I could hear her murmuring to someone. She then led me into the bright white living room where a carefully groomed woman who had been ensconced on an immense sofa rose to greet me. "How lovely to see you. Do come sit down," she said.

The sofa, big already, seemed to grow as she spoke. It looked like a whale, a big white brocade whale. I looked down at the equally white carpet and discovered two feet almost black with dust. At the same time, I was suddenly acutely aware of my homemade flowered dress, the straw hat held on with a faded ribbon, and the glass rosary with a tin medal of Padre Cícero that hung about my neck. The woman in white smiled resolutely and held out her hand to me. She was very careful not to eye the dress, the hat, the beads, the dust between my toes. "Daniel's told us so much about you and your work," she said graciously. "We are so pleased to meet you." I wanted to say something gracious in return but all I could think about was how I could avoid dirtying that whalelike sofa. Trying to smile, I felt my lips move into that sheepish grin.

City Steeple, City Streets

While still recording pilgrim storytellers in Juazeiro, I became curious about the relationship between the miracle narratives I was hearing and others that might exist in quite different settings with a similar folk-literary tradition. So, when a friend later told me about a group of stories surrounding a Granada-based Capuchin friar roughly contemporary with Padre Cícero (Fray Leopoldo de Alpandeire, 1864–1956), I decided to travel to southern Spain.

Accustomed to the northeast Brazilian interior, I was suddenly surprised to find myself doing fieldwork in a place that boasted computer terminals, nightclubs, and department stores and restaurants happy to take credit cards. There were cafés in which to dawdle over the morning newspaper, bookshops, travel agencies, movie theaters, and laundromats. And, instead of stringing up a hammock in someone else's house and living out of a suitcase, I found myself renting a furnished apartment in a complex with a swimming pool and supermarket next to the church housing Fray Leopoldo's crypt.

As one might expect from these striking differences in context, the devotion to the friar diverged in important ways from the pilgrimage. Whereas, for instance, I had found no one in Juazeiro who did not have an opinion about Padre Cícero, some residents of Granada had trouble identifying Fray Leopoldo. Then too, most visitors to the friar's crypt displayed a restraint unthinkable in the Brazilian backlands. Time and again I was taken aback by what I saw as the distinctly low key nature of the devotion as well as people's apparent tolerance for radically divergent points of view.

Furthermore, although sometimes their tales were all but identical on the surface to others I had recorded in Juazeiro, storytellers in Granada seldom displayed real passion in regard to Fray Leopoldo. Not infrequently, an individual who had begun by describing the friar's actions would switch in mainstream to a catalogue of now-antiquated customs or an extended account of the political upheavals that had ushered in the Franco era.

Because the Brazilian stories focused very closely on their protagonist, whom their tellers customarily described with great emotion, Spanish storytellers' tendency to expand and transform accounts of the friar into more general treatments of his epoch surprised me. When the people I asked about Fray Leopoldo began talking about seemingly unrelated matters, I would try to nudge them back to the original subject. They would often humor me by responding to specific questions about the friar. Minutes later, however, they would once again be reminiscing about outmoded traditions, denouncing various abuses associated with Franco and the Franco years, or arguing about the sequence of events in the Civil War.

Not just the fact of these apparent digressions but also their length and frequency perplexed me. Could something be wrong, I wondered, with my way of asking questions? Or did the problem lie instead with Fray Leopoldo? Why did he seem to be so much less compelling to storytellers than his Brazilian counterpart? Perhaps the saints had lost their force in an increasingly industrial society; perhaps the tales were mere survivals doomed to extinction in the not-too-distant future. At least that's what I had half-concluded until a conversation late one cold spring afternoon with Doña Hortensia.

Ninety-two-years old and the oldest resident of the Fray Leopoldo Home for the Elderly, Doña Hortensia had been born into a wealthy family in the north of Spain. Having decided at an early age that she would rather see the world than marry, she moved to Granada with her parents after completing her studies in a French university. After the Civil War, she became the treasurer of a lay religious association known as the Third Order of St. Francis and in this capacity had numerous dealings with Fray Leopoldo, whom she came to regard as a saint. Although Doña Hortensia was now crippled by arthritis, her memory remained unclouded. On the chilly April day in question she spent well over an hour recalling in detail a whole string of once-proud landmarks that one by one had disappeared over the last few decades.

The older Granada that Doña Hortensia was evoking had a certain fascination, and yet, listening to her, I heaved a large inward sigh. What was going on? Hadn't this lovely old woman known Fray Leopoldo? Didn't she insist he was a saint? And if so, why wasn't she describing him and his various miracles instead of a collection of long-vanished buildings?

When the nurse appeared to take Doña Hortensia to dinner, the latter squeezed my hand. "Come back tomorrow and I'll tell you some more stories about Fray Leopoldo," she said enthusiastically.

"But Doña Hortensia," I objected with a smile that I hoped concealed my frustration. "You weren't talking about Fray Leopoldo. You were telling me about the way Granada used to be."

Doña Hortensia looked startled for a moment before squeezing my hand again. "But of course I was telling you about Fray Leopoldo," she assured me patiently. "I was telling you all about the way things were back in his time, and now, just look how they have changed." "Just look," she repeated. And suddenly I saw. Could not Fray Leopoldo be important to people precisely because he was for them the symbol of an era that had ceased to be? Might he for this reason be a springboard into a Granada and a Spain that no longer existed, a way of talking about immense changes that had affected both the nation and individual lives? Was he appealing to them not just as a holy figure but also as a focus for what would otherwise be an overpowering mass of memories and feelings? The dinner bell was ringing. I thanked Doña Hortensia and promised her I would, indeed, be back tomorrow.

Dance of the Dolphin

[handwritten margin note: least successful of the bunch.]

When my students in a course on Brazilian civilization at Berkeley asked for readings about the Amazon, I unearthed great amounts of information but no overview of the sort they wanted. Surprised by this lack and increasingly curious about this vast expanse of land and water, I decided to see Amazonia for myself.

As soon as I stepped off the airplane before dawn in Manaus, a city of some one and a half million in the midst of the rain forest, my eyes began to water. "It's the factories," the taxi driver said. "But you get used to them."

I had no intention of getting used to the smog and smokestacks of

Manaus. This was the Amazon and I expected trees. After a few days, I boarded a boat for the small city of Tefé. There I would begin by looking into a messianic community about which an anthropologist had told me. Certainly, I would like Tefé far better than Manaus.

Almost three days later the boat chugged into the harbor. Soon a kind friend of a friend was driving me about town in search of the community. When we finally discovered the group's location, Líbio parked his jeep. We clambered over a hill and leapt across a stream fed by a sewer, landing in the mud where a tiny chapel stood. I pounded on the door and an old lady appeared. "You two can talk and I'll be back for you," Líbio told me, leaping back across the stream.

The old lady received me warmly. She told me all about the leader of the community, who had died four years ago, outlined the rules he had established, and recited numerous prayers. She gave me the addresses of the other branches of the community, told me how to get there and explained who I should contact once I had arrived. No researcher could ask for more. The only problem was that although Tefé was, indeed, very different from Manaus, my original bad humor had in no way dissipated. I didn't like the heat, I didn't like the sewage, I didn't like the Amazon, I wanted to go home.

When Líbio reappeared I thanked the woman profusely. "Come back again!" she said. "When shall I bring her?" inquired Líbio and the two settled on an hour and a day while I balefully observed the putrid stream out of the corner of my eye. "It's time for lunch now," Líbio asserted. "Let's make a list of things you want to do tomorrow," he said.

Líbio's good cheer made me feel ashamed of my own intractability. Chastened, I made a list for not just the next day but the next week. I would visit a local priest who worked with the parish in which the community was located. I would contact a doctor who worked in the neighboring town where the community had a mission. I would check on boat schedules for trips to the other towns the woman had mentioned. In short, I would make the best of things and get down to work.

Early the next morning while I was waiting for the faithful Líbio in the lobby of Tefé's one small hotel, one of the young engineers from the national oil company called PETROBRAS struck up a casual conversation. He and a number of his co-workers were about to fly back on the company plane to Manaus after two weeks on the outpost about half an hour by air from Tefé.

He described his work, the wildlife and the Indians who lived on the edges of the outpost, the effects of ever-increasing development on the future of the forest. "Well, I guess that's the airport van now," he said. "I've enjoyed talking with you. Good-bye." "Good-bye and good luck," I said. And then, much to my own surprise, "Can I come too?"

Half an hour later, forty engineers and I were crammed into a tiny airplane headed for Manaus. What would I do there? Wherever would I go next? What must the good-hearted Líbio be thinking? The cabin was hot, the motor loud, the flight low and choppy. I closed my eyes in the hopes of easing the headache that had started as we left Tefé. I wanted nothing more than to catch the next plane to the U.S.

"Look," said the young engineer who had arranged the trip for me. He pointed out the window. "The Amazon."

I had seen the river before. Hadn't I just spent almost three very long days on a boat? I nonetheless opened my eyes slowly and peered out the window through the clouds.

Having grown up around oceans, I had never given much thought to rivers. They were lines of water between two lines of land. But what now appeared below us was no line, but instead a mass of curves and long ellipses, land embracing water, water embracing land. The river was an enormous, living Slinky spiraling out into a forest that extended as far as I could see. "So what do you say?" demanded the engineer.

The plane began descending. Soon we would be in Manaus. I still had no idea of what I was going to do. But I did know that I would not be on the next flight to California. "Is it different from what you had imagined?" the engineer inquired.

On Second Thought

Their continuing sharpness singles out the four moments I have recalled from a multitude of others. Even though the first occurred almost twenty years ago, it seems to me no more remote in time than do any of the others or, indeed, the sultry days through which I moved at a snail's pace this last, Amazonian summer. The incidents described here, however, are more than particularly vivid memories. They have acquired, or I have imbued them with, an emblematic force. Looking back over my own descriptions, I find myself returning time and again to the intensely visceral quality of fieldwork as well as to the psychic dislocations and, often, real discomfort it implies.

In underscoring the resolutely physical nature of fieldwork, I am thinking of far more than the heat of northern Brazil or the rainy chill of Andalusian winters. Clearly, sounds, smells, textures, tastes, and images are all part of what has become known as "being there." The dance of which the *cordel* poet José de Souza Campos speaks, however, is far more than a conglomeration of sensations useful in evoking a larger, ostensibly more important story about the ways that other people organize their lives. Above all, it is a rhythm or a series of rhythms not apprehensible through will alone. Although it is possible to isolate and to analyze many of the components of these essential rhythms, the perception of movement and the ability to move in step are often separate things. I would have difficulty spelling out exactly what I learned in looking down over the Amazonian forest or in confronting that whalelike sofa in the well-appointed sea of a now-distant living room. However, the distinctly tactile quality of the experiences that signaled turning points in my own research suggests that much of fieldwork has to do with literally, and not just figuratively, seeing things in a new light.

This straining to envision inevitably involves a measure of discomfort. Here, once again, I am thinking less of the midday sun or chill spring rain than of my anxiety at whether I was really doing research, my frustration with the embarrassed silence of pilgrim storytellers, and my bewilderment at the Spanish storytellers' seeming lack of interest in the protagonist of their own tales. I am remembering my own astonishment at the force of the culture shock I experienced—and still regularly experience—each time I set foot in the Amazon. According to the saying, practice makes perfect. But even the best-written manuals rarely convey the extent to which even the most seasoned fieldworker is always a beginner.

Today, some degree of reflexivity has become acceptable, if not obligatory, in most ethnographic enterprises. As a result, contemporary writers are considerably freer than past authors to acknowledge just how many false starts and awkward pauses lie behind a page of relatively graceful prose. Even so, most accounts of on-site research still dwell far more upon eventual insights than on the hesitations, disappointments, and, often, outright failures on which these insights often depend.

The limits of participant observation and the essential untranslatability of cultures have inspired a growing multitude of books and articles over the last decade. Much of the work by authors such as James Clifford, George Marcus, Clifford Geertz, and Vincent Crapanzano focuses on the rhetorical strategies underlying ethnographic writing, emphasizing the identity of field description as a quite particular sort of narrative that emphasizes certain details while excluding others. As a result, virtually all of today's often heated debates about the nature and limits of field description begin by acknowledging the extent to which even the most painstakingly documented account is necessarily a partial fiction.

At the same time that they insist on "writing culture" as a recognizable literary genre, many contemporary authors emphasize the process through which research subjects become the objects of often subtle, sometimes violent, transformations. Salutary in many respects, this stress on the potentially pernicious effects of an objectifying gaze has the drawback of obscuring the very real effects of the observed on the observer.

The current emphasis on the power of what Mary Louise Pratt has termed the imperial eye also tends to invest field investigations with a purpose and direction they do not always possess. In my experience, fieldwork is, above all else, surprising. Often tedious and physically demanding, it is also intensely exciting precisely because of its fundamental unpredictability. No matter how carefully researchers map out their investigative strategies, no matter how well they fortify themselves with theories and background readings, they are all but certain to find themselves confronting challenges to assumptions they didn't even know they entertained.

The image of the fieldworker as lonely seeker in pursuit of Knowledge—a sort of laboratory scientist in dusty blue jeans—has a certain romantic allure that makes the wait for boats that never arrive and the nights thick with mosquitoes easier to bear. It is comforting to think that perseverance and a steadily growing store of knowledge will allow one to decipher in a modest burst of light the puzzle that is another—or one's own—culture. The moments I have described, however, fail to support this fond belief in moments of revelation as academic Just Rewards. My sudden insights into the people and places I had set out to study attest far less to my own powers of analysis than they do to the ability of these same people and places to effect profound changes within me. Although I could not have arrived at these junctures without extended, systematic effort, they happened without warning and, often, despite myself. No dramatic climax, these instants of secular grace were in every case a new beginning. As such, they stand as invitations to an ever-changing dance.

References Cited

Clifford, James. 1988. *The Predicament of Culture: Twentieth-Century Ethnography, Literature, and Art.* Cambridge: Harvard University Press.

Clifford, James, and George E. Marcus, eds. 1986. *Writing Culture: The Poetics and Politics of Ethnography.* Berkeley: University of California Press.

Crapanzano, Vincent. 1992. *Hermes' Dilemma and Hamlet's Desire: On the Epistemology of Interpretation.* Cambridge, Mass.: Harvard University Press.

Geertz, Clifford. 1973. *The Interpretation of Cultures: Selected Essays by Clifford Geertz.* New York: Basic Books.

———. 1988. *Works and Lives: The Anthropologist as Author.* Stanford: Stanford University Press.

Marcus, George, ed. 1992. *Rereading Cultural Anthropology.* Durham, N.C.: Duke University Press.

Pratt, Mary Louise. 1992. *Imperial Eyes: Travel Writing and Transculturation.* London: Routledge.

3
Inquiry and Epiphany in the
Culture of Capitalism
Dan Rose

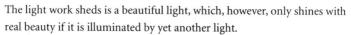

The light work sheds is a beautiful light, which, however, only shines with
real beauty if it is illuminated by yet another light.
—Ludwig Wittgenstein (1980: 26e)

here among them the americans this baffling multi people
extremes the variegations their noise restlessness their almost
frightening energy how best describe these aliens in my reports to The
Counselors

disguise myself in order to study them unobserved adapting their varied
pigmentations white black red brown yellow
—Robert Hayden (1985: 192)

I was driving my Chevy through a late spring evening on the rain-slickened
streets of South Philadelphia, down the narrow, wetly shining streets boxed
by three-story row houses. My wife, Karen, was sitting in the front seat next
to me and the moving shadow from the windshield wiper stroked patterns
on her face as we drove under the streetlights. We were listening to the news
on the radio and waiting for the weather report, hoping that tomorrow
would not be as miserable as this night. I told her that I would drop her off
at the apartment and look for a place to park so that she wouldn't get
drenched. We had just been out to dinner and as we entered the block where
our apartment was located I started to watch for a parking spot. I passed
one in front of the illegal numbers bank near the end of the block and only
had to drive a little further on to our place.

That was 1971.

We had lived in a neighborhood for a year and a half, and as a cultural anthropologist I had been studying the life of our neighbors, who were black and who were pretty much working class or on welfare, although there were many who were young and unemployed. Our neighbor across the street was a truckdriver; I worked for a middle-aged mechanic who had started his own business just the year before; other people we knew in the area were longshoremen, merchant seamen, and construction workers. One of the women who lived next door sorted vegetables in a food distribution warehouse.

I was trying not to skid on the slick steel rails of the trolley tracks as I pulled up to the apartment and braked the car to a stop. Karen, trying to dodge the raindrops, quickly ran to the door of the row house that led to our second-floor apartment. She unlocked it and disappeared up the stairs. After the door closed I turned around to look through a veil of rain washing down the rear window and backed the car slowly up the street near the numbers bank to the parking spot I had seen. I eased into it and never even noticed the black car which pulled quickly up behind me and stopped in such a way that I could not leave.

As I started to get out of my Chevy, a cop, one of the elite Highway Patrol, commanded, "Up against the car." There were two of them and I had no chance to do anything. They caught me completely by surprise, and I had been looking in the direction from which they had come; it was perfectly timed. I hoped they would not find an item I was carrying, because if they did I would be spending the rest of the night, and probably far longer, in a Philadelphia jail; there was absolutely no bargaining, I knew, in this situation. As I'd seen in movies, I turned and put my hands on the roof of the car and spread my legs.

The one cop started to search me. He patted my chest under my jacket. I was wearing a short Levi's denim jacket that had a pocket over each breast, a short western style jacket that was meant to protect from the wind, but was no good for cold rain. I had it in the right breast pocket. As he patted my waist and down each leg to the ankles, the other cop, seeing I was giving no trouble, walked in what seemed a deliberate swagger around to the back of the car.

Although they moved quickly they did not act rushed and I caught a good look, my first, at Police Commissioner Frank Rizzo's dreaded Highway Patrol. I say "dreaded" because these were the elite cops, the ones who were lean and trim, who were noted for their sophisticated beatings of black men. They dressed in black leather, their boots—like storm troopers'—up to the knee.

The cop in back called out, "Hey, these are Wisconsin plates."

I found my voice and figured that they had missed what I had desperately hoped they would not find and felt some remnant of confidence. It had all happened with phenomenal quickness and I had not been afraid at all. I am sure I did not have time to be. I had just gone with the flow of events until I could get my voice into it.

"What's going on?" I asked.

"Drugs," the guy next to me said.

The one who had looked at the license plates came up to stand next to me and asked, "What are you doing here?"

"I live here. I just left my wife off and found this parking space. I'd like to get out of the rain."

"What about the plates," he insisted.

At that point I broke what had been until then my complete silence locally as to why I was living in South Philadelphia. Karen and I were doing ethnography as anthropologists—I was the anthropologist and she was helping by taking notes on her observations and involvements. None of our black neighbors had been told that I was conducting ethnography, we had not mentioned to anyone we lived near why we were there, I had gone to work for Telemachus Combs in his hole-in-the-wall repair shop, then we had moved into the apartment next door. The first year we had just lived there and I had worked as a mechanic and the second year Karen had begun to manage a sheet music business and I did some mechanical work and pickup jobs on the street. But to the cops I blurted out immediately, "I'm a graduate student at the University of Pennsylvania and we live here while I'm finishing my graduate project."

It was not quite true. I was living off a doctoral dissertation grant from the University of Pennsylvania while finishing dissertation research for my Ph.D. degree from the University of Wisconsin. Right then I was completely happy that I had not changed my license plates from Wisconsin to Pennsylvania. The cops bought my story and left satisfied with what I had told them.

They had not found the automatic pistol I carried with me all the time. It was a .25 caliber, which that evening I had slid into the right breast pocket of my denim jacket, the safety off, six bullets in the clip and one in the chamber. I had gotten it the year before because I had felt that I was in too many life-threatening situations with men my own age who carried pistols not to be armed like an equal. I had no license to carry the pistol and am certain that the Highway Patrol would have locked me up. In Philadelphia one can usually obtain a permit to carry a gun if one routinely transports large amounts of money in the course of one's work. I had been told by people wise to the vagaries of acquiring permits that I would not be qualified for one. When I called my brother (who was underage and then had to ask my father) and asked him to buy me the gun, I was too impatient to wait for the permitting process. I reasoned that if I were turned down, the local cops would watch out for me if I then carried an illegal weapon. At that same time a friend was studying Rizzo's cops. When I later told him that the patrolman failed to find my gun he told this to some of his friends on the Highway Patrol. He then reported to me that they couldn't believe that a couple of their best had missed a trick.

The more fateful possibility, however, is that I would have been sentenced to a five-year prison term. Carrying a weapon without a license is something that the cops and the courts take very seriously because too often guns are used against cops. I am uncertain that I would have been let off even with the reasons I could have claimed for myself. I was more than a little relieved that they missed the pistol in their search. Ethnography, as I was conducting it, was treacherous, and I had exaggerated the dangers to myself by carrying an illegal weapon.

Although I was not dealing drugs, I was intimately part of an underground economy, and of something far more interesting, something that I saw as a vestigial precapitalist system in black American urban life. The underground economy, a world without licenses or taxes on economic transactions, sheltered the kind of monetary and nonmonetary transactions that I am calling precapitalist. The black people whom I knew—mostly men—conducted a form of exchange that did not, does not now, closely resemble the capitalist mode of exchange of the north European and American middle classes.

Through this story I want to introduce the reader to black South Philadelphia, from which vantage I began the tracings of autobiography that move outward to embrace white America. It is as if I stood inside a resistant, unincorporated black world and began to discover as an anthropologist a white world to which it was nevertheless fused. And then as I returned to white middle-class life, I made the effort to discover the hidden order of American life and concentrated unconsciously at first on its legally incorporated existence, and the effects of that existence on the spatial order of Philadelphia and its hinterland.

I worked in South Philadelphia in a black man's illegal or nonlegal shop, something both in and out of legally constituted America. For two years Karen and I lived with black people, then moved to the countryside outside of Philadelphia. A little more than a year later we moved back into the city to a white working-class neighborhood and there our marriage broke up. I took the opportunity of being single once again to stay in the field as it were and studied a coal mining community, an agricultural area undergoing suburbanization which edged an upper-class estate area. It was as if I were undertaking to move as a native observer in an upward spiral of curiosity through cultural strata and trying to comprehend how we have evolved our national cultural space. These sites were within commuting distance from the University of Pennsylvania, where I joined the faculty in 1974. Throughout the 1970s I engaged in continuous fieldwork. In retrospect, those studies can be seen as a kind of personal and professional quest for America visualized through anthropological eyes.

Our life with black people had exaggerated my concern with American culture, because I felt the exclusion and alienation that results from racism and class differences. It was evident everywhere that racist stonewalling had achieved its agenda of keeping many blacks from realizing their potential in American cultural life. In one of my field notes written when we were living in South Philadelphia between 1969 and 1971, I wrote that I needed to understand how the country was organized. I felt, as I lived and worked on the street, too remote from the organizational system of American society to comprehend firsthand how blacks were often excluded from the rest of the everyday life of the country.

Boycie was one of my friends in South Philadelphia. We had gotten to know each other by drinking together. He had taken me uninvited to a wake and later, on another occasion, I was present when he had publicly argued with his landlord in front of a local crowd in what had amounted to a local lawsuit. On a hot August day, short of money, he and I had panhandled for quarters so we could go out drinking that evening. We were neatly stationed between the Martin Luther King Jr. Plaza, a highrise slum clearance building, and a small corner grocery store. A steady stream of people left the plaza to pick up items of food or drink and we were in their way, not too far from the entrance to the convenience store.

Boycie had been a mechanic in the Korean War and, after his discharge, returned to Philadelphia, the city where he was born. His mother, and his mother's sister, and other relatives I knew about, lived scattered throughout black South Philadelphia. He was one of the few people I knew who had lived all their lives in the city. Our other neighbors seemed mostly to have migrated up from the Carolinas and Virginia. By the time I knew Boycie, he had fathered several children by a woman who lived in the plaza. He told me that he turned over his entire disability check from the army to her. When he needed money he *scrambled* for it. His right ankle was badly mangled, apparently from the war, and did not on the surface much resemble an ankle at all. For all that, he neither limped nor complained about the pain. He was an excellent, intuitive mechanic, but he drank too much. He seemed to spend most of his time in the evenings in speakeasies, the unlicensed little enterprises usually run out of a woman's kitchen where one could buy a drink of beer or wine, and on rare occasions a platter of food.

I think Boycie lived several places at the same time. One evening he took me over to a weathered three-quarter-ton Ford pickup truck. I asked him if it ran. He said it did but it needed *juice,* a battery. That night he wanted to show me the books he had stored in the truck, religious tracts of various kinds and a Bible. He said that he slept there, but I had trouble believing that he did it very often in winter because the cab of a pickup is very cold. I know that for a while he had a room in a boardinghouse. He lived for a time in a white businessman's storefront, and his clothes were stored—after he was evicted from his rooming house—at our place and at an old couple's house a block behind the plaza. He might have slept there too, but he never slept at our apartment. The man for whom I worked in the auto repair shop, Telemachus, told me not to let Boycie keep his suits up in our apartment because he would try to move in. I let Boycie do it anyway, and he didn't try to move in. I know that Boycie's mother refused to let him keep much in her rooms. As far as I know the only thing of his she permitted there was a Polaroid picture of Karen and me that Boycie insisted he wanted to keep.

Boycie was probably an alcoholic, although I could not think of him in that way. When talking to Boycie and the other black people I was living with and studying, I felt as if I were lying on my back in the basement of our culture crushed by the weight of the stratified and affluent middle classes somewhere above me. I could not reach up to them, they were beyond my grasp.

A boy about eleven came by as we sat there, and Boycie asked him if he had any change. The boy by way of response said that he was on his way to the store which implied he had no change, only bills. Boycie turned away from the boy and he and I continued to talk. A man in his early twenties stopped to talk. He carried a Bible and several other books. He asked Boycie if he wanted to buy a book that commented on the Scriptures. Boycie told the salesman that the books he had sold Boycie earlier were still in the pickup truck and he was reading through them slowly and had not finished. They talked for a few minutes and the man walked on. Boycie greeted others and asked for quarters. I sat next to him quietly when he talked to people he knew and was his conversationalist when there was no one nearby.

The same eleven-year-old boy returned from the store with groceries in his arms and Boycie asked him for any change he had. The boy said he had to take the change home to momma. Although he was not yet out of earshot Boycie turned to me and said, "That's my son. He's doing the right thing." Boycie was proud of the fact his son had not given him any change, which showed that the boy minded his mother. He entered the project and disappeared from sight.

We collected enough quarters to get drunk that night on cheap, sweet wine.

Begging for quarters, I suppose, would be defined by the United States Internal Revenue Service as a part of the underground economy, but Boycie, *scrambling* on a daily basis for what he needed to live, engaged in a local circular flow of money, goods, services, and communications that for the most part existed outside the purview of white society. In the literature on blacks, particularly in the autobiographies of pimps and players, this mode of exchange has been termed the *hustle,* and it connotes a con game in which the mark is taken. I want to expand thinking beyond the term and what it evokes. Because I lived on the street, entirely within the underground economy, except for my modest stipend from the university, I came to play with others according to the discourse of give and take. This form of inter-personal trade seemed to me to be language-like, a lingua franca among black people that could be found in western urban Africa, the Caribbean, and America's southern and northern black communities. When people needed and asked for something that another had, they received part of what they asked for. And when first parties wanted a return on what they had given, they only received partial repayment. This kernel of the exchange constitutes the heart of the hustle and of everyday exchange relationships in which vital elements such as food and sex were given and received. This kernel interactive feature, which bound people up in larger and larger net-works, was understandable to anyone engaging in them, but at the same time, everyone expressed their dissatisfaction with what went on. No one was satisfied. Neither those who gave nor those who got. As a result people expressed hard feelings.

Along with the negative emotional tone to the constantly discounted trades, an instant credit system was instituted. It seems unlikely that peo-ple unhappy with what they had received would return for more, but that is exactly what did happen. Since both those who gave and those who re-ceived were continuously complaining to the community at large about how they had been shortchanged, they constantly sought to obtain more from their exchange partners than they had received on the last round of give and take. I came to believe that lower-class blacks, and certainly urban ones, could meet perfect strangers and in nearly any locale engage people there with the rudiments of the discourse of exchange I have just outlined. In-deed, the shop where I worked was run along the lines of the street hustle, and I came to understand what went on from hard experience even if I failed to develop a fluent ability to conduct the round of trades and expressions of hard feelings and demands for further consideration which the hustle exchanges required.

I would like to stress the instant credit quality of the hard feelings mode of the face-to-face economy. This is the way people became bonded over long periods of time. Because people felt they were owed by others, they were always, as it was said, *in one another's face.* Incredible intimacy was created by these exchanges by the hard feelings and the endless discussions that attended them. Finally, there were no third parties who could, like some supreme judge, decide between competing claims. For this reason in part, I think, people were armed—and everyone was. Persons had to be their own collection agency for what was owed and had to be their own judge in the litigations that often enough attended the buildup of hard feelings over unsatisfactory trades. No one seemed afraid to argue, and weapons were faced with an impunity that, as I witnessed with great sadness, ended all too often in death.

Here was an America that had not been completely infiltrated by middle-class modes of exchange or formal institutional frameworks, such as the courts, that evolved to control them.[1] I was in an invisible zone of American life, as Ellison would understand; it was simply never glimpsed by whites in the middle classes. If working-class whites in contact with blacks knew about it and learned it, they did not write it up as contributions to ethnographic literature. I think part of the phenomenal resourcefulness of the black community in light of staggering relative scarcities in a capitalist consumer society is due to the instant credit quality of the face-to-face economy that involves everyone every day. Due to the barrier between races, a black cannot use the hard feelings mode of exchange with whites (or is the barrier there so blacks cannot?). You have to be in the community to feel the demand, pay what is requested, and ask for what you legitimately need at some later time.

Now, seventeen years later while living in a village that since World War II has been transformed into a suburb of Philadelphia, one of the people I have gotten to know recently is Gaetano Ciccione, who lives a couple of blocks away. I think Gaetano has moved here to distance himself from his family, which in the last generation moved from South Philadelphia to the suburbs near the Main Line. Three generations ago they were Sicilians. I cannot ask him if he is attempting to put space between himself and his relatives, but when I am with him I feel he has made that choice. One day he picked me up in his car and drove to show me the suburb where his uncles and cousins live and another suburb where his father lives. He has removed himself from that proximity by moving here. They all still work together, unhappily, in the same family firm, a very large kitchen utensil manufacturing plant in South Philadelphia. His maternal grandfather started the company and his father married into it. On his father's side there is a consanguineal closeness to a recently murdered Mafia family head from South Philadelphia, about which people speak only quietly, if at all, and about which he says nothing to me.

Last fall I was over at his house at dinnertime and he invited me to stay for pasta. I was happy to stay, and afterward we went into the basement, which has a garage at one end. Gleaming under the electric lights was a white 1961 Ferrari Testa Rosa. He opened the doors and hood and we looked into the interior and engine compartment. I asked if I could get in. He said, "Sure." My stereotype of the Ferrari was of an expensive, unreliable automobile, but my naive belief was soon shattered.

"Let's take the T. R. for a ride," he said. I could hear the enthusiasm for the idea in his voice. But he tempered the fun, or perhaps increased the pleasure, by explaining that he had imported it for a cousin who lived in Italy in order to sell it here, and it was not licensed or insured. He had a bank note on it and needed to sell it quickly in order to pay off the note. The bank had expressed a little reticence in advancing him the money as it was. But I said okay anyway, not having ridden in anything as exotic as this car. My only experience with high-priced vehicles had been to ride briefly around Moline, Illinois, with the chairman of the board of John Deere and Company in his Rolls-Royce.

The Ferrari was nothing like the Rolls. As we drove into the night at a street corner not far from the house he said, "Watch this!" He put the car into first gear and slammed the accelerator to the floor. We accelerated like a rocket. I had never before felt anything like it in an automobile. By the time we arrived at the first turn off the road, less than a quarter mile, he had just shifted into second. He quickly braked, and downshifted, and then took the corner under power. "We were doing better than a hundred back there," he said. I found it plausible, but still incredible. It was indeed a world-class machine and I began to understand the wild enthusiasm, the seductive power, the addictive quality that captivates the Ferrari purists like some sweet opiate. He told me that every Ferrari has a registered pedigree and is documented through the course of its existence, something like yacht registry. An owner can look up a vehicle in Gerald Roush's *Ferrari Market Let-*

ter, a de facto American catalogue raisonné of Ferraris, and not only find out where it's been and who has owned it but know as well that what fate holds in store for that car will one day be recorded in that book.

When hockey season rolled around, Gaetano asked me if I would like to go with him to a game. He said we would eat at Dante and Luigi's restaurant in South Philly and then go to the Spectrum to catch the Flyers. I liked the idea but did not anticipate before going that the seats at the game and the dinner were provided by the company. We left our suburb and he drove us down Philadelphia's treacherous Schuylkill Expressway. We turned off the expressway and cruised in his big Mercedes into South Philadelphia. It was as if I had been suddenly transported in time back to my fieldwork there fifteen years before. Then I had associated only with black people; I had not allowed myself to get to know whites, including the Italian-Americans. I had not gone exploring in white residential or commercial space. My research had the qualities of island ethnography, but my island had been inside black cultural life. Now I was cruising into South Philadelphia from the other side, from the white side. I was within a block of where I begged with Boycie, then as we drove to the factory, where he showed me around before dinner, we were only two blocks away, but there was simultaneously a universe of cultural distance from the place where I had lived for two years and feared for the quality of my life from cops, co-workers, and adventurous neighbors. The epiphany was like some suddenly opened sky, some revelation that swept through me. Here I was in corporate America, in the white manufacturing, commercial, and residential space of the Italian-American community, and I realized with new intensity that there were two worlds: the private, chartered corporate life of those who manufactured and ran businesses, and those who in remarkable and distressing contrast hustled on the street for the necessities, people who, like Boycie, *were essentially and in nearly every way outside corporate America.* This polarity cut through the black working and welfare class. Gaetano's family owned their own business, and it seemed that nearly all the families of the nearby Italian Market had a legally incorporated concern whether it was large or small scale, or trafficked in legal or illegal goods. And there seemed at that moment in moving from white to black, driving into South Philadelphia as a white person and not as a black person (which in a sense was the way I had absurdly moved fifteen years before), I was confronted with a fine but un-

Secrecy
false-pretenses

giving dividing line between the street hustles and face-to-face exchange economy of Boycie and most of the others I had known, the theatrical life of performance on the street, and the world of the white shop and corporation owners that began a mere block away.

For me as for other naturalistic observers who spend much of their lives studying people, the epiphany of realization was not an indulgent or even psychiatric *aha* phenomenon. Rather, it was, in the case just recounted, a sudden formation of connections between fieldwork experiences and the immediate sense of a larger cultural order. The reader will legitimately ask what an ethnographer does with a moment of epiphany. In my situation there has been for the past decade a concern with the forms of American life that organize our culture: in a word, *corporations*. I use the moment of realization to try to come to terms in a provisional way with the range of field experiences I have had in this country: black with white, lower with middle and upper class, urban with rural, and the unincorporated or partially enfranchised with those who are fully accredited members of the American corporate polity and mainstream cultural life.[2]

Notes

1   For a fuller account, see Rose 1987.

2   I have pursued this epiphany in recent work. See Rose 1990 and Rose 1991.

References Cited

Hayden, Robert. 1985. *Collected Poems*. Ed. Frederick Glaysher. New York: Liveright.

Rose, Dan. 1987. *Black American Street Life: South Philadelphia, 1969–1971*. Philadelphia: University of Pennsylvania Press.

———. 1990. "Quixote's Library and Pragmatic Discourse: Toward Understanding the Culture of Capitalism." *Anthropological Quarterly* 63:155–68.

———. 1991. "Elite Discourses of the Market and Narrative Ethnography." *Anthropological Quarterly* 64:109–25.

Wittgenstein, Ludwig. 1980. *Culture and Value*. Ed. G. H. von Wright, trans. Peter Winch. Chicago: University of Chicago Press.

4

I'm Going to Say It Now:
Interviewing the Movement
Alessandro Portelli

A Paradox: The Missing Oral History of 1968

When the Italian student movement broke out, between the end of 1967 and the beginning of 1968, I was not around. I had just completed my law degree and was serving my stint in the air force. But precisely because I was in the service through the first few months, I could identify with the anti-authoritarian spirit of the movement; and even through the biased reports of a generally hostile press, I could tell that its essential meaning was a huge battle for free speech. Young people were tired of being talked about, they were determined to speak for themselves.

The movement spoke to itself in countless meetings, great and small, and addressed the outside world mainly by means of the megaphone and the mimeograph. These forms of communication suggest that the speakers were many, perhaps as many as the listeners, and that their acts of speech were intended to be quick and ephemeral: a leaflet and a speech in a meeting are easily made, and easily discarded and forgotten. The movement's words were meant to be accessible now, not to last forever. When Phil Ochs sang "I've got something to say, sir, and I'm going to say it now," the key word was *now*. And although Ochs referred to the Berkeley Free Speech Movement, his song is also applicable to the Italian situation.

This has important consequences for the historical perspective on the movement, and especially for its oral history. Much has been written about the student movements of the 1960s and 1970s, especially around the twen-

tieth anniversary year, 1988; but there has been little serious historical research, and hardly any oral history. The bulk of this literature was composed
of ambiguous reminiscences: leaders' autobiographies, a few controversial
pamphlets, a great deal of discussion on whether the student movement was
anything but the breeding ground of terrorism, or whether terrorism was
a betrayal of the movement. The exceptions were few, and hardly any used
oral sources. Luisa Passerini wrote a fascinating book (1989), combining
autobiography, oral history, and the history of her own historical research,
on a path of self-discovery through the critical rethinking of those years.
Her work was part of an international project on the history of student
movements which resulted in the excellent book (Fraser 1988) that failed
to find an Italian publisher. I had included some interviews with student
activists in my oral history of Terni (Portelli 1986), which was, however, as
peripheral to the movement as those interviews were peripheral to the book.
Cesare Bermani and the radical history journal *Primo Maggio* regularly
published interviews and conversations with members of the New Left, but
concentrated mostly on the working class and on the 1970s. Autobiographies
and books of interviews by and with former terrorists also included reminiscences of 1968, but always in the perspective of what came later. The
archival situation is also disappointing: while this is true for the whole oral
history situation in Italy, the history of the 1960s is especially scattered and
undocumented.

Now, this is a serious paradox. Oral history, at least in the shape it has
taken in Italy, can be considered in many important respects a product of
1968. Of course, it existed before: Gianni Bosio, Danilo Montaldi, and Rocco
Scotellaro had used and been aware of oral sources, in different forms, since
the late 1950s. After 1968, both Bosio and Montaldi joined (again in different and almost antagonistic forms) the broad New Left originated by the
student movement (Scotellaro had died years before). The political tension
and the focus on subjectivity that have characterized most of Italian oral
history in the 1970s and even in the relatively quiescent 1980s, both in and
out of the academic field, can be traced back to these origins.

I will try to discuss the paradox of the missing oral history of the
movement with reference to two aspects: the formation of sources (the
expression of 1968), and the collection of sources (research about 1968). The
most important factors influencing the formation of sources are the tech-

nology of the word, the social composition of the movement, and the movement's forms of discourse. The most important factors concerning the collection of sources in historical perspective are those which make up the classical parallelogram of forces of all interview situations: the relationship between observer and observed, and the relationship between narrated self and narrating self.

The Formation of Sources

Let us begin with what I have called (lifting a phrase from W. J. Ong), the technologies of the word. The student movement of the 1960s is the first mass movement entirely originated in the electronic age. It is also the first mass movement whose entire membership is highly literate, by definition the most highly educated portion of the population. Therefore, the student movement did not entrust its collective memory to the individual memories of its members, or, at least, did so to a much lesser extent than earlier mass movements. Oral narration and memory, storytelling and reminiscence were, rather, restructured within a general reorganization of the technologies of the word. This process runs through all of the modern age, beginning at least as far back as the invention of printing, but it undergoes a sudden acceleration in the years of the movement. I would describe this process as one of focalization and intensification of certain forms of orality: the very presence of printing and writing encourages the uses of the word, and therefore (as all literate cultures do), the movement reads and writes obsessively but also speaks a great deal, and does not worry about having to save its words for the future.

Since other ways of preserving words are now available, the voice is no longer needed to transmit identity and memory through time. Rather than certifying and consolidating identities, memories, and events, orality is free to improvise, to converse, to interact loosely on the spot, reacting to the immediate situation. Liberated from the burden of public functions, orality is made available for the expressive functions of the individual self. For the first time, the speech of a mass movement reserves so much room for informal, ephemeral, personal expressions of subjectivity.

Hence, a problem for coeval fieldworkers. A movement was being created under our own eyes, and we had the machinery to record it (the 1960s were also the age of the relatively inexpensive portable tape recorder), but we didn't know *what* to record. Like Bob Dylan's Mr. Jones, we knew that "something is happening here," but we didn't know what it was. Unlike Mr. Jones, we reacted by listening, and keeping all our organs and instruments indiscriminately open.

One of the effects of 1968 on me was the decision to go back to school (to study literature, this time); the other, to buy a tape recorder and join the Istituto Ernesto de Martino, a Milan-based group of independent radical historians, folklorists, and musicians. On purchasing the tape recorder, I received from my two Istituto de Martino mentors, Franco Coggiola and Gianni Bosio, the two pieces of advice which were to be all my training previous to undertaking fieldwork: don't place it on the table unless you want to pick up the engine's hum, and never turn it off. I sometimes forgot the former; the latter, never.

The rule of keeping the tape running at all times descended from the political nature of the Istituto's origins and work: it was interested in people's lives, rather than in their folklore, and by keeping the machine open it signified to them that we were interested in all of what they had to say, that we did not break the contact. But in the environment of 1968, this approach had an additional value: we did not discriminate because we had no framework for discrimination. The recording of the movement was linked to what, at that time, we referred to as the question of "urban research." The Istituto de Martino took its name and impulse from the work of the historian and ethnologist Ernesto de Martino, who had been the first to tie ethnological research with the advent of popular movements in the rural south of Italy and in the Third World. Bosio's idea was to carry de Martino's insights to the industrial north. The methodological background of the Istituto's work, therefore, came from the experience of ethnological and folklore research in the rural south; but there was very little folklore visible in the urban industrial environment. Therefore, although we did collect and store everything (including scores of personal narratives, anecdotes, oral histories), what we knew to look for and to work with were the formalized structures of expression we had found in rural contexts: folktales, rituals, songs, proverbs, and so on.

This emphasis on form was also related to our unconventional reliance on sound rather than writing as our prime form of communication. The Istituto de Martino was one of the motors of the Italian folk revival, through the Nuovo Canzoniere group of musicians and songwriters; much of Bosio's own historical research was published in the form of long-playing records rather than books (I followed his lead: my work with the Rome homeless people's movement produced a record of songs, sounds, and sayings, rather than a documentary book). In spite of our extreme austerity, by selecting concerts, rallies, and records as our prime form of communication, we had to make allowance, if not for entertainment values, at least for aesthetic ones, and for forms which could retain the attention of an audience.

None of these were forthcoming in our first approach to urban situations. The homeless people's movement, in which I was active, was an exception, since it was made up mostly of rural southern immigrants, who still used the traditional folk forms. But the city itself was something else, and the industrial city par excellence, Milan—which is where our ultimate target, the working class, was more concentrated—was much harder to crack than a basically southern metropolis like Rome. I recall a tape in the Istituto de Martino archives, in which someone in Milan had simply stepped down to the corner and turned the tape recorder on: we don't know what to look for, so let us just start listening to whatever sounds the city makes. This was quite something else from going to some country person (or southern immigrant) and asking them to sing "Lord Randal" (which I did collect in Rome): from the full formalization of folk culture, we were going toward the apparent formlessness of the urban environment, and were not yet ready to distinguish between noises, sounds, words, speech, discourse, form.

Thus, we used the tape recorder much like a candid camera. We would just automatically shoulder it and turn it on wherever we went. Gianni Bosio taped the incidents in Milan in 1969, in which a policeman was killed and the student movement was blamed. His tapes proved that it was not so, but they were not admitted as evidence in court; and no one bought the long-playing record of noises, police whistles, screams, snatches of conversation that he created from those tapes (Bosio 1970). I hid my machine under a loose overcoat and taped the policemen who were evicting the squatters in Rome; the record (Portelli 1970) had some songs in it (one was later a folk hit of sorts) so it found a few buyers. We were recording events, but were not interacting with them. And, contrary to positivistic myths, interaction is what makes research meaningful, because it implies a project, a perspective and interpretation—flexible, replaceable, open, but always there. The paradox is that, since we *were* helping organize the squatters or demonstrating against the police, we were in fact "interfering," as activists; but our mixture of positivistic ideology and radical criticism of the division of labor and roles induced us to step back and disappear, as researchers. In Bosio's phrase, we were creating the sources for future history; but we were not doing historians' work yet. *any implied propaganda.*

We recorded situations, collective and public events: demonstrations, meetings, sit-ins, and dozens of long, drawn-out, free-form conversations, in which there was no distinction between the person behind the tape recorder and those in front. The political, social, personal homogeneity of the fieldworkers with the movement prevailed on the distance which is as necessary to fieldwork as empathy is. We were not participant observers, because our participation overcame our observation; which was also due to the fact our observation was obfuscated to begin with by our lack of a clear idea of what we were supposed to observe (one consequence is that the mass of taped documents we collected became very hard to index or describe, and has, therefore, been used much below its potential). I did dozens of interviews with squatters and Bosio and Cesare Bermani with radical working-class activists and leaders, but no one thought of doing interviews with movement people: the sense of otherness, which is inherent to the interview approach, and which we felt in terms of class and/or generation with labor or homeless people, was missing in our relationship with the student movement (even though all of us, including myself, were at least slightly older). It would have been like interviewing ourselves.

The magmatic shape of the movement's urban discourse was not, indeed, totally without form. Some of these forms were precisely the ones we had always looked for—songs, for instance. On March 1, 1968, the students in Rome, for the first time, fought the police in front of the School of Architecture at Valle Giulia. When Paolo Pietrangeli (a member of the Nuovo Canzoniere) wrote a song about it, it did not merely glorify the event but also expressed very vividly the subjective changes which had made it possible:

> And your eyes looking at me seemed tired now
> But more important things were going on:
> Down with the bourgeois schools,
> Down with the bosses . . .

The song voiced the collective discovery of the *personal* meaning of politics (the reverse of the political meaning of the personal, which characterized the 1970s): a tired love relationship was less important than an incipient revolution (I'm afraid at the time I reacted negatively to the song because it was too "subjective," not political enough . . .). We had been looking for folk songs, and "Valle Giulia" was clearly not a folk song. It had not been created by the working classes or the rural proletariat—conspicuously absent at Valle Giulia—but composed by an educated middle-class individual. It had not gone through oral tradition: as soon as Paolo composed it, we printed it on vinyl and distributed it in record stores. There were long discussions on the nature of these new protest songs and their relationship to the tradition of radical folk music; and we were gratified when another of Pietrangeli's songs, "Contessa," spread orally through the movement and became a collective property. But we were not prepared to analyze the relationship of vinyl to folklore and mass movements, or to think of these songs as an expression *of* the movement, as inherent to it as Joe Hill's to the IWWs, rather than a commentary *about* it. Once more, something was happening, but we didn't know what it was; on the other hand, let it be said in fairness, whatever it was, we were the ones who created, sang, printed, and distributed it.

Slogans are another example. In all respects, a slogan is a "folk" expression, from oral transmission and variation to formalized rhetoric and metrics resembling the proverb and the "stornello" down to the closest thing that ever existed to Gummere's communal creation (by the "demonstrating throng"). Yet, we never took them seriously. I remember some desultory conversations in the late 1960s, and then I never thought about them again until ten years later, when I wrote an essay, and tried to make a record, about workers' (not students') slogans.

The most collective form, however, was the movement's speech itself. The discovery of "Left-ese" by the conservative media in the 1970s was one of the most effective tools of the deconstruction of the movement: the first step in our defeat was the ridiculing and stereotyping of the way we spoke. This was made possible by the fact that the movement itself had never seriously thought about its own linguistic creativity. When this cultural aggression came, it found us unprepared, without data and without a theory (besides, we had just discovered "irony," and thought it was a good and healthy way of laughing at ourselves), and it literally silenced us.

The Collection of Sources

I have done no systematic interviewing about the student movement. But I know that the very cornerstones of the interview experience were very different from my previous or current fieldwork with Italian steelworkers and Kentucky coal miners.

I said that oral history, in Italy, is to a large extent a result of 1968. This means that whenever oral historians tackle 1968 they are involved in something akin to autobiography—maybe not personally, but scientifically, inasmuch as we are dealing with the roots of our scientific identity and method. Even though I was not present at the "battle" of Valle Giulia, I am doing autobiography when I interview people about it, because it was one of the events which molded the very tools I am using, my very approach to reality. Since so much of the political debate about 1968 has to do with its legitimacy (was it terroristic? was it totalitarian? was it anticultural?) by exploring 1968 I am exploring the legitimacy of my own work. This is why Luisa Passerini was so right in her book, twining together her own autobiography, the history of 1968, and her own collecting of that history.

The other difference of which I am acutely conscious concerns generational distance. The longer I work with oral history, the more I realize that something has changed. For one thing, I am getting older: when I began, there used to be at least thirty, often fifty, years between myself and the narrators; now, the distance gradually flattens and tends to disappear. Indeed, when I interview movement people, it is usually reversed altogether: they are younger than I. My whole relationship to this history changes: I am no longer collecting memories of events that happened before I was born, but versions of events that I am old enough to remember; I have less a sense of the past, more a sense of contemporaneity.

Even with miners or steelworkers, I found that being of the same generation means sharing many experiences and memories. Not only did we listen to the same records, we belong to the first generation that made listening to records a form of collective identification. The dialogic nature of all interviews is made even more tangible when there is so much in common. Interviewing the movement belies the theater of abstraction and detachment, the "playing dumb" which is so often exchanged for a good objective interviewing technique. It may make sense for me to ask a Kentucky coal miner "What happened in Evarts on May 5, 1931?" or a Terni steelworker "Who won the local elections in 1920?" (a battle between miners and gun thugs; the Socialist party): the narrators can assume that I don't know the answers, because I am a foreigner, or so much younger. But when a movement activist says "My initiation was Paolo Rossi" (a student killed by the Fascists at the University of Rome in 1966), it makes absolutely no sense for me to ask "who was Paolo Rossi?" The inevitable reply would be, "Who are you trying to kid? You were there, or you should have been."

The interviewees' relationship between narrating and narrated self is also different. The activists of 1968 have gone through a very peculiar phase of history. In these twenty years, history has been much faster than at other times, the pace of change much quicker. Can we really remember ourselves before women's liberation, before the environmental movement, before color TV?

These twenty years have also generated deep changes in the way people look at themselves. The "me decade" was not as intense in Italy as in the U.S., but the politics of private life, the auto-analysis approach learned from the women's movement, the role of imagination and subjectivity, the new legitimacy of mass culture have all given us a different outlook on ourselves. Many of the people we talk to have gone through traumatic experiences and radical personal changes: yuppism and success have created as many fragmented identities as jail, terrorism, the crumbling of many pillars of our faith and actions. To some, 1968 is a faded memory, to others a gnawing guilt.

Finally, the very process of remembering has come under attack in these years. On the one hand, the "now" culture of the mass media combined with the political propaganda which depicted 1968 as a whole big mistake which was best forgotten. On the other, certain influential thinkers and groups on the extreme left actively fought against memory as a piled-up, ossified burden of tradition hindering the revolutionary new. The two approaches were not as separate as they might seem; they often overlapped and communicated and fused in the name of "modernity": the only "good" 1968 was the "modernizing" one, especially with reference to lifestyles, the one which gave us divorce and rock, abortion and a new look.

The distance between narrator and narrated self is, for comparatively young people, immense. A miner or steelworker in his seventies has less difficulty remembering the 1920s than many a forty-year-old ex-activist has remembering the 1960s—not because the change has been less wide (steelworkers have color TV, too), but because it has been more gradual. And, most importantly, because the change took place at a different time in the personal life cycle.

The student movement was a movement of adolescents; its members were eighteen, twenty years old; they were in a personal state of flux while all these social changes were happening around them. It all took place at a time in history when the definition and duration of adolescence were being stretched to unprecedented limits. Old steelworkers or miners can remember what they were doing at the age of seventeen, because in most cases they were already engaged in their adult occupation, working at the mill or the mine. But for student activists, the combination of osmotic but constant biological change with dramatic historical change makes it difficult to stabilize in memory the forms and times, the very terms of the change that has occurred.

The Battle of Valle Giulia

Different personal histories influence recollections of the same event. The "battle of Valle Giulia," on March 1, 1968, was a traumatic experience, almost an initiation, for a generation of students: for many, it was the first confrontation with the police; for all, it was the first time that the students fought back. As Paolo Pietrangeli sang: "Suddenly, a new thing happened: we didn't run, we didn't run anymore." All narrators focus on the moment they first saw the police; but their perceptions and memories diverge sharply:

> *Massimo.* And then we reach via Gramsci, in front of the School of Architecture, and we see the police and the *carabinieri*—more numerous than we expected, ready for war, organized.

Lucio. They were few, and not very warlike. Indeed, what really struck me was that they were old, or at least that is how I remember them. Old, and few, and relaxed, too, like us. We stepped on to the gate as if it were the most natural thing in the world, and suddenly they attacked us.

Raul. I mean, they were really no good—they were funny, they were ugly—they looked like they had their asses on backwards . . . they wore those heavy overcoats that hindered them running.

The recollection is influenced, first of all, by the subjective state of mind at the time. According to Massimo, as the students walked toward the School of Architecture, "it was a demonstration without slogans, tense and silent." "The demonstration," says another narrator, "was like a holiday, relaxed." Everybody remembers the slogans; a verse of Pietrangeli's song repeats them. Massimo, apparently, came prepared to find a state of war (and comparatively prepared to fight back: "it's not as though we hadn't foreseen violence—but throwing eggs or something. I mean, that was the level of violence then"); Lucio was taken by surprise. Massimo was tense, while most of the others were in a mood of celebration. This confirms a finding of all oral history work on collective events: masses of people may be involved, but individuals always came with different reasons, expectations, states of mind.

The other influence is later personal history. It would be silly to attempt deterministic interpretations of these contrasting recollections; it strikes me, however, that of the three witnesses Massimo is the one who has changed least since then. He has always been associated with the most "unruly" ultra-left element, which made almost a cult of fighting the police; therefore, his vision of the movement's history contains a large military element. Valle Giulia is a historical event but also a founding myth, and it sustains this militant identity. Lucio, on the other hand, was active in the same groups as Massimo for a few years; he was later arrested and tried (some of us say, framed) for terrorism, and found innocent after spending a couple of years in jail awaiting trial. He sees Valle Giulia in the perspective of the violence and repression that came later; perhaps, he also tries to project an "innocent" image of 1968, as opposed to those which see it as the seedbed of political violence and terrorism. Certainly, he has given the question of violence more thought than all the others. Raul, finally, was always identified with the moderate wing of the student movement; he plays down the role of physical repression in order to emphasize the cultural and political struggle. A final paradox: according to Sandro Medici, an expert journalist who has studied the police records on that day, the police presence at Valle Giulia was "a small but powerful and well-trained army. . . . It was a true military operation." It seems that Massimo is right after all.

While these three versions are, at least partly, a matter of opinion and judgment, two other testimonies differ in terms of facts:

> *Roberto.* I can still feel the impact of the tear gas cans they shot, way up in the air, very naively, in a curve. This was the first and last time I saw tear gas that didn't go further than fifteen or twenty feet. In 1977, they were shooting straight at face level.

> *Maria.* [At Valle Giulia] It was bad, because they were shooting straight and low. I had never seen tear gas cans, and they were deadly.

Quite possibly, the police did both: they sent the cans up in the air to spread the tear gas, and they shot them straight and low to hurt the demonstrators (at least one person was killed in this way in the 1970s). The difference between Roberto's and Maria's testimony may simply be one of point of view, of where they were in the "battle." But the recollection is also influenced by their subjectivity, then and now. Roberto instinctively compares Valle Giulia with 1977 ("In memory", he says, "all these things overlap. Things don't come out unless you compare them and bounce them reciprocally"), a year in which shooting, on both sides, was definitely at face level. He was active in the movement then, and, like Lucio, sees Valle Giulia as a rather tame affair when compared with the battles of nine years later: "It was a violent morning, but not one of those days when you expect to be shot." On the other hand, Maria's subsequent political history is much less militant (though her ideas may be as radical to her), so Valle Giulia stands as the primal encounter with violence. While both Roberto and Lucio had some small political experience before Valle Giulia (they had been in the Communist youth movement), this was Maria's first demonstration; she still identified with her middle-class student status, and recalls being shocked at the sight of policemen beating up members of her own class like they did workers. Ironically, though they stand at opposite ends of the political spectrum of the Left, Maria's state of mind while walking to Valle Giulia was similar to Massimo's: she was in the process of breaking with her own class, and sees tension in what others see as a holiday ("In those days, demonstrations were all very tense, nervous.") Narrators seem to have a hard time separating their state of mind from objective events—perhaps because the real events and changes were talking place in the mind.

Thus, the stage of personal life cycle at which crucial events take place influences recollection and representation. In another article (Portelli 1991), I have remarked how working-class activists in Terni always thought of working-class history as a series of missed opportunities, but each set *the* crucial opportunity that was missed at the time of his own most intense involvement in historical events. The battle of Valle Giulia stands, clearly, as a beginning ("un fatto nuovo," "a new thing"), a sort of collective initiation. At the individual level, however, its image depends on whether the encounter with political violence and the question of responding to it were being raised for the first time or had been faced before. Thus, Raul's rather ironic view of the events at Valle Giulia must be seen not only in the context of his later political history but also of what came before: "My initiation, I mean the shock, was not in '68, but [the death of] Paolo Rossi. This is what turned me into a comrade, because I saw the fascists, I got beat up, I first thought about fighting back, because they were professionals, some of them would hold you and the others beat you up, a very scientific and shocking thing. And much more shocking to me, who after all was nothing but a democratic young man, was turning to the police for help and discovering that they were in league with the fascists."

The tendency of many narrators to represent the "battle" as less dramatic than it really was introduces the question of narrative forms. There is an implicit relationship between autobiography and irony: in both cases, the speaker steps outside and looks at him/herself as at another person. In the narratives of 1968 this ironic element is accentuated, symmetrically with the greater distance we have described between narrating and narrated selves. Thus, one recurrent narrative mood is steeped in irony and the mock-heroic style. The following is the history of the occupation of a high school in Terni in 1968:

Walter. In this first phase of the student movement, our demand was freedom of assembly. We wanted the students to have a room in which to meet, in every school. And, we carried out one of those actions—heroic, in quotes—which led to the occupation of a wing of the Technical Industrial Institute. I mean—to give you an idea of the conspiratory style of those days: we, the leaders, initially planned to occupy the building by climbing the outside wall with ropes at night, and barring the gates in the morning. And, I remember that the expert was supposed to be comrade Sandro Berarducci, because he was a member of the Alpine Club or something, so he was supposed to be an expert in knots, ropes, and all. Then, fortunately, rationality prevailed, and we followed another strategy. We were going to wait for the bell to ring the end of classes and then the comrades who were in school were going to have chains, nails, wrenches, and hammers in their bags, and they would hide in the toilets and after everybody had left they'd come out and bar the gates. We had to give up this solution, too, because our strategy was so secret that everybody knew about it, so our comrades were watched. In conclusion, at 3 P.M. we finally invaded the Technical Industrial Institute by walking in through the main gate—which had been closed earlier, very accurately, because everybody knew there was going to be an occupation; but we were able to sneak in, because a truck arrived carrying fuel for the heating system or something—so the gate was opened and we, thirty bold and daring young men, we walked in and barricaded ourselves inside. And we opened a meeting of struggle and protest. And the whole thing was, under certain aspects, comical. Under others, I don't want to exaggerate, not tragic, but dramatic.

The mock-heroic narrative style links the movement of 1968 with later student rebellions, including that of 1990. Fausto Ciabatti, a 1990 activist, describes his own testimony as "stories of ordinary mental dissolution about the very precocious senile dementia that the occupation generated. [I] wanted to show how in those moments lucidity just waned" (Arcidiacono et al. 1995).

As we already noted (and as Fausto's reference to Charles Bukowski confirms), this is an educated movement. Its rank and file have gone to elite high schools, so the mock-heroic mood is often heightened by parodic references to heroic examples drawn from classical history. When the police broke into the first sit-in at the School of Humanities in Rome, Raul is reminded of the first barbaric invasion of the republican Roman Capitol— "We waited for them like Roman senators, all seated, very decorous"—and the humorous contrast is enhanced by the fact that the police did not treat them "decorously" at all. Another mythical episode from ancient Roman history (the battle between two sets of brothers which settled the account after the rape of the Sabines) shapes Massimo's recollection of a scene at Valle Giulia: "It was getting hot, and the *carabinieri* were getting tired. I was running with three or four other comrades, and we stopped and turned, and there was only one of them left behind us. So I shouted: one of you against one of us, let's take off our coats and fight like men. He thinks it over for a second, and then starts taking his coat off to play the Curiatius."

But they were also young people of the 1960s, shaped by mass culture as well. They played soccer and read sports papers, they had grown up on a fare of western movies. And they were just out of childhood, too. The "conquest" of the School of Architecture at Valle Giulia is the crowning of the formative experiences of football, hide-and-seek, cowboys and Indians:

> *Raul.* At last we entered the School of Architecture. There were a few policemen in the hall, and Oreste [Scalzone, one of the leaders] made a very amusing speech—amusing, to think about now. That is, he granted them immunity if they went out with their hands up. Literally. Don't be afraid, he said; you shall not be hurt, just stick your hands up and leave. The cops were kind of surprised, too. It was fun. And it wasn't militaristic; it was the power of politics against the power of weapons; because we were completely unarmed but—the feeling was, we had won, we had made fools of them, we were home free.

References Cited

Arcidiacono, Micaela, Francesca Battisti, Sonia Di Loreto, Carlo Martinez, Alessandro Portelli, and Elena Spandri. 1995. *L'aeroplano e le stelle. Storia orale di una realtà studentesca prima e dopo la Pantera.* Rome: Manifestolibri.

Bosio, Gianni. 1970. *I fatti di Milano*. Milan: Dischi del Sole. Sound recording.

Fraser, Ronald, with Daniel Bertaux et al. 1988. *1968: A Student Generation in Revolt*. New York: Pantheon.

Passerini, Luisa. 1989. *Autobiografia di gruppo*. Florence: Giunti.

Portelli, Alessandro. 1970. *La borgata e la lotta per la casa*. Milan: Dischi del Sole. Sound recording.

———. 1986. *Biografia di una città. Storia, memoria e immaginario. Terni 1831–1984*. Turin: Einaudi.

———. 1991. "Uchronic Dreams: Working-Class Memory and Possible Worlds." In *The Death of Luigi Trastulli and Other Stories: Form and Meaning in Oral History*. Albany: State University of New York Press.

5
Living Dolls
Nancy Kalow

On a warm March day in 1987, I was on location in San Francisco shooting a documentary video on runaway kids. Waiting on a grungy bench at the corner of Market and Powell, I looked like a tourist with a small 8mm camcorder. I alone made up the entire production crew; I had no expenses to speak of, and no deadline. Perhaps there would be no documentary, either. At that moment, I was indeed a tourist, an outsider to the group I was trying to document. It was lunchtime, and I was hungry and restless. Where were the street kids who usually hung out at Market and Powell? Maybe they were headed to another part of the city, I thought to myself, to justify packing up and quitting for the day.

In the beginning of the project, a few months earlier, I would go off on my own to escape street people, to eat well, and to see old friends. I slipped away from the very people who were the subject of the documentary, which effectively turned my field trips into vacations. My first set of interviews barely scratched the surface; the street kids were talkative and charming, but I had no idea why they had run away from home. The kids hinted at their reasons for escaping seemingly normal, middle-class lives: "You'd rather be cold and hungry and living on the streets than being at home." "Home is a torture chamber." The writer and social worker who introduced me to members of one street "family," Grace Roberts, had told me that they were victims of physical and sexual abuse perpetrated by their parents. Grace acted as a mother hen for the runaways and eventually became foster mother to two, Juan and Tommy.

The pure luck that kept me at the Market and Powell bench decisively changed the progress of my fieldwork. That afternoon, a frightening encounter with the San Francisco police led to a deeper relationship with the runaway children. As I learned more intimate and painful details about their pasts, the gap between filmmaker and subject developed new contours, new bridges. I began to shun mainstream San Francisco on my visits to work on the film, and lived, ate, and spent all my time with street people.

At Market and Powell, Grandma Lasagna joined me and started to set up lunch. Now both of us were waiting for some runaways to show up. Grandma had a bucket of tuna salad for them. She brought food every day, dispensing a message from God with each serving. Finally, a group of kids approached, one on a skateboard. Several of them wore heavy makeup and Day-Glo mohawks, others were dressed in dirty sweatshirts, with baseball caps almost hiding their eyes. Their average age was about sixteen. They ate Grandma's tuna and chatted with her. A few in the group began to spare-change the tourists. The panhandled money didn't buy food; instead, the group drifted to a liquor store and someone old enough bought cheap red wine and 40-ounce bottles of beer. Then they paraded to an alley south of Market, just a few blocks from Union Square. The alley wall was covered with graffiti, mostly of their street tags: Mad Max, Poser, Tan Monkey, Misfit, Terry-Bash, Delphi. Broken glass, discarded clothes, and excrement were on the ground. It was Juan's fifteenth birthday, and they were having a party for him. No one minded that he didn't show up for his own party; they asked me to tape birthday messages for him. They started drinking and showing off. They sang songs like UB40's "Red Red Wine" and Run-D.M.C.'s "You Be Illin'." They performed songs and raps they had written. The mood was a happy one. Suddenly, three motorcycle cops burst into the alley, their sirens screaming. The party was over. Escape was blocked by police vans. My camera batteries were dead so I couldn't videotape the hush and terror of the scene: several officers roughly frisking fifteen children spread-eagled in a row against the alley wall. I was frustrated to miss the chance to capture the moment for my film and bewildered by my first experience with the brutal side of law enforcement. I faked an air of self-assurance, stepped up to the officer in charge, and shook his hand. I looked at my reflection in his mirrored shades and found myself saying, "Hello, I'm Nancy Kalow. I'm a folklorist from the University of North Carolina." I explained that I was working on a film about the folk culture of street kids. The officer's scowl was derisive; the other policemen turned to look me up and down. The kids still stood along the wall, but were watching with interest. The officer in sunglasses was put on the spot, so he responded to my words with a threat: it was illegal for minors to drink and everyone, including me, would be arrested for disturbing the peace. Bluffing desperately, I offered to play the police my videotapes to prove that the kids weren't drinking. They must have known I was lying; nevertheless, all of us were simply told to leave and the police disappeared as quickly as they had arrived. The kids were about to head back to Market and Powell anyway. They had run out of beer and wine. More kids had gathered there meanwhile, and they hung out until enough beer money had been panhandled again.

The kids changed their attitude toward me after I "negotiated" on their behalf with the cops in the alley. They didn't care if they were arrested or not, but it was someone actually standing up for them that counted. They were warmer and less polite with me, politeness based on Grace's recommendation that I was "OK." Now, they wanted to take an active role in the documentary, give advice, and endlessly watch themselves in the raw footage.

As I began to get to know the kids better, they seemed surprised that I was twenty-six. "I thought you were nineteen!" Margery said; she was sixteen at the time. I went through a fieldwork "honeymoon." For example, I looked for (and saw) only the best aspects of each individual. Many were articulate, creative, intelligent, and generous, especially to members of their street family. Later, the honeymoon was over: I saw their casual cruelty to one another. Similarly, the kids impressed me for being self-sufficient and capable. Later I saw their extreme fragility. I was optimistic that they would get off the streets and off drugs. Naively, I believed drugs and alcohol to be the problem; later it was apparent that living on the streets and drug use were the only ways the kids could cope with years of abuse at home.

Their loyalty to the street family initially seemed strong and unshakable. I thought that the emotionally stronger kids could help the more troubled ones. Tommy, a leader known as the "granddaddy" of the group, was especially adamant about the meaning of the family. "We all stuck up for each other, we all did things together, we all did things like a family would. We'd drink together, some of us would sleep together, and everybody looked out for each other." Margery, who used go out of her way to help other runaways and show the new ones the ropes, said "I felt that Tommy was my brother and that City Baby was my daughter." The street family seemed a viable replacement for uncaring parents. As Juan said, "People that care about you consider you part of their family, because they don't really have a real one."

The first indications I got that the kids couldn't take care of each other came during in-depth interviews. The intense identification that certain kids felt for their chosen role models surprised me. Margery, for example, felt remarkably close to Marilyn Monroe and read and reread her autobiography. She had an even closer bond with Nancy Spungen, who was killed by her boyfriend Sid Vicious, a member of the Sex Pistols. Both women, like Margery, had terrible childhoods and felt unloved. Margery's friend Jake was obsessed with concentration camps. Half the time he felt like a victim of the Nazis, and half the time like a member of the S.S., dressing up accordingly. Juan identified with Alex in *A Clockwork Orange.* He had seen the movie so many times that he had memorized it. "Alex was aggressive and insecure. In a way his parents never really loved him." Juan also compared himself with Bugs Bunny: "He talks shit to everyone, he fucks with everyone, he makes everyone look stupid, and he's skinny like me." The kids were trying to tell me something about their pasts when they told me about these characters, something they didn't feel comfortable telling me directly. Their profound hurt at being mistreated and rejected by their parents was something they did not like to admit.

I began to see that they couldn't play the role of parents when they so badly needed real parents. They fiercely defended the street family in concept, so I was shocked to see how easily it could betray itself and fall apart. At a time when Tommy had deteriorated and was sleeping in a construction site, members of his street family kicked him and pushed him as he walked by them. Some even beat him up and stole his clothes. Tommy, their "granddaddy," frightened them. He was what they would become if they stayed on the streets too long: he was desperate. He was doing "hot shots" of gasoline because he couldn't buy methamphetamine, known as crank. He was doing a lot of dates, often picking up johns who turned violent. He had a liver ailment, an abscess on his arm and plenty of other diseases. Tommy looked terrible on the day that Juan and I met him at the crowded McDonald's at Market and Powell. He was barely recognizable, spoke in a mumble, and warned Juan not to become like him. Irrationally, he insisted that he had to have $25 to buy a Filo-fax-type appointment book. "There are a lot of things I have to do that I can put in that book." He put handfuls of sugar and ketchup packets in his sweat-shirt to save for his next meal. For the next several days, Juan dwelled on Tommy in a series of interviews, as if he was trying to sort out in his mind what had happened to his "big brother."

Tommy's condition frightened me too. But I was lulled into optimism again a few months later on my next field trip. Tommy was on a tempo-rary rebound, again living at Grace's apartment. He was trying to stay off crank and start a new life, maybe go back to school. I was confident that he could. I spent most of a week with Tommy, during which I learned why he was prone to dramatic swings from stability to hopelessness. Tommy's off-hand comments and everyday behavior revealed more to me than his vague references to an abused childhood. What Tommy did say about abuse at the hands of his parents was painfully corroborated by his therapist in an in-terview for the film.

While I was grocery shopping with Tommy that week, he asked me to buy him some pacifiers. Tommy opened the packages before we got to the checkout, and chewed on one so vigorously that it fell apart. He popped another pacifier into his mouth, then two more, rolling them around hap-pily. I videotaped him with his pacifiers; he showed no trace of embarrass-ment. In contrast, he hated to be photographed by a still camera. It remind-ed him of how he was exploited as a child. He'd say, "Don't take my picture! There are a million pictures of me naked." I filmed Tommy playing card-board drums and an old guitar. Jimi Hendrix was his idol, but he also was greatly moved by some Black Sabbath songs about drugs. "'Push the Nee-dle In'—that's me in that song!"

He was terrified of being in public at that time. He was a speed freak trying to break his cherished habit. Tommy smoked pot throughout the day, so he could get by without the urge to shoot up speed. But being high all the time made him paranoid that everyone would notice and that the cops would bust him. He refused to stay at Grace's apartment except to sleep, because Juan was also visiting. Tommy and Juan, foster brothers, no long-er spoke to each other and the resulting tension was impossible for all. To keep the boys separated, I drove Tommy around the Bay Area, now and then stopping at the drive-up window of a Jack-in-the-Box (Tommy slyly referred to it as "Jack-in-the-Crack"). We stayed on the road for hours each day, returning to the apartment briefly and leaving again when Juan picked a fight. My rented car became littered with fast food cartons, crumbs, and ketchup. But Tommy could not, would not, get out of the car. While we drove around, from time to time I got the impression of something happening on the passenger side of the car. I'd look over, and Tommy would be looking out the window—all seemed normal. But I saw people in other cars looking strangely at ours. I realized that Tommy was somehow attracting attention; he was sending out some signal, seductive or mocking, that they were picking up. Once, four shirtless men in a pick-up decorated with Confederate flags started following us, yelling and making gestures. They took pains to make sure we saw them writing down our license plate number. They followed us closely through town after town in the Silicon Valley until they finally drove off. "What did you do to them?" I asked Tommy. "Nothing—I just looked at them," he insisted.

Tommy had spent five years on the streets by age sixteen but he was the least "streetwise" person I had ever met. Obviously, Tommy's parents never gave him that universal admonition, "never get in a car with a stranger." Diving into strangers' cars was part of his day-to-day life. Probably only a tiny segment of the Bay Area's population liked to hit on little boys, but it seemed that a lot of them found Tommy, or he found them. Tommy's behavior in my car showed he was completely open, with none of the protections I normally take for granted. Instead of avoiding people's gaze, he brazenly looked at them, sometimes working his mouth in a nervous fashion that could be read as obscene.

Back home in Chapel Hill, I would hear from Grace about Tommy's repeated cycles: degradation and illness on the streets followed by ever-briefer periods of calm normality. It was the same for many of the kids. Margery, whom I also got to know well, endured her own sorry pattern of crash, recovery, crash. Margery had originally seemed like one of the strongest of the street family, but she was actually the most vulnerable. She taught me the most about life on the streets and the painful reasons why the runaways left home.

The first time I met her, she was staying at Grace's apartment in an attempt to get off the streets. She was interested in the documentary but wary of being interviewed on camera, preferring to discuss her life with audio-only recordings. Her stories showed her wit, her love for the street family, and her disappointment with all the adults she had ever come into contact with. She explained how to forage for food in dumpsters and where to find a safe place to sleep. Then she began to describe the "sadobaby" dolls that were created by many of the runaways:

> A sadobaby is basically a doll that's been rejected by a factory. Actually, I found my sadobaby at a garage sale. I cut its hair on the side and I gave it a Mohawk and I put it up and I put some makeup on it and a few safety pins through its head. It lived in the trunk of [a] car for about nine months: a homeless sadobaby. My sadobaby's done quite a few things. Sadobaby has friends. There are a lot of sadobabies. Each individual person designs their own sadobaby. If they get mad they can throw their sadobaby against the wall. They kind of like it. They're masochists.

I knew the dolls would be a key element in the film, but I didn't see a sadobaby at all during that first field trip. A few months later, when I saw Margery again, I asked to borrow her doll to videotape it. The doll was dressed and coiffed to look exactly like Margery during her punk stage, three years earlier. Juan and Margery were now a couple, although she was living on her own in an SRO hotel called the Broadway Deluxe, and he was at Grace's apartment. When Juan saw Margery's sadobaby, he wanted to be videotaped with it. Juan theatrically launched into a sadobaby demonstration by enthusing, "This is what sadobabies are for!" He played with, taunted, insulted, scolded, kicked, and punched Margery's doll, while his friends, looking on, laughed knowingly.

Margery appeared to be doing well. She had dyed her hair blond, from bright blue, and was the lead singer in a band called Baby Alive. In interviews, I learned that she recently had several blows at once. Her father, the source of so much of her misery, had come back into her life, which disturbed her greatly. She feared that he would molest her younger sister as he had once molested her. Her mother and grandparents had made it clear that she was not welcome at their homes. She was trying to get away from certain old friends, but they kept harassing her, trying to get her to use drugs. I videotaped her on Market Street with two of these friends, young men hiding shotguns in long green coats; one of them gave her some jewelry. Margery also had something to hide: she secretly earned money by picking up tricks in front of a grand old hotel near Union Square. I accompanied her shopping one day; she bought what she nonchalantly called "whore boots": tight and high-heeled.

Margery's relationship with Juan disintegrated one evening at Grace's apartment. Margery confessed to Juan that she was a drug addict and a prostitute. Acting horrified, he bolted out the door, and stayed away for several hours. Margery asked me to drive her home to the Broadway Deluxe. She was calm but grim. A friend of mine, a stand-up comedian named Ed, accompanied us for the long drive. Always a discerning reader of his audiences, Ed got Margery to laugh, and the two of them told stories and jokes the whole way. Margery fixed us tea in her small room at 3:00 in the morning and talked about plans for her rock band.

Several months later I visited San Francisco again, staying at Grace's place. Juan and Tommy had moved out; now Margery was staying there. She was thin and pale, wearing oversized clothes and a new blond wig. Mysteriously, she wore a long tube of black fabric covering her left arm, like the torn-off sleeve of a leotard; she kept it on even under her nightgown. During my trip, I videotaped her in the empty Polytech High School building where her street family had lived. A city official concerned about the homeless came with us into the boarded-up school and asked Margery all sorts of prying questions, such as, "How do you live with the memories of your father sexually abusing you?" My video camera recorded Margery's faraway look as she replied, "I cut on my arm. Or I do a lot of drugs." Recalling her life at Polytech High made Margery excited and exhausted; by the end of the afternoon, she was almost in tears. The next day, she fell apart because of something that happened to Tommy.

Margery was the only member of the street family who still cared about Tommy. She helped Grace find him that day because he needed medical attention but wouldn't get it himself. The abscess on his right arm had rendered his hand paralyzed and was the size of a golf ball, bright red and horrible under the skin near his elbow. He was wandering around Union Square without his usual baseball cap, his outgrown mohawk dirty and straggly, wearing clothes three sizes too big for his emaciated sixty-seven pounds. In a surreal moment of cinema verité, I videotaped Tommy's drug dealer approaching him and then disappearing into the busy street after Tommy shook his head no.

He also said no to the idea of going to the hospital. When he finally decided to go, we couldn't get there fast enough. It was slow going along Market Street; we stopped at every traffic light and behind busses. Tommy wheezed and coughed, but also snickered at my driving. He sang out the foods he craved: "Make a left here and get me two tacos . . . I want McDonald's . . . gimme some gum." We got him a soda, then pulled into the emergency room drop-off. It was Friday night and the place was packed. Tommy said he was over eighteen and gave an assumed name, Brian Smith, afraid that his mother would be notified. Seeing Tommy lying on a stretcher in the waiting area, a woman asked, "Is he dead?" We stayed with him for three or four hours until he was treated. When we got back to Market and Powell, everyone already knew he was in the hospital. Apparently, other street people in the emergency ward got the word out.

The next day, Margery came to visit Tommy in his hospital room. He was in a great mood, blowing smoke rings and doing Humphrey Bogart imitations. The operation went well. He laughed when he told us one advantage of his drug abuse: "When they put in the IV, they found my vein right away." His girlfriend had just brought him some crank, but Tommy told Grace and me to "beat up anyone who uses drugs." He didn't like being an addict. He had every reason to lose patience with an uninvited visitor, a pipe-smoking narcotics counselor named Lloyd. The hospital gave Lloyd the run of the IV drug and alcohol abuse ward and he made the most of it, sitting next to a patient's bed for hours, talking about the twelve steps to quitting and the "higher power" we must all acknowledge. The guy was smarmy and arrogant. Tommy hated him so much that I took Lloyd to the hospital cafeteria for some coffee, just to get him out of Tommy's room. Unfortunately, Margery came too. She was familiar with this type of do-gooder who had all sorts of easy answers and who was not interested in any underlying causes for substance abuse. To them, addiction was a stand-alone problem that could be wiped out with a little willpower. Margery—already overloaded from the tour of Polytech High and dealing with Tommy's poor health—sat perfectly still while Lloyd lectured us and told us the merits of his techniques to reach the addicts: "I confront the shit out of these people in a really loving way." His thumbnail psychoanalysis of Tommy: "You see his tattoos? Brian has a love of death." When I saw Margery beginning to shake, we left the cafeteria. "He reminds me about everything I hate in the system—right down to his blowing smoke in my face. I want to knock him in the mouth. He's so sure he's got the only way to do things. Tommy's not some fuckin' person who stole mommy's lunch money!" Back at Tommy's ward, Margery paced in a small waiting room, getting more and more frantic and angry. She raged against "the system" that so inadequately dealt with runaways like herself and Tommy: the psychiatric hospitals, the group homes, the parole officers and courts, the cops, the counselors, and the rest. She trusted no one because all of these people, and her parents most of all, had betrayed her.

Later that night Margery was found in a bus station ladies room with fresh razor cuts on her left arm; she had been making small slashes under her black leotard sleeve for days. Twenty-three cuts, from her wrist past her elbow, required stitches. Although Margery checked into a psychiatric facility under the care of her longtime doctor, she said she would run away the next day to resume cutting on her arm.

Margery's physical wounds were terrifying evidence of how she felt about herself. Her internal pain was expressed on her arm while her overall appearance was angelic compared to her days as a shaved-head punk. Back then, she told me, "I made myself ugly because I felt ugly from my family. I'd be obnoxious on purpose. Because I'd be so fucking mad at everyone. Because I felt victimized and I thought other people should suffer." Other people did not end up suffering; instead, she did: she started cutting on her arm and taking drugs.

I flew back to North Carolina, sure that Margery was going to die (she didn't). A direction for the film emerged from my sorrow and determination to try to make a statement about the street family and their life that Margery would have endorsed. Through her eyes, the harshness of the streets always had a humorous and creative side that "normal" people never saw. To her, the "normal" people were the weird ones, always selfish and materialistic, always ready to exploit someone else's weaknesses. When dealing with runaways, the mass media focused on teen prostitution and drugs, not the underlying causes for running and certainly not the realities of day-to-day existence. TV news interpretations sounded one note: that the runaways were somehow to blame, not the adults. I could do something different and more true to the group of kids I knew. In the documentary, I decided to show street life solely from the point of view of the kids. I also highlighted the cops, the tourists, and the psychiatrists as examples of the adults who continually interact with the runaways. I was at a loss, however, in conveying the truth about the all-important relationship of the kids to their parents. I turned to the editing room to find what I needed in the footage; the messy and inspiring process of editing gave the film its direction.

At home, I started reviewing all the footage I had shot, and was taken aback to realize what I missed. A one-person crew has many advantages, but holding the camera while conducting the interviews created a big problem for me: I didn't "hear" what was said. One of these interviews, with Juan, turned out to be especially significant. During the editing process, I juxtaposed his conversation with his sadobaby doll batterings, allowing me to absorb what he was saying about his parents and childhood. During the interview itself, I saw Juan's light, couldn't-care-less attitude but didn't hear his words. Now, it was heartbreaking to watch him laughing on the videotape while telling me he is an alcoholic, that he likes to drink because it helps him put up a wall when sleeping on the street. In an offhand way, he explained the effect of incest on kids: "A lot of parents don't love their kids. If someone who gave you birth and who you look to for trust and protection, if they just beat you up or sexually molest you, you know what that does to a person? It makes them really insecure. It makes them have a wall that they hide behind. They show a tough outside but they're very fragile inside." Not five minutes later in the interview, he said, "I usually have this wall up above me. I was insecure." And as transparent and obvious an admission as this was, I didn't get it until I started editing.

In the same interview, Juan said of the runaways that "a lot of us are so fragile, like a porcelain doll." He also spoke about his own life before running: "My mom didn't really want me around. Plus my stepfathers would beat me up and she would just sit there and watch. Like I've had boards hit me across the head, pipes, I've had my tailbone cracked because of it, I've had ribs broken, I had my head thrown through a plate glass window, had my head smashed against walls, I've been kicked in the back. I mean I've had a pretty good childhood. She went through four husbands, and three out of four used to beat me up. The other wouldn't even talk to me."

I also reviewed the sequence of Juan playing violently with a sadobaby. He punches it, hard, while shouting, "Why aren't you at home? You're drunk. Who says you could drink? Where were you? Get to your room.

Don't sleep when I'm talking to you, stand up and take it like a man. What—get in the house right now!" Juan's tirade is a replay of what his father and stepfathers had shouted and done to him. Juan was the sadobaby. I found that each child, like Juan, performed scenes from his past with the dolls. Sadobaby "play" brought to life the abusive words and methods used by their parents. It was the central image for the film, and I discovered it, finally, in the editing room. The image was there all the time, but the meaning became clear only when I pieced it together in a sequence with other scenes.

In the final edit, I didn't include Juan's comments about the porcelain doll and his description of the injuries his stepfathers inflicted. His words made the connection between the sadobabies and the kids too direct and obvious. I edited to make sure viewers would come to the same discovery, that the kids themselves were the sadobabies. The structure of the completed film makes the sadobaby image especially potent by first pulling the viewer into the lives of Margery, Juan, and Tommy.

6

From Home to Prison:
A Personal Narrative
Carol Burke

In north central Indiana the fields run on like extended metaphors. Farmers, comfortable in their religion and Ford pickups, gather for coffee and conversation at "the Elevator." These hard-working people are proud of their Germanic past, proud to be forty-eighth in the list of states receiving federal aid, proud of their Mister Basketballs and Miss Golden Girls, proud of Purdue University, where even during the sixties you could send your son and know he'd come back to the farm.

In 1975, fresh out of graduate school, I moved from New York to Indiana with my husband, who had accepted a teaching position at Purdue, and for the next four years I interviewed families who lived on the surrounding farms and in nearby villages. In senior centers, in offices, in living rooms I gathered reminiscences from men and women who worked this rich black soil.[1] Reclaimed from bogs, this land once supported diverse crops and livestock. Now most of the cattle, the wheat, and the oats are gone; the traveler who passes through on I-65 can see at one time all the variety there is to see—thousands of acres devoted to the efficient, profitable production of soybeans and corn. The weather is still the farmer's most benevolent friend as well as his cruelest foe; but the weather now has formidable rivals for preeminence: the lobbies of Congress, the laboratories of universities, and the exchanges in Chicago and New York. No matter how much they have conserved, no matter how much they own, no farmers in this part of the state can hope any longer to live solely off the land.

In their stories, these farmers recalled a time when they were, of necessity, closer to the land: when the weather was forecast by the signs, when there was no insurance for crops. Residents of Wolcott, Remington, Reynolds, Chalmers, Brookston, and Monon shared with me stories of little money and much work, of school pranks, of chivarees, and of dates on bobsleds.

Nostalgic, they reconstructed a past rich with sentiment and suffering that somehow both justified and diminished their present prosperity. Their narratives celebrated times of scarcity when they'd burned corncobs because they could afford no coal, when they'd saved rather than borrowed, when they'd gathered together in threshing rings of twenty men to do the job that today requires two people and a $100,000 machine.

At first, their tales were reassuring: I knew I was in the land of genuine folk and authentic lore, replete with legends, tall tales, and accounts of pranks, remedies, superstitions, and cures. But after a couple years of hearing comfortable tales in comfortable living rooms, I seemed to sense a disjunction between these stories and the land itself, which to me appeared frighteningly open, too wide for a frame. I sought in their narratives some image, I guess, to coincide with my own of the danger or the fear of living in such geographic openness.

I remember driving on a narrow two-lane road after a morning collecting holiday traditions from a grandmother who still drove the tractor in the fields. The snow had been falling lightly all morning, but by the time I headed back to Lafayette it had thickened to what the farmers called a "white out." With no way to distinguish the blustery sky from the wavy white fields, no way to find the thin line of pavement once limiting it all, blinded by the white, I steered only by feel as my right tires slipped on and off the tarmac. But for such a precarious anchor to the land I could have been riding through sky.

And the springs could be as fierce as the winters. One spring a tornado chased me home. The oppressively heavy air silenced the streets of Wolcott; doors were shut, windows secured. The sky turned a strange mustard green as I headed down a deserted interstate, past the newly plowed fields—some deeply ridged, others disked smooth and ready for planting, but all rich and enticing to the violent swirling storm. The farmers said that the churning up of the soil in preparation for planting spawned these savage winds till they'd spin a great cord that would sweep the ground clean.

On this May afternoon I got back to Lafayette in time to pick up my ten-month-old daughter from the sitter's across the street. The sky cast a pale mauve; the air stood still as if anticipating its bruise. As I climbed the porch stairs of our white clapboard house, its siding strangely pinkish, I heard the loud tornado alarm warning all of us with basements to take refuge. Throughout the city everyone sought shelter: some in their carpeted, paneled basement rec rooms and others, like my daughter and me, on lawn furniture in the damp for over an hour awaiting the all-clear alarm when we'd surface into the fresher, cooler air.

As they emerged from their seclusion and their fear, my neighbors would compare notes on fallen limbs, loosened shingles, and past storms: "You should have seen the damage to the 7-11 on Sagamore Parkway last year." "I remember what it looked like in Elkhart after the Palm Sunday tornado; nothing could compare to that!" After such storms the next day's paper would inevitably detail the massive destruction of a trailer park. The front page would carry a picture of the rubble—roofs ripped like paper from their frames, pickups upside down. Trailers always seemed to be the lightning rods where tornados invested their passion. Always, though, amid the accounts of disaster were the stories of uncanny privilege: the shed lifted one hundred yards down the road without as much as a hammer out of place, or the doghouse deposited in the middle of the street, its dish still brimming with Purina chunks—evidence of grace in what was otherwise arbitrary violence.

But my informants spoke seldom of this violence, granting me no glimpse into the eye of the tornado, of either its beauty or its horror. They doted on the past, excusing its misbehavior and its ugly moods. Even after four years, I was still the outsider from the present, greeted kindly but cautiously, entertained with family folklore as fresh as the new quilts made by the local craft guild.

What I saw only later was that the guardedness they showed me was one they also adopted toward each other. So fearful of local criticism was one rural high school that it kept books by black authors off the shelves and instructed librarians to draw clothing on the scantily clad models in magazine and newspaper underwear ads, as if blacks and sexuality were equally alien to the community. What startled me about this latter practice was not the obvious prudity but the extra labor it took to draw little magic-marker blouses and skirts rather than simply to obscure the whole ad.

Not ashamed enough to destroy the white robes and hoods, costumes of fear, some still kept in attics, they nevertheless hesitated to speak about the secret rites. The rage silent in their tales resounded one warm summer night in 1978 when several gathered in a parking lot behind the town hall to burn the science books of their children and grandchildren, books that taught evolution. The rage blazed in a fiery cross on the front lawn of a teacher who'd assigned *The Diary of Anne Frank* to her sophomore English class.

The folklore I collected from these people lacked this strain of rage fueled by fears, at once richly violent and unpredictable. Whether it lay on the other side of language, articulated only in fraternal rites that take place in the dark, or whether it remained simply one of those truths forever concealed from outsiders, I could not tell. Whether these residents ever talked of such events in local bars and coffee shops, I never learned.

Suspecting first that I would never get beyond the warm reminiscence and fond recollection of family life to focus more sharply on the lives and beliefs of these people and secondly that what I was seeking might, in fact, be of my own invention, I eagerly took advantage of the opportunity to begin fieldwork with a different group of people: inmates of the Indiana Women's Prison. Such a switch reinvigorated my quest for the exotic, the extraordinary, and the dangerous. North of picturesque Bean Blossom and Bedford, south of the infernal fires issuing from the refineries of Gary, Indianapolis is the middle ground in a middle state in the middle west—the golden mean of America and first state capital to be constructed at the perfect geographic center of a state. Mapmakers simply sank their compass into the state's center, and Indianapolis was invented.

Indiana Women's Prison was the first separate prison for women in the country. Once on the outskirts of Indianapolis, now in a poor white neighborhood on the east side of the city, the walled, wooded block is a relic of the nineteenth century. Since its opening in 1873, the women's prison has housed women convicted of the most violent crimes—multiple murders, armed robbery, manslaughter—and has been a way station for those chronic alcoholics and drug addicts who periodically come to the prison to dry out. Within its walls have been the psychotic, the retarded, the habitual criminal, and the shoplifter.

In my transition from farmhouse to prison I discovered a new ease on the part of the women I interviewed, an eagerness to tell their stories. Many of them needed no questions to prime their memories. I allowed them to chart the direction of their narratives, and they told life stories with such fluency that they appeared to have been rehearsed. These autobiographical narratives fell into two types. First, there was the story of the life of crime. The narrators of these stories spent a great deal of time recounting their childhood, characterizing themselves as high-strung babies and irascible children, more interested in spending their days running with the boys and hanging out with the warehouse derelicts than in attending school or engaging in what they refer to as "girls' play." Theirs was the often comical picaresque tale of the rascal making her way through life more by her wits than her industry.

The tellers of these life histories were sometimes regarded as "the old girls," women who had been in and out of institutions since childhood. Their narratives, a series of episodes—adventures and misadventures—had little plot. What tied these episodes together was the often witty, sometimes wise, voice of one who had endured and who would, in her own feisty way, continue to do so.

Sixty-two-year-old Anna May was such a woman.[2] At the time I began my fieldwork she was serving a ninety-six-day sentence for disorderly conduct. Although she'd spent several short stints in county jails and the state prison (the first at eighteen when, drunk and angry, she "busted up" the front hood of her lover's Chevy), what was most interesting were her stories of life out of prison and her days as a member of the "Moon Light Hawaiians," a country and western band who dressed in white crepe outfits with orange and purple lace and performed throughout Ohio and Indiana. Anna May told me that on the night she and fellow band member Roy Aikens decided to leave the group, he cut his name on the top of her breast. "Well, I just let him do it—blood and all! I just let him do it." The story of Anna May's life was a litany of violent episodes; in some she was the aggressor, in others the unfortunate victim: "I been had three men and got the fourth one now I'm not married to, and all my guitars they've torn up."

Completely without self-pity, Anna May was a witty and warm narrator who related a zany life story with little introspection and no self-analysis. Delighting as much as I in the crazy details of her life, she told me of the hard work she'd done as a girl helping her sickly Aunt Mabel and crippled Uncle Russell at the filling station. Recovering from the removal of one lung, Aunt Mabel kept the ribs the surgeon had removed in a jar near her bed. As a kid, Uncle Russell had broken his hip in a fall from a second story window: "His mother tried to grab him by his clothes, but when she saw it was gonna drag her out the window, she let him loose." Always matter-of-factly and often humorously, she told of a bizarre world in which even the closest relationships were marked by lurid violence and strange chance: children fell out of windows, women slept next to jars of missing ribs, men carved their names in women's flesh.

A variation of this picaresque narrative was told by young women in their late teens and twenties. Theirs was the story of adolescent depression (sometimes the result of a family crisis) leading to a rebellion against the control of parents and the authority of the law. The protagonists of these stories, the young Huck Finns, often ran away from an abusive, sometimes alcoholic, father in search of adventure, and they traveled down the streets of their cities encountering hustlers, pimps, dealers, and conmen ready to initiate them into a fast and exciting world, a world of intense action where someone was always "getting it over" on someone else. These were women who manipulated the men in their lives by their cleverness and their sex. There was always a "john" they could hustle; there was always someone they could con. They often took pride in their exploits and the skill they had acquired in the criminal "trade."

Take Pat, for example—a tall, slender, freckled blonde who married at sixteen to get away from home: "He was a real nice guy. I only lived with him for six days, and then I left him. See, there was this other guy I really liked. I lived with my husband for six days, and then I left and went with this other dude. Hey, we went out partying and having a good time!" But after a few days, Pat returned to her new husband, who sought her mother's help in keeping the sixteen-year-old at home. Pat's mother called the police.

> They took me down to detention. I said, "Hey, you can't hold me; I know you can't hold me for this." They held me for an hour or so, long enough to throw me in a cell, and then they let me go. They had to. But my mom was gonna try, since I wasn't gonna

live with my husband. She said, "Well, then we're just gonna send her to reform school. We just have to send this child to reform school 'cause there's no help for her." See, I couldn't of just left home. I figured I'd be caught sooner or later. I was a juvenile, and it'd be inevitable that I'd be sent to some school or somewhere. But if I'm married, then I could be released from their custody and couldn't nobody say nothing. I thought this was a better angle for me to work because I would be protecting myself. No, I didn't want to just take off and maybe be caught and go to reform school for a runaway.

After that Pat worked as a go-go dancer, turning tricks on the side, posed for nude portraits on black velvet, turned new girls out in northern Kentucky, and worked for a pimp until she soon discovered that she preferred to work on her own, traveling across the country stopping at "respectable houses" where the product was quality sex at high prices. Pat named her own schedule ("two weeks on and two weeks off") and never wanted for work because she was not only young and pretty but specialized in kinky sex: "I prefer to turn strictly freaks because that's where the money is. You can take men that just want straight sex—they know what to spend. They spend a limited amount. The only way they're gonna spend any more is if they're in love with you. But now freaks, they know that they're weird, and they know that they have to pay extra. You can usually charge them whatever you want to. Once they tell you what they want, they feel committed to pay you whatever you ask." For an undertaker's assistant in Akron she'd soak in an icy bath till she got real cold. For others she'd play the parts of little girl or mother. Pat spoke fondly of her young clients:

> I always like the little guys, too. A lot of them would lie; you could tell they were lying. They'd say they were eighteen in order to get in, but they were sixteen or seventeen. But I always felt like I was helping them, showing them what they were supposed to be doing. They would have one little, crumpled twenty dollar bill they'd saved. They'd immediately want to start kissing and all this, but I'd say, "We're gonna sit down," and I'd talk to them like my child, "You're giving me a hard time. Don't do that 'cause I ain't gonna give you no hard time." They'd always listen and be OK.

It was only after my afternoon with Pat that I began to see these prison narratives as responses to the world of nostalgic and repressive domestic harmony evoked and lived by my rural informants. It was a world that bred outsiders. As I had left it, so, with greater reason and far graver consequences, had she. Pat could not stand home, and in order to be free of it she married, but when she fled that domestic relationship, husband and mother colluded to imprison her, if not in either of their homes, then in the state "home" of corrections.

The countryfolk's suspicion of outsiders was a futile defense against the inevitable realization that the price of staying inside the home was an alienation so severe that it imposed on some women the single choice of continued violence to oneself or explosive violence to others. Over and over women told me of abuse in the home and of their conflicting responses of anger and fear—subjects of the second major category of life stories I collected. The life stories of these women were the gothic inversion of conventional lore; they recounted not the good wife at her hearth but a heroine paralyzed by fear before the monster in the home. Theirs was often a private terror, knowing that they could expect periodic and certain mistreatment if they remained in their marriages but dreading even greater abuse directed toward them and their children if they tried to leave. The plots of these tales had uncanny uniformity; their tellers were amazingly similar: imprisoned at home, released by the murder of a husband or lover, and then imprisoned by the state. Most were women with no previous convictions whose crime was the cataclysmic act in their lives, the first and perhaps last independent action they would ever take. These women did not think of themselves as criminals or outcasts, but as victims: victimized by parents, husbands and lovers, and the legal system. They had once tried to escape the confinement of home through marriage, sometimes because of early pregnancy, sometimes just to be free of parents. But in marriage, they found no freedom, just a greater and often more brutal constraint:

> Several things might trigger my husband's violence. I'll give you an example. We could never leave a light on or water running. That was cause for real anger. The kids and I were always very cautious. When we left a room, the light had to be turned off. There were never two lights on in a room. We never used any

more electricity than had to be. Our bills were lower than any-body else's anywhere, I know. We were many times charged the minimum, and this is with a family! That's probably unheard of.

Anyway, my son went into my daughter's room once and was watching TV. This was Tommy, my youngest, watched TV in my daughter's room and went to sleep with it on. This would normally initiate a good slapping around, into your room, restriction, a lot of hollering. It might last for days—just over going to sleep with the TV on. But David, my older son, saw that Tommy had gone to sleep with the TV on so he went in and turned it off and was waking Tommy so that he could go to his own room and go to bed. Tommy, because he was sleeping, made a fuss. My husband heard it, went in and grabbed David, threw him down the hall into his own room, took out his belt (he wore a heavy belt), and just started beating. He beat David, and beat David with the belt doubled. David only had on a pajama bottom, and the belt came undoubled. He was just beating him; he was out of control. He was beating him with the buckle end. He just kept beating him, and beating him, and beating him. I was trying at this time to stop it, trying to grab the belt, trying to stop my husband. I don't know if I made him more angry, I don't know if I could have stopped him even with more interference in what he was doing. He just kept beating David until he was wore out. David was black and blue all over from the belt buckle. His skin was open. He just swelled up all over. It went on and on. He beat until he couldn't beat any more. Then my husband went into his room, lay down and rested. I stayed with my son as long as I could. I couldn't stay out very long once my husband went to bed.

These desperate women attempted to stop the brutality with gun, poison, or hired killer.

From one perspective, their crimes may be considered the revolt of the repressed, but whatever "liberation" they accomplished was, ostensibly at least, ephemeral. The act against society was summarily punished by society. Despite their violent divorce from the past, these women had merely exchanged the arbitrary brutality of home for the systematic discipline of the indifferent penal machine. No strangers to confinement, they did well in prison. They married it, and with some success. After all, they had more rights in prison than they ever did in their homes.

By the end of my first year of weekly visits to the women's prison in which I would interview two inmates a day, I dreaded interviews of this type. The cast of characters in each family drama was always the same: older, brutal husband/father, teenage wife, children beaten if they were boys, sexually abused if they were girls.

But finally, it was one meeting with Officer Verna Brown that made sense of it all. Early one April morning I checked in at the prison gatehouse and was escorted up to the sewing room where twelve prisoners mended the khaki uniforms of the male prisoners from other state prisons. Every time I entered the sewing room I reflected on the irony of women, even in prison, tasked with men's mending.

Veteran of twenty-two years, motherly guard and reputed clairvoyant, Verna Brown ran the sewing room. Most of the staff regarded her as eccentric; most inmates saw her as caring about those she governed and possessing an uncanny knowledge of things to come. Despite their belief or disbelief in her psychic ability, no one viewed her as harmful. Even the skeptics heeded her predictions, "just in case she might be right."

I had chatted informally with Officer Brown and even conducted three more formal interviews in which she told me of a divine calling that instructed her to come to the women's prison and about her knowledge of spirits, which assisted her in a ministry that aimed to ease the suffering of those under her charge and to maintain order in the institution. The easing of pain and the maintenance of order may seem contrary missions, but Verna Brown overcame the contradiction between the impulse to nurture and the necessity to control through her contact with a spirit world which aided her in both roles. Although unable to transform a harsh, inhumane place into a home, she chose to view her role as guide rather than jailer.

As maternal spiritual guide to those under her control, whom she viewed as wayward or disturbed children in need of nurturing and discipline, Brown took her instruction from a powerful spirit, her Indian guide. Although she had previously mentioned this spirit guide, she had refused to answer any of my questions about this mysterious figure. For several weeks he had instructed her to remain silent about his identity, but at the conclusion of our conversation the preceding week she had promised to discuss him on my next visit.

She was true to her word and told me that her Indian guide warned her of dangers to come both to herself and to others and instructed her in the making of secret cures and small packets to ward off evil. Although he had appeared physically to her, his presence was more often discernible by touch; she would feel his fur against her skin as she walked through a doorway. A benevolent force, this warrior reassured and protected; his warnings and instructions enabled Brown to control and to nurture those in her charge. This threshold figure mediated Brown's two worlds: the wing of prisoners she governed and the superimposed spirit world whose forces governed her.

As the Indian spirit guided Brown, so her story taught me. As I left that small supply room off the sewing room and headed back to the gatehouse, I thought what an institutional couple Brown and her spirit guide made: strong protective father who keeps his family secure and nurturing mother whose expressions of kindness and concern were rare among officers, who seemed to fear that any expression of sympathy would make them appear unprofessional to their superiors and vulnerable to prisoners. Learning to be a folklorist was, for me at least, discovering that, although spirits may only appear in stories, stories often appear like spirits—guiding us beyond ourselves, healing the splits in our selves and our natural lives that in the long run make no more sense than the supernatural.

I had fled the homes of north central Indiana two years earlier in search of the strange and the turbulent and had discovered much that was odd and violent in the lives of my new informants. But what I had not counted on finding in prison was the domestic. Not only did an officer, in her peculiar way, reconstitute the family in prison, but older inmates routinely "adopted" younger prisoners and served as their "prison mothers," offering sound advice, comforting them, and keeping them out of trouble. Occasionally, "studs" (masculine partners in prison lesbian couples) played father and uncle. Sometimes stern but never abusive, they reprimanded their daughters: "Watch your tongue." "Don't talk to your mother that way."

I realized, too, what should have been obvious to me all along: that these women were the daughters of those Indiana residents whose family traditions I had spent four years gathering. In seeing the homeliness in the prison, I could look back and see the prison of the home, a home which had seemed natural but was, in fact, as artificial as the fields.

Notes

This essay appeared previously in Carol Burke, *Vision Narratives of Women in Prison.* Copyright © 1992 by the University of Tennessee Press. Used by permission.

1   These reminiscences are collected in Burke 1983 and Burke and Light 1978.
2   Since even a simple personal disclosure can sometimes be used as a subtle weapon within prison, I have substituted pseudonyms for the names of my informants. Each quotation is from a tape-recorded interview in my possession.

References Cited

Burke, Carol, ed. 1983. *Plain Talk.* West Lafayette, Ind.: Purdue University Press.
Burke, Carol, and Martin Light, eds. 1978. *Back in Those Days: Reminiscences and Stories of Indiana,* special issue of *Indiana Writes* 2:4.

7

The Genius of Palermo
Michael Buonanno

On the Feast of the Immaculate Conception, I vowed to leave my books aside for the day, to let authority give way to experience, to witness those spectacles and hear those stories which are to be found only in the streets and public squares of Palermo. The route of that evening's procession was laid out in arcs of multicolored lights and the continuous rush of economic development (marked most notably in Palermo by an endless crunch of traffic) was momentarily halted. For the time being, I had the run of the city.

One envisions Palermo, both historically and architectonically, as a series of foreign occupations: Punic, Roman, Arabic, Norman, Spanish, Bourbon, Italian. Palermo has rarely belonged to the Palermitans. The city rises from the Conca d'Oro, the Golden Shell, an alluvial plain wedged between sharp limestone peaks and the Tyrrhenian Sea. It is centered upon a rocky spur which runs down to Palermo's harbor, La Cala, and was once bordered by two rivers, the Kemonia and the Papireto. Its historic center is divided into four somewhat irregular quarters by the Corso Vittorio Emanuele, built along the rocky spur, and the Via Maqueda, which crosscuts the spur as well as the ancient riverbeds (Sciascia and La Duca 1974: 24–30). Where the two intersect, at Quattro Canti, four ornate facades mark the spiritual center of the city with allegories of the four seasons in the first tier, four of Palermo's Spanish kings in the second, and the patron saints of the four adjacent quarters in the third. These streets are straight, wide, and notably higher than the narrow, winding streets of the quarters (which are centered on the depressions left by the Kemonia and Papireto) and the monuments of Palermo's officialdom cluster about them (though some are to be found dispersed about the quarters). Another distinguishing feature of these main thoroughfares and of the winding streets of the quarters is that Italian is the dominant language in the shops and cafés of the former while Sicilian is the dominant language in the sprawling markets (such as the Vucciria and the Ballarò) of the latter.

It is Palermo's Norman architecture that distinguishes it from any other city of the world. These sprawling citadels of massive rock, softened only by the gentle ornamentation of the city's Arab craftsmen, contain the traces of Palermo's Punic, Roman, Byzantine, and Arabic occupations. Here, slender lancet arches and geometric inlays of colored stone adorn the stark walls. There, clusters of red domes rise above the heavy crenellations. Within, one is liable to find rich Byzantine mosaics of gold and lapis lazuli. Norman architecture gives way to a number of Gothic styles patronized by the Normans' Swabian, French, and Catalonian successors. Stark lines are broken by rose windows, slender colonnades, and delicate spires. Under a newly unified Spain, the heavy Renaissance gates and palaces, tiered and varied through the use of Doric, Ionic, and Corinthian flourishes, transform the city but these in turn give way to the plateresque facades of Imperial Spain. In the statuary of this period, angry prophets raise their fists at the city while the gentle patrons shed quiet tears over it. With a single blast of Gabriel's horn, plump cherubs fall from the clouds and angels supplicate the Immaculate Virgin with hands extended in mournful prayer. Here Emperor Carlo V strides into the city in the guise of a beggar. There he presides over the city in all his imperial majesty. Renaissance architecture gives way to a rich baroque, preferred by the Bourbon court at Naples, and finally, the neoclassicism of a newly unified Italy fills out Palermo's architectural scheme with its grand theaters and ornate kiosks.

With the Spanish occupation a curious depiction, found most often in the winding streets of Palermo's quarters, begins to appear. It is a sculptural theme called the Genius of Palermo. A duke sitting serenely on his throne permits a serpent to feed at his breast. There are at least five of these statues scattered about the city (one discovered only in 1988 behind a decrepit wall). In at least one instance his throne rises from a scallop shell (the Conca d'Oro) and in another a dog lies obediently at his feet.

On this particular morning I took my coffee at a small bar where I had stopped a few times before. The bar was rather quiet, the day being a holiday, and the owner was less harried than usual. He gave me a free coffee and asked what brought me to Palermo.

"I'm here to study the puppet theater," I answered.

"Bravo! And why the puppet theater?"

"It's the only place where the Carolingian Cycle is still being told."

He thought for a moment and said, "The Normans brought the Carolingian Cycle here, you know." He then added somewhat solemnly, "But they didn't take it back with them." He was intimating that the stories of Charlemagne and the Paladins belonged to Palermo now, that they had somehow become Palermitan.

"And what will you do with your studies?" he asked. "Are you writing your thesis?"

I told him that I was transcribing tape recordings of the puppet shows and translating the transcriptions into English. He was horrified.

"But you'll ruin them by writing them down, in English no less. They're not meant to be read. They're meant to be heard."

I explained that my transcriptions would take into account the oral qualities of the stories, that each time the puppeteer paused I would start a new line, that I would show the cadence of his lines through the capitalization or elongation of stressed words, that I would explain certain peculiarities of voice by various notations like in the script of a play. He was only partially reassured.

"Well, they might be beautiful," he said, "but not really beautiful."

I had already learned that some of my most important understandings of the puppet theater were to be had in some of my most casual conversations. This was lucky because the puppeteers had lost their traditional audiences (men and boys from Palermo's quarters who were willing to follow the adventures of the Carolingian heroes for months on end [Pasqualino 1982: 17]) in the mid-sixties and it was no longer possible to study the puppet theater's social contiguity from the performative context. Today's audiences (primarily Palermitans but also tourists who view special episodes of the Carolingian Cycle during city festivals) do interact with the puppeteers but not necessarily in a manner that the puppeteers understand or even approve. It was possible, however, to understand the social ramifications of this last tradition of chivalric narrative through the puppeteers' compositional techniques, the manner in which the puppeteers actualized their stories, and in this task my various encounters helped me for they taught me how to listen to the puppeteers' narratives. It is a credit to the puppeteers' declamatory art that a rather thorough knowledge of the Carolingian Cycle is diffused throughout the city of Palermo (this despite the fact that the cycle is performed in some 270-odd episodes).

What the owner had suggested to me was the fact that it was not *any* version of the Carolingian Cycle that I was studying but the version of the Palermitan puppeteers and their direct forebears—the popular press of nineteenth-century Sicily, which put out chivalric narratives serially, and the *contastorie* (storytellers) who told the stories of Charlemagne and his knights on the public squares of Palermo until the mid-twentieth century. He was moreover telling me that what differentiated the puppeteers' version from the Old French, Franco-Venetian, and Italian versions before it was the fact that this version belonged to the city of Palermo. I was beginning to understand this but I was unsure how the city became inscribed in these chivalric narratives, how these narratives somehow signified Palermo itself. Yet people were giving me hints all the time.

One of the first conversations I had about the puppet theater was with a shopkeeper on my street named Maria. She was about sixty years old and she insisted that I take milk with my coffee, as it was winter. When I told her I was studying the *opera* (i.e., the puppet theater) she immediately told me who to like and who to ignore. "Don't pay any attention to Orlando [Roland]," she told me. "He's no good. There he had a perfectly good wife at home, Alda the Beautiful, and he ran around starting fights over Angelica, even with his own cousin, Rinaldo. Rinaldo is the good one. Pay attention to him. He always acts honorably." Maria's privileging of Rinaldo over Orlando is standard procedure in Palermo, where Orlando is nicknamed Cross Eyes (in fact, Orlando's painted eyes are always crossed) and Rinaldo is nicknamed the Mafioso (Cammarata 1970: 6). But what was most striking about Maria's statements was the fact that her interpretation of the *opera*'s narratives centered on characters and their attributes; as a friend from a small inland village who would see the puppet shows once a year at the village festival told me, "That's because these old people think those characters are real." A better way to explain this circumstance is to say that the *opera*'s narratives in the not so distant past were understood as histories: histories with marvelous elements added but histories nonetheless.

An interpretive technique which centers on characters and their attributes has one special ability: allegory. The *opera*'s characters are always literal (self-referential in their words and deeds) at one level but they are always and equally allegorical (referring to various others through their words and deeds) on another. This penchant for allegory (which may be universal to those stories understood as histories) was pointed out to me by a friend who upon seeing an infant Orlandino (diminutive for Orlando) wrapped in swaddling clothes said, "See? The swaddling clothes! See? He's born in a cave!" (The cave is the traditional setting of Christ's birth in Sicilian nativities.) "A shepherd is there! Get it? It's one of the puppeteers' tricks!"

Maria often told me about Charlemagne, Orlando, Rinaldo, Ganelon, and Angelica and I once made the mistake (I had not been in Palermo long and did not yet know much about the *opera*'s audiences) of asking her which theater she had frequented. She was taken aback and said, "I've never been to one of those places." I found out later that the *opera*'s audiences consisted exclusively of men, except on those occasions when a saint's life or the *Life and Passion of Jesus Christ* was being performed. Maria had learned all the stories from her brothers.

Other conversations gave me further insights into the *opera*'s major characters. Orlando was mainly disliked because he too often took the side of Charlemagne when the sovereign banished Rinaldo due to the various calumnies of that archtraitor, Ganelon. But Orlando was not completely disliked. "When he's rescuing damsels or killing Saracens everyone cheers for him," one man told me. "It's just that Orlando tends to be a little flat, too one-sided, always doing what he's supposed to. There are more sides to Rinaldo's nature." What was flat, then, was the perfect knight: a curious admixture of the loyal soldier and the martyr-saint. What was multifaceted on the other hand was the knight who had the audacity to revolt. He was at once the rebellious baron of Old French epic, the bandit of Sicilian popular narrative, and the mafioso of the Palermitan streets.

In fact, I was coming to find that all the *opera*'s major protagonists were multifaceted, being constructed from more than one genre of traditional narrative. The puppeteers' repertoire, before the early nineteenth century, consisted almost exclusively of farces derived from the *commedia dell'arte:* the seventeenth-century theater of improvisation which centered upon such masques as Harlequin, Columbine, and Punch (Pasqualino 1978: 191). It is probably from the *commedia* that the puppeteers derived their technique of keeping small notebooks containing manuscript plot summaries which they could amplify during the performance through the proper concatenation of themes and the creation of appropriate voices. The puppeteers did not however replace the masques in their pursuit of chivalric material in the early to mid-nineteenth century. Rather, they augmented them. The masques remained to comment upon, burlesque, even insert themselves into the new chivalric narratives. Thus, masques and knights came to inhabit the same narrative space, epic themes and voices played off their farcical counterparts, and the knight's significance became a function of his relationship to the masque: the knight became a representative of the Palermitan aristocracy because he fought, while the masque became a representative of the Palermitan people because he worked. Knights and masques were soon to be joined by saints and bandits who bore with them the habitual themes and characteristic voices of their own particular genres of Sicilian popular narrative. The saint was a permutation of the knight: noble but with a voice more aptly characterized by prayer and supplication than the apostrophe and the challenge. Likewise the bandit was a permutation of the masque: vulgar but with a voice better characterized by the boast and the hyperbole than parody and the pun. What resulted from this peculiar convocation was a chivalric narrative at once multigeneric and dialogic: multigeneric because chivalric narrative was now constructed in the themes of epic, farce, saints' and bandits' lives; dialogic because knight, masque, saint, and bandit each spoke in his own particular voice. The kernel of a social classification thus began to be formulated in the *opera*'s narratives but the *opera*'s major protagonist, the knight, was unwilling to inhabit just one slot of that classification. In their youths, both Orlando and Rinaldo are represented as admixtures of the overzealous young knight and the bumbling masque. As they grow into manhood, Orlando is variously represented as the traditional knight and/or saint, while Rinaldo is variously represented as the traditional knight and/or bandit.

The puppeteers actualize their stories through a quite limited set of themes. And not all of these come from the epic progression of Council (the speech of the sovereign before his knights), Announcement (the entrance of a soldier with news or a letter), Audience (the appearance of an ambassador or the reading of a letter), Dispatch (the sending off of an ambassador or letter), and Battle. As the youthful Orlando and Rinaldo descend among the people they are temporarily caught in the simpler, farcical sequence of themes: Entrance, Encounter (the chance meeting of two vagabonds), Brawl, Alliance (the ceasing of hostilities between the two vagabonds), and Exit. If a knight (most likely Orlando) attempts to convert a dying pagan, certain themes from the Sicilian saints' lives (which in fact form a part of the puppeteers' repertoire) such as Apparition (the appearance of an angel with orders from the Lord), Miracle (the appearance of baptismal water), and Glorification (the ascension of a soul to heaven) will be borrowed. Likewise, if a knight (most likely Rinaldo) is found in revolt against the sovereign, certain themes from the Sicilian bandits' lives (also a part of the puppeteers' repertoire) such as Theft and Abduction will be borrowed. More importantly, the youthful Orlando and Rinaldo are often caught talking in the idiom of the masques: a familiar form of Sicilian rather than the knight's polite and refined Italian. And when Orlando, in manhood, is caught in a saintly act he will inevitably speak in a particularly saintly prose. Likewise, Rinaldo in the perpetration of a theft will speak in a manner more consonant with the speech of a bandit.

I popped back up to my room for a moment, where a singular tragedy was unfolding. I was living in a set of rooms rented out by Tunisian immigrants to Palermo and one fellow from Togo named Mohammed. Mohammed, having the day off from work, had bought a chicken at the Ballarò and just as he was preparing to butcher it (in the same sink where I brushed my teeth) the bird flew out the window. "That stupid beast," Mohammed swore as I was coming up the stairs. "It has the mind of an animal." And, indeed, it looked pretty stupid standing out on the roof unaware that stray cats (who sometimes availed themselves of my bed) lived there and fed for the most part on incautious birds. Mohammed and I climbed out onto the roof of ancient and precariously slanted tile and began chasing the chicken. I was gaining more respect for this beast which would let us come within inches of her and then flutter off gobbling and clucking to a point just beyond our reach. She was teasing us. As we climbed back into the window and over the sink Mohammed swore, "That stupid beast! I was trying to save its life!" (In fact, he wanted to eat it.) The chicken clucked and strutted off, oblivious to the dangers which awaited her.

As I was running back down the stairs, a Tunisian woman came in. Her son and husband were still at work. She had learned all the possible complaints in Italian and decided that day to use them against me.

"Good morning, Signora."

"Oh, what a life full of misery. My stomach hurts and my tooth still aches. These Christians are so bad here. They take advantage of us and don't care if we live or die. Only the French Christians are good. I wish we could go back there, or to Tunisia. Moslems are always good people. They take care of one another." As she was winding down she asked me to go to the market and pick up some bread. She gave me some money and I hopped off to the Ballarò.

Is it fair to learn something from Mohammed and the Tunisians and apply it to Sicilian narrative? Does it break the rules of ethnographic verisimilitude? Mohammed, the Tunisians, and I were not always communicating through words but quite often through speech acts. Mohammed's speech act was syncretic, as much African as Palermitan, and I am unsure why he claimed to be saving the chicken's life, but the signora's speech act was functional, Palermitan, and immediately recognizable; it was the lament, the spoken symbol of poverty, not only in the streets but also in the puppet theater. I once heard Orlandino (in response to his mother's warning that he should no longer beat up young nobles) cry:

> But I am unable to accept their insults
> simply because I am poor;
> These rich men don't care if I live well or in misery.
>   (Cuticchio and Cuticchio 1987)

Perhaps due to my curious living arrangements, perhaps due to the nature of fieldwork itself, I was coming to see that the puppets' voices were varied through the translation of typical speech patterns (Italian, Sicilian, supplication, irony), specific speech acts (challenge, parody, lament, boast), and various figures (apostrophe, pun, conduplicatio, hyperbole) from the streets and public squares of Palermo to the *opera*'s narratives and that when a character in the *opera*'s narratives changed his voice, he himself did not change but the thing to which he allegorically alluded did. An example of this variation involved the differentiation of speakers through their use of the polite and familiar forms of address. On the streets and in the public squares this variation emplaces a social continuum which differentiates relations familiar and egalitarian on the one hand from relations characterized by deference and respect on the other; in the narratives of the *opera* this variation serves to demarcate various characters' generic affiliation. The familiar (*tu*) form of address demarcates the masque, while the polite (*voi*) form of address demarcates the knight. The variable use of Italian and Sicilian is in effect an extension of this concept. While Italian is the language of the shops and cafés of the great boulevards (the Corso Vittorio Emanuele and the Via Maqueda), products and namesakes of Palermitan officialdom, Sicilian is the language of the winding streets of the four quarters' market districts (such as the Vucciria and the Ballarò), home to the Palermitan people. Once again, the variation refers in its narrative context to different generic affiliation. The masque speaks Sicilian, while the knight speaks Italian.

Other examples of speech patterns that are borrowed from the historic center are the prayers and supplications which center the voice of the saint (we hear them during the processions on the various feast days) and the boasts and bouts of irony which center the voice of the bandit; I heard them when I was trying to convince another foreigner that the men robbing the storeroom in her apartment building were not robbing the storeroom and that it would be best to continue upstairs (as everyone else was doing) rather than engage the "new men" (who admittedly used metal clippers rather than keys to get into the storeroom) in conversation as they seemed quite busy.

I wandered here and there throughout the morning and early afternoon, just having a look around, until it was time for the procession. The procession began at the Church of San Francesco, home of the Immaculate Virgin, with a benediction, a release of white doves, and the ringing of bells. Bits of blue and yellow paper were dropped from the balconies above. They fluttered in a syncopated tumble, catching the light of the sun on each half turn, blanching and blushing as they fell. Hands stretched up to catch them for they were prayers; they read *Viva Maria Immacolata!* Long live Mary the Immaculate! A bell rang once. The penitents caught hold of the bier. It rang again. The bier was shouldered. It rang once more and the penitents lumbered along the Via Paternostro; each locked one arm around the bier, the other around the man ahead of him. The Virgin, gilt in silver and gold, moved in a smooth, effortless progression, directing her gaze here and there about the adulatory crowd as a band of flutes and drums, trumpets and violins began to sound.

As she crossed Vittorio Emanuele, I ran ahead of the procession in order to arrive at the church first and see the procession enter the square, but as I cut through the Vucciria, I caught my first glimpse of the Genius. I thought it was a man being attacked by a serpent and I momentarily lost interest in the procession. I asked some other people cutting through the market what the statue depicted but they didn't know so I trailed along to San Domenico where the procession stopped before a tall column supporting another Immaculate Virgin. Here, with the aid of a fire truck's hydraulic ladder, a bouquet was presented to the Virgin on the column and I began to realize that this Virgin was the same as the one down on the square, immaculate, and that it was not any Virgin that could be honored on this day, but only the Immaculate Virgin. In this case, Mary's attribute was not intercession, motherhood, nor pity, but only immaculacy. Those other attributes belonged to other Marys and could only be addressed on other days, under different contexts.

The procession continued on, pausing momentarily in the Quattro Canti to catch the beneficent gaze of the four patrons. One of Palermo's most famous legends, that of the Beati Paoli, opens just at this point of the procession in the early eighteenth century: the innocent orphan Costanza (secretly married to Corrado, who is noble but, as the second son of his family, penniless) is accosted by a certain Prospero who in the ensuing scuffle is wounded in the cheek by Corrado's sword. That evening as Corrado flies to Costanza's home disguised in the cape and beret of his manservant, he too is accosted. He gains the better of his assailant and chases him without the walls of the city. He finds himself in an open field where a group of men dressed in capes and berets like himself are gathering. He is herded along with the others into a secret chamber and thus finds himself in the midst of the Beati Paoli: a nocturnal convocation of men of the people whose sole intent is to avenge the injustices of the aristocracy and curb the excesses of the Inquisition. Among the petitions that Corrado witnesses that evening is one against a prince who is keeping the young son of a peasant locked up in his dungeon and administering daily beatings, another

against a minister of the Inquisition who is attempting to "ruin the reputation" of a good family through pressing too insistently on a young daughter, and finally Prospero's petition against Corrado himself (Linares 1980:
21–54). This treachery in the people's tribunal leads to the demise of the
Beati Paoli, but the group is to this day thought of as consisting of men of
honor, the true purveyors of justice in an unjust society. I understood this
when a woman said to me, "Up north there are the terrorists. Here we have
the Mafia. The terrorists will kill anybody. The Mafia will only kill you if
you do something wrong. Which is the more honorable? Excuse me. I think
the Mafia. I'm talking about the true Mafia, the Mafia when it was more like
the Beati Paoli."

The procession continued along Vittorio Emanuele and culminated
in a triumphal entrance into the cathedral, another benediction, and then
(for me, as I lived just a few steps away) the vision of the procession moving steadily back to San Francesco amidst the occasional stirrings of flutes
and violins.

In the following days I tried to find out more about the Genius but
asking around was useless. Everyone knew the statue but no one knew what
it signified. In this case I had to resort to authority and return to my books.
Giuseppe Pitrè, Palermo's illustrious folklorist, collected the following account of the Genius: a rich lord who sailed about the world simply for pleasure was tossed during a tempest upon the Conca d'Oro. He fed on the fruits
of that abundant plain until he was restored and decided to found a city
there. He gathered engineers and masons who constructed the city which
was named, after the lord, Palermo. "The same engineers and masons who
built the city sculpted the marble statue of this rich lord, father and patron
of the city, when he was already old. And this statue is the one found in the
square of the Old Market" (Pitrè 1888: 348). Pitrè says of this story that it
must surely be older than the statue and that seems likely. Who would com-
mission a statue (much less five) without allusions to a narrative in Palermo? But this story contains no mention of the serpent and thus is only a
partial explanation of the Genius.

The Genius in the Old Market is probably the most popular inasmuch
as it was used to display notes of protest during various insurrections. It was
in fact thought to so much represent Palermitan rebelliousness that it was
removed from the Old Market by the Bourbon government. Only after the

unification of Italy (1860–70) was it replaced. The Genius which today stands near the Quattro Canti admits a further explanation for it carries the inscription *Panormus conca aurea, suos devorat, alienos nutrit* (Palermo, golden shell, you devour your own, you feed the foreigners). In effect, then, the serpent represents the foreigners who feed off the fruits of Palermo's abundant plain while Palermitans starve. While such sentiments certainly must have existed they could hardly have been patronized on five separate occasions through the commissioning of these statues. This inscription is of the nature of the less durable protests attached to the Genius in the Old Market. The only feasible explanation, I believe, is the one I finally heard from a fellow student in Palermo. She claimed that the duke represented the Palermitan aristocracy while the serpent represented the Palermitan people. Therein lies a narrative which could receive official patronage for it propagated the necessity of the aristocracy in a manner consonant with the ideology of the people. The people feed off the aristocracy.

A curiosity of the symbol involves its arbitrary character (i.e., definition of things through that which they are not) and its polyvalence (i.e., ability to symbolize various things at one time). A symbol is formed on the authority of a perceived similarity of attributes; the knight fights as does the aristocracy. Therefore the knight represents the aristocracy. The masque works as do the people. Therefore the masque represents the people. The saint espouses the *lex Christi* ("turn the other cheek," etc.) as does the cleric. Therefore the saint represents the cleric. The bandit espouses the vendetta (the Palermitan analogue to the *lex taliones* ["an eye for an eye," etc.]) as does the mafioso. Therefore the bandit represents the mafioso. Yet symbols (which are also fully developed characters) are often defined by a number of attributes and may therefore find further *significants.* For example, the knight commits himself to obedience as does the angel and therefore represents the angel. The masque lives as does mythological Man and therefore represents Man. The saint dies as does Christ and therefore represents Christ. The bandit rebels against his sovereign as does the David of Judeo-Christian mythology and therefore represents David. It is at this point that the peculiarity of symbolic formation comes into focus. Once the knight has come to represent both the aristocracy and the angel, these two *significants* are narratologically altered so that the aristocracy is redefined as obedient and the angel as a warrior. Once the masque has come to represent both the Palermitan people and mythological Man, mythological Man works and the Palermitan people live. Once the saint has come to represent both the cleric and Christ, the cleric becomes a medium of death and Christ the sponsor of a deadly law. And once the bandit has come to represent both the mafioso and David, David becomes the patron of the vendetta and the mafioso comes to be perceived as a rebel.

There is much that is arbitrary in this. In and of themselves knight and masque have no real relationship. They belong to two different genres of narrative: the one to epic, the other to farce. Yet once they come into coincidence, once they come to inhabit the same narrative space, they are redefined. The knight represents the aristocracy because he has encountered the masque, and the masque represents the people because he has encountered the knight. Likewise, the saint represents the cleric because he has encountered the bandit, and the bandit represents the mafioso because he has encountered the saint. Symbolic formation creates in a body of narrative a social configuration which lays the groundwork for a number of narrative progressions.

Through the variation of his voice, effected by the variation of typical patterns of speech, various speech acts, and the figures which control and contain the puppeteers' formulas, the *opera*'s major protagonist, the knight, becomes a masque, becomes thereby of the people, becomes a bandit, becomes thereby a mafioso, becomes a saint, becomes thereby like a god. He ranges about his narrative space, incorporating the various personages who populate it, citing them in their own distinctive voices, and creates of the social configuration a psychological division. It is his movement between the various integers of this division which creates the narrative. If the knight works, he is a masque and the narrative involves the knight's descent among the people. If the masque fights, he is a knight and the narrative involves the recognition of the masque's royal origins. If the knight dies, he is a saint and the narrative involves holy war, but if he rebels, he is a bandit and the narrative involves just retribution.

I think narrative is distinguished precisely by these shifts, these metamorphoses, these reversals. Social configurations are evoked in other modes of discourse, likewise psychological divisions, but the movement within the various configurations, within the various divisions, is the particular province of narrative. It provides the recognition, the sudden flash of insight, the epiphany, which ultimately defines (and perhaps even informs) the major social relations of Palermo, those very relations which determine the interactional basis of the aristocracy, the people, the clerical class, and the Mafia. I am suggesting here that narrative itself formulates social relations, that it creates logical connections where none have as yet existed. If it were otherwise, multigenericity (the convocation of characters from disparate genres of narrative) and dialogism (the citation of real voices by these disparate characters) would achieve no dramatic force.

On my first visit to the puppet theater, a young boy, his face brightening with surprise, said to me, "But you speak like a soldier!" He then turned to his friends and reiterated, "But he speaks like a soldier!" I did not understand it at the time, but he was telling me that my Italian was like that of an outsider, like that of someone not from Palermo. When that understanding finally came, several weeks later, there came fast upon its heels another: when the soldier is the very model of the foreigner, the city is in a state of occupation. Curiously enough, that young boy, one of the first of my Palermitan interlocutors, had particularly emplaced me so that I might understand the function of epic to Palermitan society.

Our major environment as human beings is social. Certainly we live in a physical environment as well, interacting with the world of material good, but this physical environment is mediated at every juncture by our social environment; our access to the material world is mitigated by our social standing, our position within a particular social structure. Various benefits that the material world has to bestow are inextricably intertwined with the people who are their owners, their custodians, their purveyors, their distributors, inextricably interwoven with political-economic relations. If our major environment is social, if so much of our existence hinges not upon material good but upon variable access to material good, it is little wonder that we spend much of our time in negotiating our relationship to other human beings, in the peculiar act of self-emplacement; we thereby negotiate our own particular store of power.

That area of thought which most completely puts one human being in interaction with another, thus emplacing both in a social environment, is narrative, which catches up alter egos (personae) and places them in interactional networks (plots). I imagine that the portion of our leisure time taken up with narrative (film, television, storytelling, gossip, accounts of daily events, etc.) is proof of narrative's ability to satisfy our abiding interest in our social environment. I further imagine that the sorts of interactions which characters undertake in narrative are determinative to some extent of the major social interactions which define a given society, that characters are essentially idioms for classes of society and that their discrete acts are the means by which they form their relationships and become emplaced in a social configuration. In other words, our abiding interest in characters in interaction (i.e., narrative) is a function of our abiding need to emplace ourselves in a social environment.

When I finally realized what it meant to "talk like a soldier," I began to understand the function of Palermitan epic; it is the negotiation of the relations between the major classes of Palermitan society: the aristocracy, the people, the clerical class, and the Mafia. Yet, by then, New Year's Eve was upon me and my fieldwork was winding down to an unnatural conclusion; I would be leaving Palermo (broke) in about a week and I simply had to close my notebooks and quit my studies with the decided sensation that I was not yet finished with them. As midnight, that moment of symbolic closures and openings, approached, I found myself on another Palermitan rooftop, a pistol in my hand, and my hostess urging me to shoot. So along with hundreds of other Palermitans, and to the accompaniment of firecrackers and bottle rockets, I shot a bullet straight into the sky. The children, two dogs, and a duck scattered about the roof and were herded back to a protective overhang by my hostess, only to press once again to the edge of the roof. As each man shot the pistol in turn, I wondered if this act were simply an augment to the noise of the firecrackers and bottle rockets, an assertion of Palermitan independence, or some admixture of both. I took the pistol again as it went the round, shot once more, and ran with the children, dogs, and duck to the edge of the roof to watch Palermo grow crimson beneath a fire-streaked sky.

References Cited

Cammarata, Felice. 1970. Introduction to *Storia dei Paladini*. Giusto Lodico, ed. Felice Cammarata. Palermo: Mazzone.

Cuticchio, Carmelo, and Giacomo Cuticchio. 1987. *The First Adventures of Orlandino*. Audiotape. Palermo: International Museum of Marionettes.

Linares, Vincenzo. 1980. *I racconti popolari.* Ed. Elio Giunta. Palermo: Edizion "Il Vespro."

Pasqualino, Antonio. 1978. "Transformations of Chivalrous Literature in the Subject Matter of the Sicilian Marionette Theater." In *Varia Folklorica,* ed. Alan Dundes, pp. 183–200. The Hague: Mouton.

———. 1982. *I Pupi Siciliani.* Gibellina, Sicily: Nando Russo.

Pitrè, Guiseppe. 1888. *Fiabe e leggende popolari siciliane.* Palermo: Pendone Lauriel.

Sciascia, Leonardo, and Rosario La Duca. 1974. *Palermo Felicissima.* Palermo: Edizioni il Punto.

8

Crossing and Recrossing the Line
and Other Moments of Understanding
Dwight F. Reynolds

●

Epiphanal moments have, for me at least, come in several different flavors. Some come with a "whoops," some with a more bemused "hmmm," and some, of course, with that characteristic "aha!" All of these are represented in the five moments I have described below. In the first I discovered a barrier I did not know existed; in the second, a barrier I had been concerned about proved not to exist at all. The third and fourth moments are of that type when a single, telling event illuminates a problematic area of thought. The last was a moment at the very end of a period of fieldwork which reframed an entire year's work.

What's in a Name?

The village of al-Bakâtûsh lies in the heart of the Egyptian Nile Delta about twenty-five kilometers from the western branch of the Nile which debouches into the Mediterranean at Rosetta. Though it is only two and a half hours by car from Cairo, and slightly less from Alexandria, its inhabitants have virtually no contact with these two metropolitan centers. Urban influence is felt, if at all, from the nearby provincial capital of Kafr al-Shaykh, or from the two large towns of Disûq and Tanta, each of which boasts major Sufi saints' festivals which many of the inhabitants of the village attend. My presence in al-Bakâtûsh stemmed from the sobriquet by which it is known throughout the province of Kafr al-Shaykh and in surrounding areas: "al-Bakâtûsh—Village of the Poets" [al-Bakâtûsh balad al-shu'arâ'], for this village is home to fourteen households of epic-singers who perform the Arabic oral folk epic *Sîrat Banî Hilâl.*[1] This is the largest community of epic-singers known in Egypt; however, when I first began collecting and recording there in 1983, and even when I returned for a year in 1986–87, it had not yet been visited by other researchers.

Though the epic, at least in rural areas of Egypt, is accorded a great deal of respect, the poets themselves are regarded with a certain amount of suspicion. They are usually of 'gypsy' [*ghajar*] origin; they are itinerant performers, though they maintain settled households in the village; and they have certain customs and traditions which differ markedly from those of the rest of the population. Thus a major part of my research was to be concerned with delineating the relationship between this small community of poets and the larger society in which they live, determining the attitudes these two groups maintain about each other and about the epic, and assessing how these conditions affect the performance tradition as a whole. As it turns out, the divisions between poets and other villagers run deep and are quite sensitive.[2] I soon began to develop the feeling that I was moving back and forth across a set of boundaries I could not see, boundaries that only became clear when I stumbled over them.

One aspect of the relationship between these two groups struck me as curious very early in my fieldwork: poets were never referred to by family names. To identify any villager, one asks for their father's name and family name. But for villagers, the poets' families do not participate in the larger ongoing genealogy of the village, they are not locatable on the intricate map of blood, conjugal, and marital ties in which all other residents of the village are presumed part. Most villagers denied that poets even possessed family names. One intense encounter in the early part of my fieldwork proved this common notion wrong, and led to a rapid change in my relationship with the poets' community.

I was spending an evening with a group of young men from the poets' families, none of whom were themselves performing poets,[3] and we began to discuss disagreements that had occurred recently between the fathers of several of the young men present. The tensions were very easy to understand: here were men in their late teens and early twenties who had little independence from their fathers, and when family disagreements arose, these often affected their only close friendships. One fellow made an offhand remark, "It's just the old story of the X's versus the Y's again" (using collective noun forms usually reserved for family names). I immediately asked what he meant, and, after hesitating a moment, he explained which of the fourteen households belonged to which of three different extended families. I tried immediately to memorize the list, for there was no question of getting out paper and pen and writing this down on the spot. This new information in fact explained a great deal about internal relations within the poets' community which I had till then not understood.

Later in the week I began to record from a poet with whom I had not previously worked. The *sahra* (private evening gathering) was to be at the home of my host family, the household of Ahmad Bakhâtî. After the poet arrived and had settled in the *mandara,* the men's sitting room, we were served a pot of tea, and began to chat. One other villager joined us (most people would not actually enter the *sahra* until they heard the music begin). I asked a number of my usual questions about repertory, family history, and other topics, and then, eager to verify the information I had received about family names, I asked the poet, "So, are you from the family of X or Y?"

The poet looked quite shocked and his face immediately registered his displeasure. He leaned over to me, and with a sharp glance at the other villager, who, thank heavens, seemed to be occupied with his own thoughts, whispered angrily, "Where did you learn those names?!" I was not quite sure what I had done, but there was no discounting the effect it had had on the poet.

I covered my blunder as best I could, but other guests began to arrive and we had to rise to greet them. I was given no opportunity during the rest of the evening to apologize or clarify what had happened.

The following afternoon I sought the advice of a poet with whom I had already worked. I recounted the incident in detail, holding back only the circumstances in which I had originally learned these names. When I reached the point where I had asked about the family names, my friend grew concerned. He felt the situation was grave and stated that if the poet chose to tell the other poets about it, things could get very difficult.

He and his wife grilled me about who had mentioned these names to me. I put them off as best I could but they eventually made up their own minds about who it must have been. I explained many times that I was not here to divulge secrets, particularly not to the villagers, and that I had been unaware these names were unlike everyone else's names. The poet's wife pleaded on my behalf: "He understands now [*huwa wâkhud bâluh dilwaqt*], and there was no real harm done."

A plan was laid out. My friend was to go visit the other poet and explain the situation. In an hour I was to drop by the other poet's house "by chance" for tea. This I did. When I arrived it was clear that all was settled. We talked the situation over, and, though the hour was early, dinner was brought out and served. There was no possibility of refusing this invitation, though I had already accepted another invitation to dinner, for it was my first invitation to eat a meal in a poet's home. As we drank tea after the meal, my friend stated once again for everyone's benefit, "He didn't know it was any different from other names in the village." Our host looked at me and smiled, "But now he knows." I never learned anything more about the subject.

One curious result of this incident was that I rapidly received invitations to eat in the homes of nearly all of the poets. One barrier had been set up, but another had been taken away. Over the months of my stay I learned that there were many aspects of the poet community that were unknown in the larger society of the village, not merely because the outside world did not care but because the poets actively withheld this knowledge from them. Part of the cohesion of their small, marginalized community lies in the maintenance of secrecy concerning some of the most basic aspects of their lives. The names and clan affiliations of poets' families are considered important secrets; the poet community possesses and uses a "secret language" (which they call *raṭâna,* a word which in Arabic means 'gibberish'), even the existence of which is unknown to most villagers; quarrels within the poet community are repressed and covered over when non-poets are present but flare up immediately in the privacy of the poets' own homes; the geographic origins of the poet families are usually played down, though when pressed publicly the poets will give an account of when and whence their families came to live here in al-Bakâtûsh.

That one moment, when I asked what clan the poet belonged to, paradoxically placed that area of inquiry out of bounds for the duration of my stay. I learned no more about the subject until I had left the field once and returned a year later for further research. That moment clarified, however, the extent and the type of social boundaries I would be dealing with, and gave me an opportunity to discuss my intentions with the poet community. The resolution of that first encounter with the poets' sense of community somehow opened up completely new terrain for me, for it was immediately after this event that the poets' homes, family life, and personal histories were all made available to me.

Poet's Apprentice

Beyond describing the social interaction of the poet and villager communities and its influence on the performance tradition, I hoped to get a closer look at the process of transmission and composition by apprenticing myself to one of the epic poets of al-Bakâtûsh. This was a type of fieldwork that had not yet been attempted with this material. In the first few months of my stay I would have to determine which of the poets I would be able to work well with and see if he would be amenable to taking on a very willing, though rather peculiar, apprentice. To do so meant running the risk that further work with other poets might become difficult; indeed I might be expected to work only with my master poet out of respect.

Obviously, I would not be learning the epic as a true apprentice would, but I hoped to acquire new insights about the traditional process of transmission by making the attempt. I had heard the poets of al-Bakâtûsh describe their apprenticeships many times over, so I knew a little of what to expect. Here is an account given by Shaykh 'Antar 'Abd al-'atî, on June 12, 1987:

> Reynolds: "When you were young how did you memorize the *sîra?*"
> 'Antar: "I'll tell you. I used to go to the *sahrât* with my father and 'support him' [*asniduh*] on the *rabâb*. My hand 'supported him' but my ear was toward him [*îdî kânit bitsanniduh wi-widnî luh*] Afterwards my father would ask me while we were walking or riding the train, 'What happened in the story last night?' And I'd tell him . . . "
> Reynolds: "But in regular words [*kalâm 'âdî*], not in poetry?"
> 'Antar: "Right, just regular words [*kalâm bass*]. The next night he'd sing the same story so I would 'drink from it a lot' [*ashrab minhâ kitîr*], I'd memorize it [*ahfazhâ*]. The next night he'd sing a different story . . . "

Reynolds: "But how did you get to the level of telling the story in words and singing it? I mean, I can tell many of the stories from hearing them a lot [*min kutrat al-samâ'*], but I can't sing poetry . . ."

'Antar: "My father would 'support me' on the *rabâb* when I first started to sing [lit. 'say': *aqûl*]—if I got lost I'd listen to him and repeat what he said [*arudd 'alay*]."

Reynolds: "How old were you when you first started to say the *sîra?*"

'Antar: "Eleven. My father used to present me [*kân biyigaddimnî*] in the *sahrât.*"

Reynolds: "But, for instance, did you repeat the story to yourself alone, make a review of it [*murâja'a*]?"

'Antar: "Of course, I'd go over the stories, looking for the right word [*al-kalima al-munâsiba*] alone [*li-waḥdî*]."

Reynolds: "And you performed at eleven—that's very young!"

'Antar: "I started supporting my mother and [4] sisters, and I married them all off!"[4]

One night in mid-March when the weather was still quite cold, we were listening to Shaykh 'Abd al-Wahhâb sing the concluding section to the episode of "Shâma, Queen of Yemen." His loyal coterie had turned up despite the weather so the room was full—there were thirteen of us in all: Jalâl the government store operator, 'Abd al-Hamîd the tailor, 'Abd al-Hamîd the poet, his son Rajab, Mustafa, Ahmad Bakhâtî (my landlord), Ahmad, Shaykh Imâm, Bakr who works in the provincial capital in the tax department, one of the local policemen, one unknown, myself, and of course Shaykh 'Abd al-Wahhâb. Conversation during tea breaks produced some amazing examples of the fine art of village genealogy of which Shaykh 'Abd al-Wahhâb is a master. It is at such moments one sees the social reversal inherent in these performance situations. Men who in daily social life are excluded and marginalized in performance are accorded respect. Though their lowly social role, their extreme poverty, and the derogatory attitudes evinced by the villagers might lead one to conclude that they are complete outsiders, they are, at another level, clearly an essential part of this community, for they are the repositories of much of its history, genealogy, and verbal art.

'Abd al-Wahhâb asked each new face that entered the gathering, "Whose son are you?" And, after the initial response, he launched into the show:

Isn't your grandfather so-and-so, and your grandmother so-and-so? And your father's the youngest of the bunch, his brothers ———, ———, and ——— are all older, right? You're too young to have known your oldest uncle, eh? Well I'll tell you he was a fine man. The whole village wept when he died. And your grandfather [pointing to somebody else] he died the next day. That week we went to the cemetery four times, and each time for a fine man. . . . Are you married yet? Whose daughter have you taken? She's your cousin that one . . . [He could go on for hours.]

At the end of the evening's performance everyone went home except for the two poets, Shaykh ʿAbd al-Wahhâb and Shaykh ʿAbd al-Hamîd, and ʿAbd al-Hamîd's son, Rajab. These were wonderful conversations, late at night, when I was the only nonpoet present. I kept the tea and cigarettes flowing and was rewarded with tales of great poets and performances of the past. Shaykh ʿAbd al-Wahhâb, however, always made a great deal of the fact that he never drank tea, only coffee. So tonight I brought in the kerosene stove and he instructed Rajab and me in the fine art of coffee-making.

While Rajab and I struggled to get the coffee just right, a conversation began between the two poets about what type of wood one should use in the making of a *rabâb* (the musical instrument epic poets play while singing)—ebony or ash. They then moved on to whether or not it was good to have mother-of-pearl inlay on the instrument. They then spoke of *rabâbs* that had been played by famous poets of the past. I was rapidly drifting out of the conversation for it was three in the morning. A new tack in the conversation, however, brought me back to a full state of wakefulness. Rajab turned and said to me:[5] "You know, when you get back to America you could perform this poetry on the lute." (The fact that I could play ʿûd [Arab lute] was always a thing of wonder, for it is an urban instrument and nobody in the village could play one.)

I responded, "But what I'd really like to do is learn to sing it on the *rabâb*."

For a moment they just stared at me. Shaykh ʿAbd al-Wahhâb chuckled, "I'll get you a *rabâb* and put you to work here beside me [*anâ hashûf lak rabâb wi-ashaghghalak hinâ jambî*]."

"By God I'd love to! [*wallâhi yârêt!*]" I replied.

Then Rajab chimed in, "Why didn't you tell us you wanted to do this. We'll get you a *rabâb* and you can go sit with Uncle ʿAbd al-Wahhâb an hour every day and he'll show you how to place your fingers."

At key turning points in fieldwork it would be nice, I suppose, to be able to say one had had deep and theoretically earth-shattering statements flash through one's mind—instead I somehow thought of Mickey Rooney turning to Judy Garland saying, "I've got an idea . . . let's put on a show! We'll use old MacGregor's barn for a stage and . . . and . . ."

In two minutes my apprenticeship had been secured, though we talked on excitedly about it for another half-hour before everyone went home to bed. What I had feared would be the most difficult transition of my fieldwork had taken place with no effort or planning on my part. Not only was my apprenticeship launched with full approval of the poets' community but there was never any question of my loyalty to my poet-teacher, even though I recorded and worked with many other poets.

Rhyme and Reason

Occasionally one simply finds the right question at the right moment and a whole system of phenomena falls into place—the classic "Aha!" This instance occurred during a performance by Shaykh Tâhâ Abû Zayd, a seventy-year-old poet who performs in a stark, almost severe style, unadorned by dramatic facial or hand gestures, but who is known for his eloquent poetic diction. We had just heard a lengthy section of the episode of "Nâʿisat al-Ajfân [The Maiden of the Languorous Eyes]" and were drinking tea and smoking. I had several times previously, using different guises such as saying the tape had "gone bad," reelicited passages from poets to see what types of variation would occur. On this night, in a moment of inspiration I asked Shaykh Tâhâ not only if he would resing the passage we had just heard but if he would do so on a different rhyme. He looked at me and squinted, a teacher looking at a precocious pupil: "What rhyme do you want?"

We had just heard the passage on an *r* rhyme [âr], so I quickly ransacked my mind for a rhyme that was quite different but that I knew to be standard.

"How about *mîm?*" (i.e., any vowel plus the final letter *m*).

Shaykh Tâhâ put out his cigarette, picked up the *rabâb* and asked, "From where?"

"From where Abû Zayd finds the horse in the desert."

With no preparation, and with apparently total ease, Shaykh Tâhâ sang the passage again on the new rhyme. I was ecstatic. Though the poets later learned that they could expect such peculiar requests from me, this first example was totally fortuitous. The overall story remained the same, even down to some of the fine detail, but the lines were each recast so as to produce the new rhyme. Here was evidence for both the total fluidity of the traditional process of composition, and the virtuosity of the performing artist himself.

When we reached our previous stopping point Shaykh Tâhâ paused and smiled. I immediately wanted to know if he would do it again on another rhyme, but the audience members objected. Several turned to me and asked, "What don't you understand about this part? Why do you want to hear it again? Don't you understand what happened?" They were oblivious to the feat they had just witnessed. Shaykh Tâhâ smiled again at me and, gesturing to the other listeners, picked up the story from there and continued.

The two texts demonstrate typical stability of the basic plot, including even a number of the smaller details, despite radical rewording of these ideas. Even more interesting in this case, however, is the fact that the poet, well realizing that I was "putting him to the test" wove a set of puns into the rhymes of the second version, that is, he not only changed the rhyme scheme at my request but proceeded to produce a more complex and eloquent text at the same time.

The following morning I went to visit Shaykh Tâhâ as usual to thank him for his performance and to hear his comments about the evening's entertainment (*his* comments always focused upon how good or bad the audience had been, not about his own singing). I mentioned the puns he had inserted into his second rendition and he responded quite simply that if I could both weigh my words and embellish them, then I would be a poet.

The process of oral composition in the performance of epic poetry has been a major topic in epic studies and folklore since the work of Milman Parry and Albert Lord in the early and mid-twentieth century (Lord 1960). Listening to, and attempting to sing, this Arabic oral epic tradition, I had no doubts that this was indeed a tradition based on oral-formulaic composition, a process by which poets manipulate a vast repertory of traditional phrases, half-lines, and whole verses, and essentially retell the stories at each performance using the rhetoric and style of epic poetry, rather than reciting a memorized text. Arabic epic, however, has a twist not found in the Homeric or South Slavic traditions in that it demands rhyming verses. The vast majority of Arabic poetry over the centuries has been cast in a single pattern: mono-end rhyme, medial caesura verse. That is, each verse ends on the same rhyme (in sequences sometimes reaching hundreds of lines), and each line has a single break in the middle. The morphological matrices of Arabic allow for more abundant rhyming than in English; however, poets in both written and oral media eschew morphological rhyme as facile and strive to produce rhymes which derive from unrelated forms.

I spent a great deal of my time that year listening to the tapes I had recorded, transcribing them, and doing initial translations of them. Some of the patterns became clear very early. The poets, for example, have stock verses in their repertory that express a key idea in which the last word can easily be substituted to render the desired rhyme. A phrase such as "and his mind from him *strayed* [wi-l-'aql minnu *tâh*]" is used to express the power of strong emotions such as anger or sorrow. The last word, in this case a past tense verb, can be replaced in order to create other rhymes:

> and his mind from him *flew*
> [wi-l-'aql minnu *ṭâr*]
>
> and his mind from him *wandered*
> [wi-l-'aql minnu *hâm*]
>
> and his mind was *absent*
> [wi-l-'aql *ghâyib*]
>
> and his mind grew *confused*
> [wi-l-'aql minnu *iḥtâr*]

Slightly more complicated changes can be used to generate rhymes easily from the basic pattern by adding images or metaphors:

> and he felt as if his mind had tipped the *scale*
> [wi-ḥass bi-inn 'aqluh fâriq il-mîzân]

and he felt as if his mind was mixed with *madness*

[wi-ḥass inn dâ ʿaqluh ikhtalaṭ bi-*jinân*]

I slowly grew attuned to these patterns, tagged them mentally during performances, and began consciously to use them in my own amateur attempts at singing under the tutelage of Shaykh ʿAbd al-Wahhâb. That first experiment with Shaykh Ṭâhâ, however, was the key to my understanding of the overall process.

Words of the Epic or Words of the Poet?

Still more perceptible, and more fascinating in effect, are moments when the poet openly manipulates the text to meld with, or react to, the performance situation. The first time I realized the extent of this creative dimension was during a *sahra* which was riddled with tension because of the presence of eight educated young men from al-Bakâtûsh, all of whom have fairly open fundamentalist leanings. The poet, Shaykh Biyelî Abû Fahmî, is the favorite poet of the younger crowd in al-Bakâtûsh; he is a lively performer who tends toward humorous and melodramatic presentation, and for these reasons claims fewer loyal fans from the older, more purist, aficionados. In this performance, however, he drew high praise from the old men present.

The young men had shown up with a guest from town, a high school English teacher whom they wanted me to meet. At the first tea break they presented their guest and then virtually took over the gathering; their conversation was energetic and soon drifted toward politics. The other dozen or so men present were displeased both with what they saw as the disrespectful behavior of the young men (who should have remained quiet in a gathering of older men), as well as by this new turn in the conversation. They were, however, constrained by the presence of an educated guest.

Shaykh Biyelî tried to steer the conversation in a new direction, but a young man cut him off. The poet spun around angrily to face the young man. "Don't you know the meaning of the word 'Excuse me' [*lâ muʾakhiza*]," he erupted. "Sit quietly!" The high school teacher intervened to calm Shaykh Biyelî, but the poet was suspicious of his ingratiating tone and his overly florid terms of respect.[6] Shaykh Biyelî picked up his *rabâb* and put an end to the matter by starting to play. The young men continued to converse and whisper their irritation. Suddenly Biyelî threw in a scene I had never heard before (and, as it turns out, never heard again). The setting is a battle in Tunis where the Banî Hilâl desperately need the aid of their mighty, but temperamental, warrior, Diyâb. Diyâb's mother, sent to persuade him to ride into battle, is guided into his tent and she removes her veil; our hero has not seen his mother unveiled since he was a child and is horrified to discover that she is incredibly ugly—which, as happens every few minutes with Arab epic heroes, prompts him to sing an ode.

The poem began with words of praise for the Prophet Muhammad. The audience responded, wishing God's blessings upon Him, and fell quiet. Then the poet sang a sequence of aphorisms in verse about how some are given great wealth by God, and some are given none, how some are given good fortune, and some are given bad, how some are given polite, hardworking wives and others ugly, rude ones. The description of the ugly wife brought laughter ("with her legs and her glare she resembles a catfish! [*lahâ riglên wi-zughrhâ tishâbih il-garmût*]"). But after many humorous lines, the poet began to comment on the man who possesses *aṣl* (nobility of character) and on politeness and respect, how some are granted sons who are born with these qualities, and others, alas, are given sons who do not know their place. The young men took this as a commentary on their own behavior and began to squirm uneasily. The poem grew pointedly critical and the tension in the room soon reached the breaking point. Those who have no schooling but are wise, the poet complained, are criticized by those with schooling who do not yet know wisdom. Just when it seemed the young men might actually interrupt the performance Biyelî alleviated some of the pressure with a quick sequence of jokes and then closed with several religious verses. Biyelî stopped singing and declared that it was time for a tea break (only minutes after our last tea break!). I was puzzled at the sudden break in the performance; clarification followed quickly, however.

Moments after the poet stopped, the young men stood up and departed without saying farewell to anyone other than myself, a clear breach of village etiquette. Their guest, caught unawares, scrambled to his feet and attempted to make a proper departure by saluting and greeting the audience en masse. The remaining listeners, all over forty-five or so, congratulated Biyelî on his handling of the situation; then, without having drunk tea, we began again. The oddly timorous hero no longer had qualms about riding into battle, and his mother was nowhere to be seen while he girded himself for war. There were no more comic sections for the rest of the evening. The encounter between the poet and the young men, however, became a comic anecdote and was retold in the village numerous times over the next few days.

Such interjected scenes and lines are part and parcel of the *Sîrat Banî Hilâl* tradition in al-Bakâtûsh; in fact, some of these spontaneous commentaries are repeated months and years after their original performance. Several lines from a performance which took place nearly twenty years ago, when a poet performing outdoors for a circumcision ceremony told the head of the village guard to get the women down off the roofs (in verse, of course), were recounted to me several times by villagers. These impromptu additions are recognized by both poets and listeners as a mark of virtuosity.

During my fieldwork, once the poet had left the room, listeners would comment on many aspects of what they had just heard: the story, the characters, the poet's voice, his playing, his jokes, and so on. Within a day or two, however, I found that audience members no longer retained the aesthetic criticisms they had offered earlier. Instead they remembered and discussed the social aspects of the performance, that is, the interplay which had taken place between the poet and the audience, and, if they could recite any of the poetry they had heard that night, it was the improvised asides and jokes, not passages from the epic! Any one telling of a portion of the epic melted into all the previous tellings. In essence, the social action within the event became their text; the epic performance was but one of many possible contexts for the enactment and interaction of characters from daily life in the village. Such was the fate of the encounter I have described above. Within days, none of the audience members could recollect aspects of that particular performance other than the witty handling of a difficult situation by Shaykh Biyelî.

Last Moments

Numerous fieldworkers have written frankly about their relations with the communities they have lived in and studied, detailing both the rewarding moments of friendship and the frustrating moments of suspicion and distrust. My own experience in the Egyptian countryside has been that the short-term hospitality and generosity is quite extraordinary, exceeding that which I have encountered in almost all other areas where I have traveled. Long-term residency, however, opened up an entirely different set of attitudes, or at least did during my stay in al-Bakâtûsh: some of these were motivated by fears of outside intrusion occasioned by my presence (government officials, the district police chief, even state police officers from the provincial capital), others derived from tensions about my unmarried status and my Christian background, and many simply were reactions to an outsider entering a close-knit community.

I never had difficulties with people who actually knew me and with whom I socialized regularly. However, for many people in the area I was merely a figure that passed by, often carrying notebook or camera, about whom they heard anecdotes and rumors many times removed from their source. The suspicions that grew around my presence and my work did not surprise me. In fact, the tightness of social alliances and the bitterness of rivalries in the village were so strong, the monitoring of people's whereabouts, purchases, and diet so intense, that I could hardly feel I was being accorded special treatment.

Each time I left the three-room house where I lived with a family of six, the mother of the household would invariably check to make sure that anything I was carrying was well concealed and out of sight. On one occasion when I had purchased material at the weekly market for a new *gallabiyya* (the nightshirt-like apparel worn by men) and was on my way to the tailor's, she seized the plastic bag in which I was carrying the cloth, took out the cloth, wrapped it in newspaper, and returned it to the bag. She chided me for giving people something to talk about. I protested that everyone already knew I had bought cloth at the market (at least a half-dozen people had offered opinions as to color and quality), and in a few days everyone would see the new *gallabiyya*. No change: avoid the evil eye and don't give people a chance to talk, wrap it up!

Another example: one late afternoon I was sitting with some older men on their *maṣṭaba,* the brick bench attached to the front of the house where much of the neighborhood's socializing takes place. As usual, our conversation was sometimes quiet, held just between the three of us, and sometimes loud, including small groups on similar *maṣṭabas* in both directions down the alley. A man passed us, greeted us, then turned down a small alleyway. Conversation stopped. Everyone in the alley was perturbed and people began to whisper: "Allah! Allah! what is this?" Finally the commotion grew to a climax and a man opposite us stood up, walked to the corner and took a long look down the alleyway. He returned and announced to the whole alley, "He's borrowing a sickle from so-and-so." Everyone relaxed and conversations began to flow again. The problem? This man had no known reason for being down that alleyway—he had no relatives there, and there were no shops, no tailor, no other plausible reason for his presence. In the late afternoon, most younger men are out in their fields, so the presence of a man wandering about the village was a source of consternation. Once his purpose was made public, the vigilant eyes of the neighborhood could relax.

For the first few months of my stay, every few weeks was marked by some encounter that seemed to belie the hospitality and friendliness I encountered face to face. The first month it was the issue of maps. So as not to get lost on my late afternoon walks through the fields and neighboring villages, I had drawn a map of the major paths that link the dozen nearest settlements to al-Bakâtûsh in my notebook. Once while I was out, a guest started rifling through my notes and translations and found the map (written in Arabic). By the time I had returned from my walk the whole village was in an uproar about the "American spy."[7] In the second month I began taking pictures—usually at the behest of the people I was photographing. Someone, however, thought I was photographing too much, for the news soon reached the district police station where I was invited to make an appearance. A few weeks later a Muslim-Christian riot broke out in the town next to us, and the village felt a resurgence of tension about my presence. A month later while I was walking through the village, a man pulled me into his doorway and whispered to me, "I want you to know that I don't believe the things they are saying about you. If you need help, you can come to me." I was shaken by the encounter and it took several days of discreet questioning to find out what the problem was. This time word was being spread that I had come to convert the young men of the village to Christianity, to lure them away from Islam.

Each of these incidents, and a dozen or so smaller ones, were handled the same way. My friends in the village (and I, on their instructions) would loudly and at every opportunity such as in the coffeehouses at evening gatherings, and in private conversations, explain what I was doing and why. It was a constant public relations campaign.

Suddenly after five months the difficulties ceased. At the time I assumed the village had finally grown used to my presence, some critical threshold had been reached, I was after all really interested in poetry and folk music. In the late summer I contracted hepatitis and had to move to Cairo for several weeks while I recuperated. Delegations arrived from the village every few days to check on my health and to bring news. When I returned to the village there was no trace of tension. People told me again and again how sorry they were that I had taken ill while in their village.

After my year of research, when my final departure drew close, I again moved to Cairo for a couple weeks. During the last visit I received from friends from al-Bakâtûsh we stayed up nearly till dawn talking and reminiscing. Before we fell asleep my closest friend, and staunchest defender in the village, asked if I knew a certain man. I recognized the family name and said so, but did not know the man in question. Everyone laughed and asked me, "Are you sure?" They then described him to me and mentioned that he was one of the village guards. I could just barely conjure up the man's face. They laughed some more and finally explained.

Months earlier, someone had seen me coming home late at night from some gathering or another and apparently coming out of an alleyway where they could not imagine me having any legitimate business. They reported it to the village "mayor" ['umda]; the result was that this man from the village guard had been assigned to follow me around the village for the ensuing months. When I went into a house, he would sit at a nearby café; when I left, he would follow. Just at the point where I had imagined my relations with the village to be relaxing and everyone's suspicions to have been allayed, I had in fact been placed under full-time surveillance. My friends were tickled that even after months I had not noticed. I, however, felt as if someone had kicked a chair out from under me. My feelings of having crossed immense cultural distances and achieved some personal understanding were being put in question. That sense of ambiguity was to linger for a long time.

I was lucky enough to have another opportunity to visit al-Bakâtûsh a year later. There were no small incidents this time to mar what was, on the surface at least, essentially a reunion of friends. Letters and photographs that I had sent, articles and photos of al-Bakâtûsh that had been published as a result of my work, had strengthened the friendships that had begun the previous year. All this bolstered the romantic interpretation of fieldwork as human contact and the search for understanding. Recollection of that one moment of discovery, however, always throws into doubt all that I think I understood, and all I encountered. It is, I believe, a productive state of doubt.

As fieldworkers we are often in the predicament of trying to turn a discordant tableau of observable behavior and phenomena into systematic description. We also strive constantly with the challenge of trying to perceive the world as other people perceive it. Our "fieldwork epiphanies" are thus quite frequently the result of successfully (we hope) encapsulating a series of observations into an analytic frame. As such they can be as much the product of our desired final objective (order, system, coherence) as they are a product of mixing our chosen methodology of close observation with a little bit of chance. But those epiphanies also act as effective reminders of the constant gap which lingers between the behaviors and forces discernible to the researcher, the researcher's means of understanding those observed phenomena, and the social, emotional world of the people we attempt to understand. They are lessons about assumption, whether conscious or unconscious, about perception, and about the power of accident.

Notes

Portions of this essay were adapted from Dwight F. Reynolds, *Heroic Poets, Poetic Heroes: The Ethnography of Performance in an Arabic Oral Epic Tradition.* Copyright © 1995 by Cornell University. Used by permission of the publisher, Cornell University Press.

1   *Sîrat Banî Hilâl* is one of nearly a dozen Arab folk epics that were in wide circulation until the nineteenth century. In the last two centuries, however, the other folk epics have all died out, leaving *Sîrat Banî Hilâl* as the last example of this genre in living, oral tradition. *Sîra* means literally a "traveling" or "jour-

neying" and is used in Arabic to refer to biographies, histories, and, as in this case, folk epics. The Banî Hilâl were a vast Bedouin tribal confederation who left their native Arabian peninsula in the tenth century, crossed Egypt and Libya, and eventually conquered Tunisia and ruled there for about one hundred years. They were then defeated by an eastward-moving Moroccan dynasty and disappeared from history in the late twelfth century.

2   The first two poet families to settle in al-Bakâtûsh arrived in the late nineteenth century; over the years the community has continued to grow. The poets were apparently itinerant before that time. Though they are permanent residents of the village, in Arabic they are referred to as the "poets" and not included in the term "villagers" [ahl al-balad]. I follow this local usage of referring to poets versus villagers in this essay.

3   In the families of the al-Bakâtûsh poets, every male going back three generations and more has been an epic poet; some were good, some were not so good, but it was the sole profession of male members of this group. In the past two decades, with the arrival of radio, cassettes, and television, the demand for the epic has dropped off sharply. The young men of the poets' families are now seeking employment in other fields. Curiously enough, a poet's son, even though he is not a poet and currently works, for example, as a plumber, is still called "So-and-so the Poet." The title is virtually an ethnic tag, not an indication of profession.

4   Shaykh 'Antar's father divorced his mother while he was a teenager; he became the breadwinner for a household of six, and a solo performer, at that time.

5   This conversation appears as I transcribed it into my field notes a half hour after the fact; it was not audio-recorded.

6   For terms of respect in Egyptian Arabic see Parkinson 1985. The poet himself made reference to the way the teacher had addressed him after the incident. The teacher had erred, as an educated, middle-class, town-dweller, in addressing an uneducated, older poet in too formal terms. His attempts to calm the poet were taken as sarcasms.

7   It must be remembered that Egypt has been at war four times in the past forty years with a nation that derives its existence from American support. I was treated hospitably and generously even by families who had lost sons to American bullets wielded by American-financed soldiers.

References Cited

Lord, Albert B. 1960. *The Singer of Tales.* Cambridge: Harvard University Press.

Parkinson, Dilworth. 1985. *Constructing the Social Context of Communication: Terms of Address in Egyptian Arabic.* Berlin: Mouton de Gruyter.

9

Absorbed in Gospel Music
Lynwood Montell

As folklorists, when we embark upon a fieldwork enterprise, we are not always aware of the full dimensions of the tradition being documented. We may begin with a project design, a plan of work, certain goals in mind, perhaps even a theory and attendant problems to be addressed. We are, however, never able to fully gauge the effects of our fieldwork on a time-honored, cherished tradition. The general assumption is that fieldwork has a negative impact on the tradition being studied, disrupting it by creating an unhealthy self-consciousness in tradition bearers. Documenting a tradition may be viewed in a positive light, feel some folklorists, only when it is done in the spirit of advocacy, helping those persons or groups of people who rely on the continuance of a tradition for economic or spiritual sustenance.

I discovered in my own research into white gospel music in south central Kentucky that the fieldwork has had neither a negative, uprooting effect on the very strong gospel singing tradition here, nor have I felt compelled to assume an advocate's role in preserving it. Instead, the singing tradition that I investigated is so well established that it absorbed my research and documentation efforts into its very fiber.

The absorption process happened in a series of stages, beginning in April 1986, when I went to a local church to document a shape-note teaching session, and culminating in late May 1989, when I stood on stage singing with the Happy Travelers, an area gospel quartet from Bethelridge, a small rural community in eastern Casey County, Kentucky. At that point, I was no longer a professional folklorist documenting a singing event. I was not even a participant observer; rather, I was one of them in full standing, assisting in the concluding moments of a religious service.

This series of events began in late summer of 1985, when I first became interested in researching the history of shape-note music and early gospel quartets in a 20-county area of south central Kentucky, and in documenting the contemporary performance aspects of gospel music as reflected in the activities of the one hundred or so groups active in the study area in the late 1980s. Thinking that the old-time music school tradition was a thing of the past, I was elated to hear an announcement over a local radio station in April 1986 that C. E. Deweese, one-time teacher for the Vaughan School of Music in Lawrenceburg, Tennessee, would be teaching a ten-night singing school at the Union Light Missionary Baptist Church, located at the northern edge of the Mammoth Cave National Park, in nearby Edmonson County, Kentucky.

I went to the church for the first session of the music school, intentionally arriving early to seek permission to tape record and photograph the proceedings. Deweese assured me that my equipment and presence would not hinder his round of teaching activities. He did, however, suggest that I seek permission from a church leader, who was actually in charge of the event.

That leader was Georgie Childress, not only a moving force in the church but a singer of many years, who has been described as having the best bass voice in the area. He was extremely cordial to me and assured me that I was most welcome to observe the proceedings of the evening. However, he apprised me of the fact that the Union Light congregation had never permitted a tape recorder or camera to be used inside the church. Moreover, he pointed out that there was not even a piano or other musical instrument in the sanctuary. "The Lord has given us the finest musical instruments possible," he assured me, pointed to his vocal chords. "All we have to do is train them," he stated proudly.

Although I was resigned at that point to forego the documentation I had planned, I still sat through that first night's session with a keen interest in what was taking place, and returned for an additional evening of shape-note instruction the following week. I was spellbound by what I heard and saw.

About a month later, I went back to Union Light, this time to witness a practice session of the church choir. Childress and the others present that evening extended to me a warm hand of welcome and friendship. We sat there and chatted for a few minutes until, as if prompted by an inner bell, Childress stood up, looked out over the twenty-five singers and the ten or so visitors, cleared his throat, and announced that it was time for the singing to begin.

The singers moved quickly to the altar area and took their regular places in front of the pulpit. They formed a closed circle in which they grouped themselves according to their respective vocal parts. The sopranos, made up of both men and women, stood to the left of the pulpit, facing into the circle. The altos stood to the right of the sopranos, facing them; the tenors filled in the remaining space on the right, while the bass vocalists stood with their backs to the audience. David Taylor, the group song leader, was stationed in the middle of the circle, facing the basses. He directed the singing of each song, but it was Childress who selected the songs to be sung and vocally pitched the tunes in the appropriate key, without benefit of any musical instrument, tuning fork, or pitch pipe.

"Tonight we'll start off by using our new song book," he announced. "Let's sing number 24. Number 24. Sing the notes, then the words."

Childress, in his late sixties then, is a singing veteran of over forty years. With near perfect pitch, he intoned the opening notes, and the other singers joined in as together they keyed the tune. Their "do, re, mis" filled the sanctuary with enthusiasm, volume, and authority. Clearly, these shape-note singers knew what they were doing and loved doing it.

Following the first song, Childress took time out to explain to those of us in the audience that the Union Light Church frequently purchases new songbooks. "We love the new songs," he went on. "Get tired of singing the same old songs all the time. We meet here and pick out new songs together. Most of us have been singing the shape notes for a long time," he said proudly, and then added without apology, "I don't know anything about the round notes."

"Number 84, number 84," he called out to the singers. "Let's sing the notes to 'Just over Yonder,' then we'll sing the words." Their talent-laden voices made the church sanctuary echo with beautiful harmony that rang loud and clear in the distinctive four-part gospel music style. Pausing only once for brief personal testimonies, prayer requests, and then individual prayers said aloud simultaneously, the singers continued for almost two hours. The session ended with the singing of "Amazing Grace" while everyone, singers and audience alike, moved around the altar area, single file, to shake hands with the others as a gesture of love and fellowship.

As I listened to the singing that evening, enthralled at the sounds produced by the singers' unaccompanied voices, I felt a strong sense of urgency to record the sound for posterity and to capture the essence of the event on film. I knew, however, that I first had to obtain permission from the church to do it and that I could win that privilege only through gaining their confidence and trust.

Following that evening's singing event, Willowdean and Georgie Childress invited some close friends from the church group to join them at their home for refreshments and included me in their invitation. Three weeks later, I returned to Union Light and sat in a pew near the front of the church. Again I listened intently as the singers shared through song their messages of God's love, spending an eternity in heaven, and the need to live right on this side of the River Jordan (i.e., death). As before, I was honored to be among those who gathered in the Childress home afterwards, an event that has become a tradition in and of itself.

By that time I felt comfortable in my relationship with the Childresses and many other members of the church. Before leaving the Childress home that evening, I sought and obtained permission to return in two weeks for a tape-recorded interview with Georgie about area congregational singing and the musical heritage of Union Light Baptist Church in particular. I had learned previously that he had no compunction against the use of tape recorders, except in the church sanctuary. As a matter of fact, he and Willowdean had a stereo record and tape player and a VCR in their home.

At the conclusion of the interview, and with the notion of recording the church choir urging me on, I asked Georgie if his parents and grandparents had sung shape-note music at church when he was a child.

"Oh, yes!" was his quick response.

"Wouldn't it be wonderful if you could hear their voices again?" I probed.

Georgie paused and then responded in a voice barely audible, "My, oh my. You can't begin to imagine how much that would mean to me."

I, too, waited a moment so as not to disrupt his emotional trip back in time, then broke the silence of the moment by gently suggesting, "You don't have *their* voices on tape, but if you let me record the church choir now, your grandchildren and their children would have the opportunity to hear you in the years to come."

His reaction to my suggestion was one of surprise, followed by a promised course of action. "Tell you what," Childress said, "I'll take this matter before the church at the next business meeting and ask them to vote on letting you tape-record one of our Friday night singings."

The church granted that permission, and Georgie called me to share the good news. Two weeks later, I was again in attendance at the choir practice. This time, I was able to set up a stereo tape recorder with the two mikes positioned in the middle of the circle formed by the singers and used a 35mm camera for visual documentation. All went well. I had been willing for things to move at a pace dictated by the circumstances rather than by my own schedule, and perhaps most importantly, I left the final decision concerning documentation in the hands of the group itself.

I had wanted a tape recording of the Union Light choir to deposit in the Folklife and Oral History Archives at Western Kentucky University as a memento of quality shape-note singing in my study area. The recording meant something entirely different to the Union Light congregation, however. They saw the tape not as some artifact potentially useful in the future but as a song ministry in the present, and began immediately to duplicate it for friends and former church members scattered across the South and Midwest. Numerous people came up to me weeks and months later to say that they had heard the tape made at Union Light.

A very poignant story emerged from the distribution of the recording. Georgie Childress himself took a copy of the tape along with a tape recorder to the home of an elderly former pastor, who lived in neighboring Hart County. The old minister lay on his deathbed and shed tears of joy all the way through the tape, exclaiming time after time, "I never thought I'd ever again get to hear the Union Light Singers."

What began as a routine fieldwork project on my part suddenly assumed new proportions. The Union Light congregation had used me, as it were, to their advantage. (Not surprisingly, perhaps, they asked me to do another recording of their group in late spring of 1989. I obliged them willingly and with great pleasure.)

Following the experience at Union Light, I actively pursued my research into other facets of the gospel music tradition, attending singings in local churches virtually every weekend and interviewing a variety of people involved in the tradition throughout the study area. In the process I became known to and recognized by the singers, who form a tight-knit group in close communication with each other, as the professor from Western studying the history of their gospel music tradition. They seemed pleased at my interest and eager to provide me with the information I was seeking about the history of individual groups. Their enthusiasm and cooperation made doing fieldwork pure pleasure. What I didn't understand at the time was that the singers were gradually weaving a web around me and my research efforts, drawing me in closer and closer to the center of their activities. I did not realize just how much they felt themselves to be an integral part of what I was doing until the second Saturday night of January 1988.

I had gone to Glasgow, county seat of Barren County, to document five Barren County groups slated to perform that night at the monthly sing scheduled at a community clubhouse. I arrived about thirty minutes early in order to set up my tape recorder. And since I was generally accustomed to patching directly from the singers' sound system, I went to Bill Jones, manager and sound man for the Gospel Crusaders, one of the groups on the program that night. When I asked if he had room for my jack, he looked at me questioningly. "Why are *you* recording?" he wanted to know. "We're taping this *for* you."

About that time, Rex Agers, president of the Barren County Gospel Singing Association, walked up and extended a cordial welcome to me. Agers explained that he and some of the singers felt that the months of January, February, and March, when gospel singing in area churches is at an annual low ebb, would be a good time to invite all the county's gospel groups to come together and sing for my benefit even though they had no idea that I would be present on that cold January evening. I was stunned! The fifteen gospel music groups of Barren County were planning to stage special performances and record them on my behalf, to demonstrate their interest in and support of my research project. This was fieldwork in reverse. It was not just me asking them for something on my terms; it was people giving of themselves to me. They loved what they were doing and wanted to share with me, a lay person interested in their music tradition.

This Glasgow episode was only the beginning of a round of similar activities carried out across the region to accommodate my research interests and to express the singers' appreciation for my paying attention to the thing they love so very much and to which they have devoted their lives. From Glasgow I went—among other places—to the Science Hill Methodist church in Pulaski County, where more than half a century of fine ensemble and congregational singing was reenacted for my benefit; to Coffey's Chapel in Russell County, where the county's annual singing convention was dedicated to my work; to Bald Knob in Logan County, where a dozen old-time shape-note song leaders demonstrated their expertise in directing congregational singing; and to Spears Chapel Community Church in Cumberland County, where on July 1, 1989, twenty-five gospel music groups came together to sing while tape recordings were being made for me that would, according to event organizer Gary Cash, "guarantee all of the groups a place in history."

Not only did the singers turn my fieldwork efforts into an outreach ministry, and involve themselves in assisting me in my research by contributing their time and talents, they also drew me into the very activity that I set about to document. This first occurred in 1987 when I was asked to serve on the board of directors of the Ohio Valley Singing Convention, an organization that stages an annual event, now in its thirteenth year, involving singers from Alabama, Indiana, Kentucky, Mississippi, North Carolina, Tennessee, and Virginia. I have since been given the title of convention historian, a new office created because of my recognized interest in preserving the history and documenting the performance styles of local gospel music.

I was both flattered and elated by the recognition accorded me by the Ohio Valley organization. When I was invited in 1988 to serve on the board of the Kentucky State Singing Convention, I was overwhelmed by this additional display of confidence. That same year, my colleagues on the board asked me to serve as vice-president, thus automatically making me the 1989 president of the State Convention—State Convention president and I don't even sing! There is no question at this point but that I had been placed by the singers themselves at the heart of the gospel music mainstream.

The Happy Travelers, a group mentioned earlier, provided me with the clearest demonstrations of the extent to which the gospel singers I studied view me as one of their own. My strong ties with the group, all members of the Haste family, began in early 1987 when I went to their octogenarian father and grandfather, Jason Haste, to inquire about the family's long-standing involvement with shape-note and quartet singing.

The story of the Hastes as a tight-knit family of singer-farmers began during the late years of the nineteenth century when four brothers organized the Haste Quartet, an ensemble that used only a tuning fork to key the songs. (This quartet is the earliest on record in the 20-county area covered by my research.) Their descendants created an additional eight quartets and/or family groups, including the Bethelridge Junior Quartet, later to become known as the Happy Travelers. Under the earlier name, the singers consisted of Jason's two sons, Virgil, age 10, and Harold, age 6, along with two of Jason's grandsons, Lewis Randolph, age 8, and Ronald, age 6. After these youngsters sang numerous times at their home church and in some of the surrounding churches, their fame was such that John Lair invited them in 1949 to sing on his All-Night Singing and Sunday Morning Gathering at Renfro Valley. Their voices were heard in much of the eastern United States over WHAS in Louisville, the station that carried the Renfro Valley broadcasts at that time.

Roger Haste replaced his uncle Virgil as lead singer and the group has since been renamed the Happy Travelers, but their high-quality four-part harmony keeps them largely uncontested as the finest singing ensemble in the region. Certainly, their teacher, constant companion, and number one fan, Jason Haste, feels that way! And when their van is packed and ready for a trip to a singing engagement, the first person aboard is Jason.

Knowing something of the rich singing tradition of the Haste family that now includes their sixth generation makes it easier to understand how I felt when I was asked to stand and sing with the Happy Travelers in June 1988. The occasion was the Haste family reunion, held at their home church, Bethelridge Methodist, an event that annually attracts family members from Kentucky, Indiana, Ohio, Louisiana, Texas, and Florida. I was there to document the event in connection with my research. During the course of the afternoon's events that involved performances by several family singing ensembles, the Happy Travelers took their turn at the podium. They sang five or six songs, then invited Hobart Haste (their father and brother) and Jason (Hobart's father) to join them for a song, as both had been involved for over forty years as members of the Bethelridge Quartet. It was at that point that Jason publicly introduced me to those sitting in the sanctuary, then wept as he asked me to join them in singing a song.

Lewis Randolph whispered something to the other singers as I proudly walked forward to join them. He had changed the selected song to "Amazing Grace," one that he expected I might know. I stood there singing with the group, holding a mike that Roger stuck in my hands. When first Jason and then Lewis put their arms around my shoulders, I was no longer a fieldworker, I was a participant in their homecoming celebration as an adopted family member.

The culminating event in the process of my being absorbed into the music tradition I was studying came on May 28, 1989, during the regular fourth Sunday night singing at Pleasant Grove Missionary Baptist Church in Warren County. I had gone there on numerous other occasions to document gospel music performance. The featured group that evening was the Happy Travelers, who had been invited to the church (a considerable distance from their home community) because of their excellent performance at the 1988 State Singing Convention.

Following three songs by the assembled congregation, the Happy Travelers were introduced by the pastor. They sang eight songs during their first set. I watched the congregation as the group began to sing, feeling that the local people would be pleased with them. Knowing that I knew the singers personally, one of the men in the congregation caught my eye, formed his lips into a whistle shape, and lifted his thumb. He liked what he heard.

When the Happy Travelers sat down, the congregation sang while an offering was taken to help defray the group's travel expenses. After five additional songs by church members and other visitors, the Happy Travelers again assumed center stage to complete the evening's program. They did four songs and were ready to sing one final number when I was suddenly pulled into their realm by Lewis Randolph who paused, looked at me, and said simply, "Lynwood, come on up here and help us sing this last song."

The invitation was totally unexpected and I was staggered. All I recall saying to the congregation at that time, as I stood up to join the Happy Travelers, was, "I can't turn down this opportunity."

Again, one of the singers stuck a mike in my hand, and again the group sang "Amazing Grace" as they had done at the Haste reunion. Just before we began to sing the final verse, the pastor stood up and said, "Let's ask these singers to stand here in the altar area so we can all come around to shake their hands and tell them how much we enjoyed having them with us tonight. And we want their newest member to stand here with them!"

I stood there singing with the group I had come to document. There was no line drawn between me, the fieldworker, and them, the performers. I was one of them. They had drawn me into the activity that they devoted themselves to every weekend.

What I had been doing as a researcher was assigned a secondary precedence with the singers. To them, I was not a fieldworker but a person drawn intentionally into their normal round of singing activities. Their music tradition is so rich and so extensive that no one person could ever hope to encompass it. They know this and thus were making what *I* do a part of what *they* do. They know and appreciate me as someone documenting the thing they love most. They see me sitting there in the congregation watching them and listening, and think, "He just might enjoy doing this with us," and then invite me to join them in song or lead them as president of their state convention.

It seems safe to say that these people do not view themselves as objects—as fish in a bowl. If anything, *I'm* the fish in the bowl, the object of *their* attention. Folklorists often describe their fieldwork subjects as "my people." Could it be that these gospel singers will refer to me as "our professor" in the years ahead?

10

On Time, Truth, and Epiphanies
Ellen J. Stekert

When I collected from "Singing" Willie Nolan in the 1950s and 1960s, I concentrated on his song repertoire for my dissertation (Stekert 1965). My major interest was how he consciously and unconsciously altered the songs as he performed and reperformed them in the specific psychological, historical, and cultural contexts of our collecting situations. Since, even then, I realized that songs do not exist in a cultural vacuum, I also collected from him, and from others in his community, a wide variety of traditions, including games, legends, and beliefs. Until I looked at it in May 1988, I had treated the legend on which I am focusing here simply as a part of the cultural context within which Willie Nolan sang his songs. Little did I realize that the manner in which I had conducted myself "within" that legend, within the performance of it, probably determined whether or not I was considered an acceptable person with whom Willie and his family could share their lives. I did not understand that the way I participated in that performance would most likely determine the future of my collection project. I was naively unaware of the political implications both of the performance and of my work as a folklorist.[1]

The legend, a personal experience ghost narrative, was recorded as we sat on the front porch of Willie's cabin in southern Indiana after a day of singing, socializing, and eating. We had finished supper and I had been led onto the porch by Willie, Willie's ailing wife, Florie, and their son, Orville. The porch overlooked a rolling, rocky field typical of this rural area. Willie's "garden" (to my city eyes it looked like a small farm) was planted in the "bottom," between the house and the dirt road along which I had traveled to get there. I had asked Willie to tell me about the times and places in which he learned and sang his songs.

It was May 1959. In the previous month, during which I began collecting from him, I had established good rapport with Willie and with those who lived in his small household. I had been put in contact with Willie a few months earlier by the ballad scholar Evelyn K. Wells. She encouraged me to collect from him, and she sent me a tape recording she had made on her last visit to Willie six years earlier. Professor Wells, a retired professor from Wellesley College, had been a teacher at the Pine Mountain Settlement School (Whisnant 1983: 291 [206 n.], citing Wells 1960). It was through this school that she first heard Willie sing, and from which she made occasional visits to his home (from 1916 to 1928), "listening hard while he sang, making scrappy notations, hoping that I was absorbing enough at the time to recall properly on paper when I got back to school, the shape and rhythms of his tunes."[2] She published a number of Willie's songs in regional publications as well as in her book *The Ballad Tree* (1950).

It was the end of a day during which I became aware that most of Willie's family had come to regard me as a friend. His sister-in-law, Mary, lived with her thirty-year-old daughter, a T.B.I. (Traumatic Brain Injury) survivor, in the same house as Willie and his wife, and it was she who had overseen the running of that household since her sister, Florie, had been in the terminal stages of diabetes. On this trip she greeted me with warm hugs and asked me to call her "aunt" Mary, not implying the literal use of "aunt" but rather as it signified familiarity, the way the term was used in eastern Kentucky.

This was the first time I had met Orville and his wife, Glacie. Glacie and I found a mutual bond in our both being teachers (I was a graduate student assistant at Indiana University; she was a primary school teacher in Salem, Indiana, who had taken classes at I.U.). As on other visits, I brought my guitar with me as well as my recording machines and cameras, and Willie and I had "swapped" songs. I think now that I sang more than usual that day not only to please Willie but also because I hoped that my singing would help Orville and Glacie accept me. I knew that singing aided my rapport with Willie and his household (almost as much as the fact that I had long hair, which was repeatedly praised). But I sensed that Orville and Glacie were key in Willie's life. Orville had appeared often in Evelyn Wells's letters; he was almost always in photographs of Willie and his mother, and his voice occasionally sang in unison with Willie on the recording Wells had sent me. I did not consciously recognize it, but it was crucial that I pass muster with Orville.

During an earlier visit when I first sang for Willie, he had commented after I finished a song, "Ah, lady, why would you go anywhere to hear anybody sing?" and after the next song, "Oh, that's fine, ain't it. That's just too good. Woman, if I could sing like you I wouldn't give a nickel to hear nobody else sing. I'd just go up somewhere on top of a mountain and set there and sing all day" (April 20, 1959).[3] And so my collecting from Willie and his household had been, at least to my mind, an interaction of give and take based in part upon mutual respect and enjoyment of one another. Each visit brought new family and new neighbors for me to sit with, talk with, eat with, and sing with. It would be many years before I fully recognized the political implications of my visits, implications brilliantly articulated by David Whisnant in his 1983 work *All That Is Native and Fine.* I now believe that Orville's concern with potential exploitation was, in large part, what triggered the ghost legend he performed that evening.

Throughout the day, Orville jogged his father's memory about songs he or his father wanted to sing. Those sessions are rich documents of a folksinger in the process of remembering songs that had fallen into his passive repertoire. We told anecdotes and talked about what life had been like back in the mountains, and what it was like being Kentucky "briar hoppers" among the Indiana "hoosiers." As usual, I kept my reel-to-reel machine on the chair next to me running almost all of the time as I interviewed Willie. I was easily able to move it with me into the kitchen and out onto the porch. I also carried a small wire recorder, which the family knew I might use. No one appeared to pay either much mind, and it seemed to me that they were accepted almost as extensions of me. It was in this atmosphere that I collected the ghost legend on which I am concentrating here. More accurately, I should say that I was told the ghost legend and that my portable recording machine collected it (and me). It was a performance quite unlike the songs which Willie had sung earlier. It was not just performed "for" me; indeed, I was *part* of it. But I was not aware of this distinction at the time, and even years later I failed to recognize the importance of it when I played the legend for my classes in the 1960s and 1970s. I finally understood as I listened to it and transcribed it in May 1988. This was the first time in the twenty-nine years it had been on tape that I had made a transcription.

The occasion for transcribing the legend was a talk about folklore that I was to give for an English department at a university in Oregon. How else, I thought smugly, does one talk about the meanings of what is considered "trivial" material by English professors if not with a text one can hand them? It would be too tricky, I thought, to attempt to explain that the "truth" of what occurred during collecting was not solely in the words on a page. Initially I would have to hand them a page of text and then depart from that familiar medium. If they only heard the tape and had nothing else to which they might refer, I knew that the poor fidelity of the recording, plus the "hillbilly" stereotype, with all its value judgments, would loom up between me and my audience, and that my subject matter would be trivialized before I began. As it turned out, I had needed this text, too.

I intended to use the legend as an example of how printed texts are deceptively simple; that their "meanings" are multiple and dependent upon the complex matter of culturally situating them. I was going to analyze the legend, relying heavily upon performance theory, to show that there were many (social, political, psychological) "texts" within a single transcription of five mimeographed pages. I was astonished at what I found. As I transcribed and analyzed the tape, I watched new meanings open to *me*—meanings I am confident were there at the time I collected the legend, but that had escaped my consciousness. Often in my career, I had felt that I had passed through a collecting experience partially, or even at times fully, not understanding what was going on, but this was a shock. Almost thirty years after the event, I finally recognized that I had undergone an initiation test from Orville when he told me this legend. I do not know how my future collecting from Willie would have fared had I flunked the test.

I will never be confident again that I have fully understood the subtleties of any interaction. I truly thought I had successfully pegged that "little" exchange, and I hadn't. Nor had I recognized how crafted the narrative was, even though the linear movement in the story line was slight. No matter how well my ears were trained, my academic eyes had to see on paper how Orville's words "looked" as well as sounded, before I could fully appreciate the extent to which he had chosen and set his way of telling this personal narrative in an artful and effective manner. He was a skilled performer of the words he chose for the narration; his command of cadences, voice, pitch, emphases, and pauses gave the story multiple dimensions of meaning. As an accomplished raconteur, he used to the utmost what performance theory people call the "emergent qualities," the creative potential, of the situation.

In fact Orville's vocal performance was so masterfully subtle that I had previously ignored the virtuosity with which he had put the words together. The taped legend had a crafted text, yet it took these new circumstances for me to recognize it for both the art it represented and the function it played. I am grateful to that small faculty gathering in Oregon for giving me the opportunity to appreciate more fully than I had these friends with whom I worked years ago.

The machine on which this legend was recorded was not visible to anyone; it was the wire recorder that I kept in a small bag which served as my makeshift briefcase. I had obtained permission from the family to use this hidden recording machine whenever I wished, and as Willie, Florie, Orville, and I sat down on the porch after supper in the twilight of that summer evening, I switched it on as Willie began to talk with me about people he had known back in Kentucky as a boy. I realize the vast complexities and ethical questions involved in the use of such equipment. These complexities remain, even when one obtains what some call "informed consent," a slippery term at best. In the past, I had been placed in an awkward situation by using an unseen recording machine (Georges and Jones 1980: 175–76). By the time I collected from Willie and his family, I felt that I had worked through the ethical problems.

It was a time for relaxing and talking. As Willie spoke to me about his life, Orville suddenly broke into the conversation and asked what *I* thought. He asked a fair question. But when I expressed uncertainty about whether or not there was such a thing as "ghosties," Orville dropped his voice and said (line 12)[4] "I definitely know they [there] is." From that point, through the telling of the legend, I was inextricably immersed in a performance of which I was a part. The following is my transcription of the legend:

Date and Time: May 9, 1959, twilight, after supper.

Place: Open front porch (stoop) of Wm. Nolan's home, Salem, Indiana (rural)

Informants: William Nolan [father, age in 70s], Florie Nolan [mother, age in 70s]. Orville Nolan [son, age in 40s]

Collector: Ellen J. Stekert [age 23]

Key: "//" indicates overlapping talk.

"\\" on either side of a section indicates unclear rendering on original recording.

"[ ]" contain nonverbal information as well as clarifications of text.

VERBATIM TRANSCRIPTION

William Nolan (WN): Do you know they, people used to always, nearly all people was, ah, used to be a little bit superstitious and they's [there's] plenty of them that way yet that have a little bit superstitious ideas about things//

Orville Nolan (ON) [sitting next to his mother on the porch with us]: //How about ghosties; do you think that there is any such thing as a ghost?

Ellen Stekert (ES): Me? I don't, no, but I know people do believe it.

WN: They [there], ah//

ON: //I definitely know they [there] is.

ES: There is?//

WN: They is, they is ghosties, now, they ain't no doubt about that.

ES: This, I've never seen one and this is why I, I, I can't say I don't know, though.//

ON: //I seen one in my life and I wasn't scared, I wasn't excited, I definitely know I seen something. [pause] My cousin was with me and we wasn't excited or scared or anything. We thought we was meeting up with a woman. It was a real beautiful moonshiny night. You could have almost seen to have picked up a straight pin—unless you was in the shade of a tree—the moon was so bright—summertime. We looked about [as] far from here [pointing across field in front of house] out across that, half way 'cross that bottom [about 100 yards]. We saw a woman coming, walking towards us with a white dress on.

Well, I thought I knew who it was,\\unintelligible\\going down
to her neighbors, Miss Shoop probably going down to Miss
Lewis's and staying 'til eight or nine o'clock at night and going
back up home about a quarter-of-a-mile. I thought that's just
what it was. I ne'er had no other idea. I told Em that's who it
was. We was just walking along. We were just boys; I was about
eighteen, I guess, eighteen years old. He was seventeen. [pause]

   Met up with her—as close as from here to that post [six
feet]; about that close—and I was just walking along looking
down and I stepped over to the upper side of the road. It was a
wagon road, or what you might say an old country, [pause]
wagon road we'd call it [i.e., sunken]. [pause, then increasing
volume] And when I stepped over this side of the road and
went to say "Howdy Miss Shoop," that's what I was going to
say; but when I looked up—I[t] stepped right over here in
front of me, right plumb in front of me, [pause] I seen by a
whole lot it wasn't Miss Shoop. Hair was [as] long as your hair,
hanging down below her [slight pause] waist. It was a pale
looking, a pale looking—something. [truck goes by on road].
It started moving, just stepping here and there in front of me.
And [loudly] why I did it I'll never know, but I just walked
right along after it. Must have been—and there was a big rock
about, we'll say as high as this porch. [to his father, WN] I
don't think that's about wrong, is it? You know exactly where
the rock was.

WN: That's about//

ES: //About three foot?

ON: //I was at the lower side of the road//

ES: //Three foot high, about?

ON: About three foot. She stepped up on that. She was barefooted.
   That's the way it looked, barefooted. And I stepped up on it,
   too, and that was out of the road. And this rock, run about far
   as from here out over to the garden, and then went off about
   fifteen feet high, or twenty//

WN: //That was at the lower end of the rock//

ON: //just went straight off, like straight down. Well, I walked out on the rock, stayed right along close to it. I don't know [loud] why I did it. I don't know, never will know why I did that. [I] Just kept looking at it. And just, it just kept moving. And it just disappeared off over that rock. And when it did that [loud] it scared me, I'm a-telling you, I never was so bad scared in my life. [pause, ES slight laugh]. You talk about two boys running. My sister lived about as far as from here across that field. And we got to the door, we didn't knock on the door but knocked that la—, run again[st] that door so hard, knocked the latch off it. [ES laughing] That's true. Now, that's the only thing I ever seen. And we seen it coming as far as from here, halfway across that field, the moon was shining just—almost as light as day. [pause]

ES: Boy, I don't blame you for being scared.

ON: We both seen it [Mrs. Nolan says something in background] Wasn't one of us imagine something. We both seen the same thing. We talked about it a lot. [pause] It just appeared the same to both of us. [pause; woman talking in background] But it looked more like a dead person only it was on its feet and [emphatically] just as plain as looking at you right there, now that just how plain I seen it. [pause] No telling me I didn't see something. I know I did. And I never got scared 'til a[f]ter it disappeared, and [loud] why I followed it out on that rock I never will know\\why\\. And when it went out of my sight it scared me to death. Boy me and him, we—you talk about two boys moving on, we moved on. Knocked the door latch off when we got to my sister's house [general audience slight laughter], we run again[st] that door.

ES: Did anybody explain who it was or why it was there?

ON: I have no idea. [pause]

WN: Well, ah, they, that place, right there at that place, you know, there's been talk for years and years that//

ON: //There'd been things heard//

WN: //Things seed [seen] and heard there. And, ah [to ON], Dave Shoop, you know, he lived up there just a little above you; he said he seen a big white horse there one night.

ON: Well, somebody else, Gilbert Lewis said he passed there one
   night and it went like chains, a bunch of chains went across the
   road//

WN: //Yes, [pause] that's just the way//

ON: //something dragging chains, didn't see anything, just made
   the sound of chains and went off under that big rock. The
   noise went off under that big rock and disappeared. I heard a
   lot of things told about hearing things, but never [WN: Well,]
   heard of anybody seeing anything.

WN: You know my daddy lived there a while down there at that
   house. And he said that he'd heard trees fall right around, just
   right nearly to the end of the house. Just go like, he could just
   hear them whoop the ground just like man had cut a tree
   down, just fall on either side//

ON: //And you know he was no superstitious man.
   [WN: no] He wasn't scared of anything.

WN: He wouldn't have nothing like that.

ON: Fear, he didn't know what such a thing was.

WN: No, he didn't know what scare[d?] was.

ON: And no foolishness. He was no, he wasn't a-feared; he didn't
   believe in no [such thing]

[End of transcript]

I felt uncomfortable throughout the narrative. Part of my discomfort
at the time was that I thought I had been foolish to declare so quickly that
I didn't believe in ghosts when I wanted to be open to what Orville had to
say. But in 1988, as I looked at the transcript, I realized my discomfort resulted from the performance as well. As we had sat there, resting on the
porch after dinner in 1959, for a brief moment I hadn't stayed in Willie's and
Orville's world. I had, as Bruce Jackson puts it, "switched codes" (1987: 80).
I had responded offhandedly as if I were back in my academic environment,
where one did not discuss (especially in earnest) the existence of ghosts,
even if one collected stories about them.

Looking at the transcription in 1988, I also realized that the "story" did
not end with Orville, but continued through his and Willie's discussion of

the happenings around that rock. I had sat and listened to them continue the discussion of strange occurrences far beyond what I transcribed. My field notes for that day continue, "then they slipped without a break to talking about magicians" and about a man who "came down to his [Willie's] house in Kentucky and hypnotized [anyone he looked at]. . . . All the man had to do was stare at you and say something and you'd be hypnotized." Willie said the man offered to teach him how to do it but Willie refused.

I knew that the flow of a conversation often indicated an associated truth. In this conversation Willie and Orville were concerned with people who had power, power they not only did not understand but which was well beyond any they had. And I think I sensed, if only briefly in 1959, that I had been in some sort of a power struggle with Orville. As I look back upon it years later, I think a good case can be made to show that the legend performance was, in part, a direct challenge to me. Orville wanted to see what kind of a person I was. Would I do what they feared, and what was so often articulated to me in my fieldwork with people in and from the southern mountains—make fun of them as "ignorant, superstitious 'hillbillies'"? Orville had every right to know if I might harm or exploit his family. After all, almost every one of my attributes, save for my being a woman, were symbols of power, and I certainly had dragged along enough strange equipment with me to draw interest if not confusion: cameras, recording machines, guitar, and a VW bug. But Orville's "initiation test," as I have come to call it, was yet more complex.

The conversation about strange powers continued more than fifteen minutes past the legend. Then Mary and Glacie emerged from the house, happy to be done with the dinner dishes and reengage in the socializing. We chatted, took photographs, went inside and sang a few songs, and talked about when we would get together again. Then, many hugs later, I was packed into my car, and sent on my three-hour drive back to Bloomington. My field notes read "I left happy and exhausted, not wanting to return to school. . . . My hair was admired all through the day. So was my singing. At least I have this much to offer them. Glacie and Orville asked me to plan to come and spend a weekend with them soon." I had established good rapport with Glacie and Orville, and I had extended it with Willie and his family, but the legend kept puzzling me.

Ghost legends are often a subset of what I call "horror" legends, many of which are personal experience narratives. Our reaction to these stories is based in part on their subject matter: they treat liminal experiences,[5] occurrences which defy categorization by the listener. Like other legends, they present us with matters that are of concern to us, or as some have said, they help us "negotiate reality." Orville's personal narrative was no different.

Orville used masterfully all the artistic tools of legend performance. His story is situated in a world filled with familiar things, but instead of giving me a grasp on "reality," they served, by contrast, to heighten the liminality of the other elements in the story that did not fit with everyday life. Orville's narrative begins ("I seen *one* in my life . . .") in a conversational tone, quiet and paced. He tells me that he was with his cousin Em, "not frightened, scared or anything." In fact the moonlight was so bright that he could have picked up a "straight pin"—unless he'd have been in the shade of a tree. Even the weather is familiar and pleasant, "summertime."

As Orville leads me through his narrative, his voice is initially authoritative and seemingly detached. But as the narrative progresses, his affect becomes that of a frightened participant. He changes roles just as the narrative brings into conjunction events and perceptions which are hardly ordinary and which are contrary to the categories we perceive as "reality." Susan Stewart points out, in her fine essay on the horror story (Stewart 1982: 42–43), that these legends move in a manner which transforms what is ordinary into the unexplainable. Things and actions whose categories we perceive as contradictory, if not mutually exclusive at the beginning of the narration, are brought together in a frightening temporal sequence. In this way, the horror narrative hardly helps the listener negotiate reality. Rather, it deals with a dark side of what we live with, showing us what and how things might be were we to lose hold of our culturally specific categories. Orville presents me with a narrative that is both believable and not believable, but he gives me no room to doubt it. He begins and concludes with blunt affirmations of its truth. I was placed in a situation where I had to believe in the reality of phenomena for which I had no category; I was asked, as all are who experience such narratives, to accept events and things which existed at the ill-defined margins, the vague no-man's-land, the uncertainties, of my cultural categories, of my life.

As a practiced legend performer, Orville knew just how much he should offer by way of commentary within the story he was telling. He knew how to use this narrative-about-the-narrative (which Barbara Babcock terms the "metanarrative" [Babcock 1977: 62]) to clarify the plot for me, and at the same time to give it some foundation in a reality in which I believed. His companion in his story is his cousin, Em; they were not excited. I am told his cousin's and his ages. The distance between things is measured out in the actual space where I sit and upon which I look. And his father, my friend, Willie, is asked to verify matters, which he does. So how am I to doubt? As Stewart aptly points out, the very essence of such horror narratives is "an abomination of generic properties" (35), for the story is neither true nor false in our ordinary sense of those words; it is *both* true and false.

As performance theory analysts might put it, the performance included statements (metanarrative) which declared its truth, while the events of the story which was told defied explanation in my, or Orville's, "real" world. So, while I listened to the verifying details within the performance, I found the events at first to be "true" or "real," but as I followed the story line, I entered into the narrative time and watched events become liminal and unreal.

If only from the skill with which he rendered it, I feel justified in believing that Orville had told this personal narrative many times before. Certainly his parents, sitting on the porch during this telling, were not at all surprised by it. Students of folklore know that each rendition is a unique event, made so, in part, by what performance theorists call the "situational context"—the specific elements which lead up to and surround that story. When I transcribed this text in 1988, I looked at Orville's story nestled within a situational context (our immediate situation) which, in turn, was contained within a greater cultural context (the social and historical context of our situation). Once I paid close attention to these layers of the story, which I had previously skimmed over in my "itemistic" concern for the songs Willie sang, I found more than I ever had suspected might be there.

The narrative was framed by both Orville and his father, and through these framings I was "keyed," as Richard Bauman would put it (1975: 295–97), to the kind of narrative I was to experience. The framing acted as a sort of communication about what was to come, a "metacommunication," which continued through the description of the setting and the introduction of cousin Em, until the "narrated" story begins: "We saw a woman coming, walking towards us . . ." It seems to me that in horror legends, more than with legends in general, it is necessary to sprinkle the narrative with generous amounts of explanations, or metanarration. In the course of this story, I was increasingly drawn into the narrative by their use: the post was the post against which I had my chair propped. The "creature's" hair was directly related to my hair, including the slight and embarrassed pause by Orville when describing its length. At the beginning of the legend performance I was directly asked about my belief in ghosts, and at the conclusion of the first telling of the legend, I was told "That's true" and "No telling me I didn't see something. I know I did," which in turn was followed by further commentary on the narrated story and a retelling (or reassertion) of it. If I ever wondered what anyone meant by saying that narration creates reality, I knew by the end of my 1988 analysis of this legend.

Perhaps the most chilling part of the narrative for me, both then and now, is Orville's use of one of the most characteristic elements of horror narrative; it is the metanarration we find in these lines: "it looked more like a dead person only it was on its feet a-moving. It looked like a corpse, pale in the face, with long black hair, and [emphatically] just as plain as looking at you right there, now that[s] just how plain I seen it." At this point in the performance, Orville had shifted from his previously detached voice, which described mutually recognized matters of the "real" world, and assumed a voice which drew me into the story where I became both the victim as well as the horrible liminal being Orville encountered. Orville had also changed from the detached teller-of-something-that-happened into the victim of his own narrative. The "situational context" of this ghost legend (that is, me, the markers of place used to give distances, and so forth) has been given what Stewart calls "a horrible life" (1982: 40). The situational context is "actualized," as Stewart would say, by the conflation of cultural categories: of the known and the unknown, the present and the past, the here (Indiana) and the there (Kentucky), the civilized (the neighbor) and the uncivilized (the undead, the "thing"), the familiar (them) and the unfamiliar (me).

It is impossible to completely separate the situational context from the greater cultural context, because the situational exists within, and is in large part defined by, the cultural. In the performance of legends, asides which appear to be part of the situation at hand often refer to culturally acknowledged truths. Ilhan Bazgöz refers to such "digressions" as "a direct line of access to the life story, psychology, and the cognitive world of the narrator" (1986: 7). He demonstrates that ostensibly parenthetical remarks are hardly peripheral, but rather contextualizing and often substantial. In the horror legend, these asides suspend skepticism about the story which is told, for we all know how far away the road is from where we are sitting; we certainly know that Orville's cousin Emmit is a truthful person; and we all have seen how bright moonlit nights can be. In addition, as members of this folk group we would have known the characters in the narrated event as members of our daily lives: Miss Lewis and Miss Shoop. And we can not deny that Willie's father was "no superstitious man." To the performer and the performer's audience there is always a world of implicit "truths" surrounding the frightening, unclassifiable events.

But when an outsider is present during (if not the very reason for) this narrative event, additional commentary is needed. The sunken wagon road and the familiar rock, about which everyone in the cultural group knows, must be explained through commentary. Bazgöz calls this "explanatory and instructional digression" (1986: 9). Unusual happenings that have occurred in the area of the rock have to be related to me, as Willie and Orville do at the end of the transcript, leaving the text open-ended. But by far the most compelling device which draws an outsider into the narrative is the use of her or his physical presence as part of the narrative itself. In this case, I and the ghost merge. I could not deny Orville's pale, long-haired, corpselike "ghost" any more than I could deny my own reality. In fact, I was directly challenged by Orville to do so and I was told that there was no telling Orville that he did not see what he said he did. I fully believe that had I resisted Orville's attempt to include me in the legend, I would have failed Orville's test, and I am certain that this failure would have caused both Orville and Willie to doubt my character and motives. In performing this legend with me, Orville was as much as saying that if I could not tolerate the ambiguities of his and his father's world, then I had no business messing with his father's art.

Although I have placed a great deal of emphasis on performance, I do not want to overlook the importance of theme in the experience of this narrative. The central concept of liminality in the legend is crucial to understanding how it acts as a test I had to pass. In several ways, to Willie's family *I* was in a liminal state when I collected this legend. First, I was a young woman assuming a masculine role, that of directing discourse and initiating visits to record personal expressive material. Second, I was both a student and a teacher, much to the confusion of the Nolans (to say nothing of myself). Third, I was of marriageable age, yet not married, and clearly determined to have a career independent of a home and family. And fourth, I was from another region (they knew my parents and my home were in New York), and another social and economic class markedly different from theirs. In several ways, the Nolans, too, were in a liminal state. During the past decade they had moved from their homes in rural Kentucky to rural Indiana. The place of the narrated event was back in Kentucky, not where we sat on that front stoop in southern Indiana on May 9, 1959.

Orville's legend was both the story of a reported occurrence and in its telling an occurrence in its own right. I had not seen that until 1988. In addition, I recognized it as an initiation test of a liminal person—me. And I could see the irony of using as a means for that test a horror narrative, itself a liminal genre, performed for a liminal person, by a liminal group, in a liminal setting (twilight), and in a liminal geographic location.[6]

When, in 1988, I finally placed this legend in both its general cultural and specific situational contexts, I understood it at last. Additional meanings emerged, some of which I, as a scholar-collector, now write in a performance for you, the reader. And just as with Orville's performance, the manner in which I perform my text on this paper will be crucial to how and even if you understand it.

Notes

1   See David E. Whisnant's superb commentary on the exploitation of the southern mountains in his book, which he describes as a "book [which] is about the politics of culture" (1983: xi). Here he observes that "externality and manipulativeness have . . . been a central characteristic of the discourse associated with almost every encounter with the culture of southern mountain people—from the 1830s to the 1980s" (259).

2   Personal correspondence from Evelyn K. Wells, June 15, 1964.

3   Bruce Jackson reports this interaction in one of the best works to date written

on collecting folklore, his book, *Fieldwork* (1987: 76). The quotation he uses is slightly different from the one I give here since I communicated it to him through my own personal folk tradition; I was certain I had committed it to memory, but now that I look at my field notes and transcription, I see that I had altered it slightly, thus illustrating Jackson's point, made earlier in the book, that "reality" is a tricky concept. The date in parentheses following the sentence in the above text indicates the entry in my fieldwork journal.

4   All lines and pages refer to the transcript in this essay.

5   I use this term differently from Victor Turner. I do not mean "liminal" as a stage *between* other stages, but rather as a state which has no culturally defined category, and which is unclear to those who experience it at the time of the occurrence.

6   Because of space limitations, the editors have deleted a major part of the author's continued political/economic analysis of this performance.

References Cited

Babcock, Barbara A. 1977. "The Story in the Story: Metanarration in Folk Narrative." In *Verbal Art as Performance,* ed. Richard Bauman, pp. 61–79. Rowley, Mass.: Newbury House.

Bauman, Richard. 1975. "Verbal Art as Performance." *American Anthropologist* 77:290–311.

———, ed. 1977. *Verbal Art as Performance.* Rowley, Mass.: Newbury House.

Bazgöz, Ilhan. 1986. "Digression in Oral Narrative: A Case Study of Individual Remarks by Turkish Romance Tellers." *Journal of American Folklore* 99:5–23.

Georges, Robert A., and Michael O. Jones. 1980. *People Studying People: The Human Element in Fieldwork.* Berkeley: University of California Press.

Jackson, Bruce. 1987. *Fieldwork.* Urbana: University of Illinois Press.

Stekert, Ellen J. 1965. "Two Voices of Tradition: The Influence of Personality and Collecting Environment upon the Songs of Two Traditional Folksingers." Ph.D. dissertation, University of Pennsylvania.

Stewart, Susan. 1982. "The Epistemology of the Horror Story." *Journal of American Folklore* 95:33–50.

Wells, Evelyn K. 1950. *The Ballad Tree.* New York: Ronald Press.

———. 1960. "Information, Please." *Mountain Life and Work* 36 (Summer): 32–33.

Whisnant, David E. 1983. *All That is Native and Fine: The Politics of Culture in an American Region.* Chapel Hill: University of North Carolina Press.

11

Strategy and Tactics in Fieldwork:
The Whole Don Messer Show
Neil V. Rosenberg

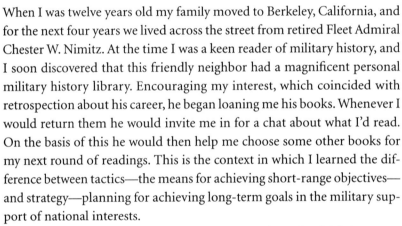

When I was twelve years old my family moved to Berkeley, California, and for the next four years we lived across the street from retired Fleet Admiral Chester W. Nimitz. At the time I was a keen reader of military history, and I soon discovered that this friendly neighbor had a magnificent personal military history library. Encouraging my interest, which coincided with retrospection about his career, he began loaning me his books. Whenever I would return them he would invite me in for a chat about what I'd read. On the basis of this he would then help me choose some other books for my next round of readings. This is the context in which I learned the difference between tactics—the means for achieving short-range objectives—and strategy—planning for achieving long-term goals in the military support of national interests.

This essay is about a fieldwork experience through which I came to understand that folklore research inevitably reveals the proprietary interests of the people studied *and* of all of us who study or are otherwise involved with them. And it is about how, in working within networks of such people to study their perceptions of musical systems, I learned about the differences between tactics and strategy in the intellectual support of proprietary interests. As a folklorist, my tactics have been methodological, and include not only decisions about how to do research but also decisions about what to study. My strategy has involved the proposing and testing of theories about the nature of folklore and folklife in order to arrive at insights for better understanding human social life.

I was drawn to the academic study of folklore through an interest in folk music. I was a performer; then and now making music had for me the same kind of necessity that sport has for many—an essential play experience that helps me take my mind off my work. When I began graduate studies at Indiana University in 1961 these musical performance interests drew me to the weekly Sunday shows at Bill Monroe's country music park, the Brown County Jamboree, in nearby Bean Blossom. Within a few weeks of my first visit I was invited to join the house band.

I soon found myself serving dual apprenticeships as bluegrass banjoist at Bean Blossom and scholar in Bloomington. By the end of my years in Bloomington I was in touch with a substantial network of musicians who played old-time, country, and bluegrass music.

Swedish ethnologist Karl-Olov Arnstberg, discussing Barbara Ward's distinction between internal and external observation, has pointed out that "An immigrant in Sweden is in basically the same position as a researcher, but he carries on internal observation—his purpose is to a greater or lesser extent precisely to 'go native'" (Arnstberg 1987: 6). In retrospect I see my apprenticeship in Bean Blossom as a mixture of going native and doing research. In order to participate as a musician I went native, internalizing many aspects of the cultural dynamics involved in performing country and bluegrass music in southern Indiana—status, role, etiquette, esthetics, history, and much more. I recognized the possibilities for research about the folk music implications of my experience but did little about them at first because like my fellow students I found most of my teachers, and particularly the director of the folklore program at Indiana, Richard M. Dorson, discouraged such research (Stekert 1987: 580). I shared their strategic goals, believing that our discipline could, through the serious and rigorous academic study of human expressive behavior, offer valuable new insights about the workings of culture. But they did not approve of my tactics. I was repeatedly told that to study the relations between what I was coming to see as folk and country music systems in research about Bean Blossom, local musicians, and the bluegrass world was "too narrow," "not really folklore," "too close to home," and so on (Rosenberg 1995).

At the same time I was discovering in the literature and ongoing debates of the discipline that there were other folklorists whose tactics were at least similar to mine with respect to this topic. Textbooks are a good measure of the boundaries of a discipline; one such work was published in 1968 by Tristram Coffin: *Our Living Traditions*. Based on Voice of America broadcasts, it included essays by Dorson and other prominent folklorists, including D. K. Wilgus. His "The Hillbilly Movement" (1968: 263–72), concluded by saying "A knowledge and understanding of hillbilly music is an essential part of the equipment of the American folklorist." It was clear to me that my interest was not iconoclastic or wrongheaded, and my resolve to pursue research on this topic was strengthened.

In 1968 I moved away from Bloomington and Bean Blossom, to begin teaching at Memorial University in Newfoundland. Now that I was teaching folk music courses to graduate students in folklore, I felt a strong need to do field research that would build on my Indiana experience and allow me to come to terms with forms of country music in their relations with folk music. My thinking was shaped by new theories about performance and behavior, and new methods which involved building models of systems and analyzing contexts.

The process of choosing a new field site began within a day of my entry into Canada in 1968. En route to Newfoundland I had traveled through the Maritimes—the provinces of New Brunswick, Prince Edward Island, and Nova Scotia. On a motel television set in Antigonish, Nova Scotia, I watched the Canadian Broadcasting Corporation's (CBC) *Don Messer's Jubilee,* a show featuring Messer's fiddling, stylized folk dancing, and old-time songs. During my first year in Newfoundland I frequently watched the Messer show, which had been on the air nationally since 1959 and was one of the most popular television shows in Canada.

Messer, son of a Tweedside, New Brunswick, farmer, started broadcasting in Saint John, N.B., in the early thirties. His first records were made in 1938. In 1939 his radio shows from Charlottetown, Prince Edward Island, began to air nationally over CBC radio, and would continue for over two decades. This, along with his television show, which originated in Halifax, Nova Scotia, was responsible for spreading Messer's repertoire and style of fiddle music nationally. It was also, in its elements, a reification of Canadian rural culture in general, and, as I came to see later, of working-class culture in Canada's predominantly rural Maritime provinces in particular (Rosenberg 1976: 5).

Messer's influence was particularly strong because his show appeared on the CBC. This nationally owned corporation has a strong mandate to maintain communications across Canada. CBC radio and television play a role in Canadian cultural and social life similar to that of the BBC in British life; it has no equivalent in the United States. Its power and the national significance of the Messer show were dramatized for me and many others when, in April 1969, the CBC abruptly canceled the show on the grounds that a "fresh new element" and a "younger look and younger orientation" was needed (Sellick 1969: 88). Sympathies ran high in support of continuing the program; thousands of letters were sent; embarrassing questions were put in Parliament; and in general there was much to-do about losing this program which seemed to many older, rural, and conservative Canadians to embody their values at a time when the mood of the times was running in favor of new kinds of consciousness and youth's demands for "relevance." But the CBC held fast. *Don Messer's Jubilee* was replaced by a version of *Hootenanny, Singalong Jubilee,* the cast of which consisted chiefly of Halifax-based middle-class folk revivalists like Anne Murray. Messer's show moved to a less prestigious private broadcasting company for his final seasons.

When I first saw the Messer show my attention had been caught, naturally enough, by a young bluegrass-style banjoist in his band. An obvious example of a recent Canadian borrowing from American culture, I had thought. I met this banjoist, Vic Mullen, four years later. In an interview he told me that as the youngest member of the Messer cast he was particularly aware that their audiences consisted of older people. Although Messer continued to perform, Mullen had left Messer in 1969 and the CBC had asked him to host *Countrytime,* a modern country format show that catered to younger country music fans. In the same interview he told me of the connections between his bluegrass banjo style and earlier traditional banjo styles in his native rural Nova Scotia. These revelations about folk and country music connections in Nova Scotia prompted me to begin thinking seriously about conducting research in the Maritimes.

My New Brunswick research began in the summer of 1972, at the Woodstock, N.B., Old Home Week fiddle contest, judged by Don Messer and his band, who were making one of their last personal appearances before Messer's death. I struck up a conversation with the winner of the contest, an excellent fiddler from Brewster (not its real name), a small logging, mining, and construction materials factory town in the center of the province. He told me of jam sessions in houses, playing at the Legion, occasional radio gigs, and so forth. I mentioned that I had some musical experience and told him that I was interested in interviewing him. Although I didn't do the interview until the next summer, this was the start of my fieldwork.

This preliminary research of 1972–73 led to a decision to spend a sabbatical year in the Saint John River valley of New Brunswick studying folk-country music relationships. I moved with my family in August 1974 to a 375-acre apple farm in the aptly named hamlet of Pleasant Villa, near Gagetown, New Brunswick.

In initiating this research I was motivated not only by the desire to answer scholarly questions but also by a new political awareness. As one of many American academics encouraged to enter the Canadian university establishment by generous government support in the late sixties, I had by the early seventies found myself at the center of controversy. Social currents of nationalist feeling had been growing since the election of Pierre Trudeau as prime minister in 1968 and Canadian sentiments against American influence were fueled by such unpopular events as Vietnam and Watergate. Canadian academics began to argue that too many unquestioned American values were being taught by American-trained professors to Canadian university students (Mathews and Steele 1969, Doucette 1993). They feared that Canadians knew more about the United States than about Canada, and that young Canadians were being educated to think like young Americans at a time when the two nations were following distinctly divergent paths. My reaction, as an American-born and educated Canadian academic, was to seek to learn more about Canadian history and culture and to orient my research toward Canadian topics.

This brought me face to face with Canada's internal cultural politics. Strong regional nativistic and/or separatist movements were under way in those parts of Canada where folklore studies were most strongly supported—Quebec and Newfoundland. Thus it seemed that to study Canadian folklore meant to study the folklore of people who didn't really want to be Canadians. In Quebec the separatists were rapidly gaining popular support and converting it into political power; the folklorists at Laval were deeply involved in this movement. And in Newfoundland, which had only been part of the Canadian confederation since 1949, a cultural nationalist movement was growing—a reaction to centralist hegemony and a feeling that Newfoundland's culture was being overwhelmed by the forces set in motion through confederation. Consequently, at Memorial University and in the Newfoundland intellectual establishment, the calls for Canadian nationalism to a large extent ran counter to the calls for Newfoundland nationalism. While I was sympathetic to both struggles, I decided to address the issue of Canadian culture.

During the summer of 1974 I was invited to teach a course in the folklore of Atlantic Canada in a weeklong noncredit summer school for the Atlantic Canada Institute (ACI) at the University of Prince Edward Island. The ACI had been created in the early seventies by a group of intellectuals, mainly academics, from the three Maritime Provinces and Newfoundland to make Atlantic Canadians more aware of their own culture. The ACI was happy to have me teaching folklore and representing Newfoundland because feelings of Newfoundland nationalism had made it difficult to involve other Newfoundland academics and intellectuals in the ACI. However, with my interest in doing research in the Maritimes, I was pleased to be member of the group. It put me in touch with local intellectuals who felt that Canadians ought to know more about their culture. My ACI colleagues could see the usefulness of folklore in the teaching of culture, and most of them seemed either sympathetic or neutral toward my interest in country music.

As I began fieldwork in the fall of 1974 I traveled from Pleasant Villa to observe local musical events, developing my contacts in Brewster and elsewhere. I met local musicians for whom music-making was mostly a matter of house parties, with occasional performances at fairs, political rallies, weddings, and other community events. My work with such performers progressed quickly, for my first contact, the contest-winning fiddler, had introduced me to his friends and I was able to join their network as a participant observer. But I was also interested in meeting and interviewing those influential professional musicians who were more extensively involved in the business through recordings, travel as full-time performers, and radio or television broadcasts.

In planning to contact these people I made tactical decisions which were shaped by my earlier experiences at Bean Blossom. I knew that my being an experienced musician wouldn't cut a lot of ice with these high profile musicians—bandleaders, stars, experienced sidemen—since they were always being approached by musicians who wanted jobs. Presenting myself as a musician was not the appropriate tactic. Even if we had actually worked together such a role would not assure the kind of status that would allow me to ask more than superficial questions. I also knew that taking a fan-type role wasn't a good idea, as the fan-performer relationship was one in which a considerable amount of distance was maintained on both sides. Finally I decided it would be best to present myself as a serious student and historian of country music who had an interest in their career. This was how I approached Vic Mullen, and I took the same approach with one of the first influential professionals I approached in New Brunswick, Art Marr (Maher). He had worked with Harold (Hal) "Lone Pine" Breau, a country singer from Maine who had been quite popular in Canada during the early and mid-1950s. In 1974 Marr was the best-known bandleader in Saint John, featured every Saturday night with his group at the city's newest country music spot, the Club XL. A number of people, including Mullen, had suggested that I interview him.

My ability to label myself as a historian of country music had been considerably enhanced that fall by the publication of my *Bill Monroe and His Blue Grass Boys: An Illustrated Discography* (1974). It had been published in Nashville by the Country Music Foundation (CMF), a spinoff of the Country Music Association, which housed in its museum that powerful trade organization's Country Music Hall of Fame.

I wrote to Marr, telling him about my past work, the Country Music Foundation book, and my present project. I mentioned that his name had been given to me by Mullen, who now had a weekly nationally broadcast country music show on CBC radio. Several weeks later I went to Saint John, located Marr in the stationery store where he worked, and introduced myself. Here is how I described the transaction in my field notes for September 26, 1974: "he said shortly and simply that he didn't have time for me—he was working here during the day and his spare time was occupied seven days a week. What leisure time he had he said, eyeing me significantly, he valued highly and spent with his family."

And that was about it. I told him I would be around for a year, and an interview would only take an hour or so, and asked if he might have some time later. But his "no" was definite and positive. I indicated in my notes that "while he was not rude or hostile neither was he overly pleasant or engaging." I asked him about other people; he suggested that I interview Ned Landry, a nationally famous local fiddler. Marr helped me get in touch with Landry by giving me his address and phone number.

I pondered Marr's refusal to talk with me. It might have been my mention of Vic Mullen, for I later discovered that some New Brunswick musicians were angry at him about something he had done or not done in connection with one of his CBC programs. Maybe the history ploy didn't work because of skeletons in the closet from the rough and tumble Lone Pine days. Mentioning bluegrass could also have worked against me, as some contemporary country musicians felt it gave country music a demeaning backwoods stereotype. Perhaps he was chary of one or all of my other various identities as announced in my letter, or didn't like to do interviews. I left with a strong impression that he did not want to talk to me. Obviously my tactic had failed.

Although I was disappointed by this rebuff, it did have the positive effect of leading me to Ned Landry. I owned some of the many records made by this man, the most famous New Brunswick fiddler after Messer; they could be found in record stores all across Canada then and are still available in cassette form today. Landry had won the Canadian National fiddle contest in 1956 and 1957, and subsequently made many records for RCA and a number of smaller companies. I wrote him as soon as I got his address.

On October 7 I came to Saint John and called Landry at his home. He wanted to know what kind of book I was writing, since I had said in my letter I hoped my research might lead to a book. I told him it was too early to say what form my work might take, and mentioned the Monroe book. He told me that he thought I was doing a good thing, that "fellows like you" could help "fellows like me," and invited me by that afternoon for the interview.

The Landrys were living in a modest apartment in an older section of town. They welcomed me cordially, showed me photos and souvenirs, and after some small talk about family, home, and neighborhood I set up my tape recorder and presented to Ned a copy of the Monroe discography. Looking through it, he told me then about a local fellow who had taken an interest in his music, had compiled a list of his records and was working to get local airplay and Nashville mail-order sales for them. Ned and his wife Celina expressed their appreciation for this person's interest and willingness to do something to help. Having thus been well coached as to the role they hoped I would play with Ned, I began the taped interview. Here is my evaluation of the interview, written the day after:

> The interview itself was not a particularly easy one. I was shooting for a life history kind of thing, whereas Ned was giving me the standard stuff for the media about the high points of his career. As a result, my attempts to get a chronological account were not too successful. I may have butted in a bit too much, for he did have a number of points that were connected in non-chronological ways. I found it hard, too, to get him to talk about other musicians and his relationship to them. On the other hand, he was happy to talk about his compositions, and my bringing along [a] fiddle tune folio [of his] was a real stroke of luck as we went through it systematically and got comments on the titles of each tune. At what I thought was the end of the interview I asked if he'd mind if a copy was deposited in the Library of the Country Music Hall of Fame and this turned out to be very much the right thing to say as he was overjoyed, and promptly performed for me a song he had written about a dream he'd had of being in the Hall of Fame.

During, before, and after the interview I gained an impression of Landry as a self-promoter. He was a proud, self-made man. A native of Saint John, he'd gone as far as the sixth grade in school before he was forced to help support the family. He told of waiting in depression soup lines to get a bucket of soup and a half loaf of bread, and of playing the mouth organ in barbershops to get money for his family's food. He was barely in his teens when he played mouth organ with Don Messer's band, then on CBC radio in Saint John, and he'd worked his way up from there to the national fiddle championship. While for much of his life he had been a full-time professional musician, he had also spent many years working as a longshoreman—a profession he shared with many of the male members of his family. He said that his national fame as a fiddler had not led to what he felt was an appropriate level of continuing local recognition for his talent, and was anxious to have me help promote his songs in Nashville so as to ensure their airplay in New Brunswick.

At the time I recognized that my tactic of stressing Nashville credentials in order to legitimize my research was perceived by him as a tactical opening for improving his career. He had access to only two modes of local cultural promotion, both involving radio and television with national influences—one predominately American, the other Canadian. To the first, the private commercial country music broadcasters, heavily influenced by American country music, his songs were not "commercial" enough and fiddle music was out of fashion. I felt he was being unrealistic to expect me to help him achieve success in gaining local recognition with them via Nashville. The second, CBC radio, might play his records from time to time, but usually his name would not be mentioned—it was just anonymous fiddle music. CBC television had (and still has) no station of its own in the province, so there was little possibility of exposure for him there; besides, he was too much like Messer. From my perspective it seemed that he did deserve local recognition as an important Canadian folk artist, and that the CBC ought to play a part in this.

Later that week one of my new ACI colleagues, Marjorie Whitelaw, came to visit. A native of Halifax, the elite-culture center of the Maritimes, she had been working for many years as a free-lance broadcaster for CBC radio, and was helping the ACI with its publicity. From a prominent local family, she was an enthusiastic advocate of the region's history and culture. This was reflected in her work with the CBC, for as a specialist in regional cultural affairs she was involved in the business of presenting the Maritimes to itself and the rest of Canada. She was in touch with or knew local historians, genealogists, writers, artists, craftspeople and various elite supporters of local culture throughout the region. She came to visit me because she knew I was a folklorist and she was putting together an hour-long program for CBC radio on New Brunswick and needed some recorded examples of colorful old-time speech. Her interest in folklore reflected the influence of Nova Scotia's doyenne of folklore, Dr. Helen Creighton, another Halifax-area native (McKay 1994).

She asked what I was doing so I explained my project in abstract terms first and then began elaborating by telling her that I had most recently met

and interviewed Ned Landry. She had never heard of him! I began showing her records by New Brunswick musicians, including Landry, banjoist
Maurice Bolyer, fiddler Earl Mitton, singer Marg Osburne, and Don Messer. Each of these musicians, I explained, was well known to country and old-
time music fans throughout Canada. I was attempting to educate her about
the views of the people I was studying, and to introduce her to the folk/
country musical system as I perceived it. Of course, Don Messer's name
came up because I had found that he was a central figure in this system:
Landry, Bolyer, Mitton, and Osburne had worked with him or been guests
on his show. I assumed that she shared my belief that Messer was an important symbol of Maritimes folk culture. As my field notes show, her response affirmed this but not quite in the way I had expected:

> She told me that she hated the whole Don Messer show and all
> the separate parts [of it]. . . . she explained her prejudice about
> the Don Messer Show. First she said that [singer] Charlie [Cham-
> berlain] was always drinking (everyone says that!), and that she
> remembered seeing him on television once and thinking, ah-ha,
> they've got him dressed up in a real "country" hayseed looking
> suit; and then discovering that he was in fact wearing his best suit
> (this was an anecdote at which I was supposed to laugh). Then
> came a statement that Marg Osburne was "kind of dumb." This
> was in line with the "Charlie's a sot" business—a back-country
> drunk and a dumb female. Don Messer himself (and the show)
> got her down, she said, because for so many years he was the ste-
> reotype of music from the Maritimes. With the various schools
> of music and composers, all one ever heard over the radio about
> Maritimes music was Don Messer, Don Messer.

This was my epiphany. What she gave me was not an expression of idio-
syncratic personal bias but an articulation of the conventional perspective
of middle-class Halifax about the hinterland culture of the Maritimes which
surrounds and is dominated by it. Here was the "garrison mentality" of
which Carole Henderson Carpenter wrote in her history of Canadian folklore studies, saying that each garrison guards "its rights, privileges, and
culture against the wilderness that the larger society is perceived to be"
(Carpenter 1979: 377–78). Founded in 1749, Halifax was English Canada's

original garrison city, the place from which came the orders for the expulsion of the Acadians. Like proud members of the urban elite in many cities, Haligonians look to larger urban centers for their models. *Singalong Jubilee* reproduced a model from New York and Toronto and was for that reason welcomed by CBC people in Halifax as a replacement for the embarrassing Messer show. This wasn't clear to me until that discussion with Marjorie Whitelaw.

My immediate response to Whitelaw's forthright statement about the Don Messer show was to fight back. I used a standard tactic of folklorist advocates of country music. I produced evidence of the connections between classic examples of folk music and the performances of modern country musicians. I played recordings of Messer and Landry doing old fiddle tunes, explaining the parallels between these and ancient ballads. I also played recordings of Marg Osburne singing Child and old Canadian ballads. She liked some things, but responded negatively to those which she perceived as sounding "commercial." She was much more comfortable with recordings of songs or tunes which were old and anonymous, and eventually taped some of those for broadcast use.

My tactic avoided the question of how this musical system pertained to folklore, and was similar to the practice (which folklorists now condemn) of collecting only the items that *we* think are authentic, rather than attempting to come to an understanding of the values of the performers and their regular audiences. Eventually I was to articulate my own view of this system, which bridges folklore and popular culture (Rosenberg 1987). But at the time my statement that I was studying a system was, for her, truly academic, and she wasn't interested in it. In my notes I somewhat bitterly summarized the impact of her statement to me about the Messer show:

Most important point here was that her perception of Messer and his show was based on the fact that his "stereotype" of Maritimes music left no room for communicating to the rest of Canada the image (or stereotype!) of Maritimes art music. Looks to me like a pretty clear-cut example of class conflict, and is the other side of what Ned Landry was talking to me about on Monday. Ned, like [fiddler] Earl Mitton [whom I'd also interviewed], was proud of his appearances on the Messer show and his associations with

Messer . . . but this pinnacle, to the M. Whitelaws of CBC, was in fact a depth.

My experiences during that one week in New Brunswick gave me new insight by forcing me to realize that each network I'd been using to facilitate my research was a unique social construct which took a proprietary interest in the cultural producers and products with which it was involved. I learned that while different networks may be involved with the same people and things, their proprietary interests and motives do not always overlap. They are often quite divergent, and can even conflict.

Marjorie Whitelaw educated me to the fact that frequently when members of local elites take an interest in their region's folklore (folklife, traditional culture, heritage, etc.), it is a proprietary interest which seeks within this perceived body of material and its performers symbols which they can understand and use in accordance with their own priorities and values. They tend to have little interest in performers who become successful without their proprietorship—like Don Messer. Although fiddlers from many parts of the Maritimes spoke to me of Messer as if he were their man in parliament, heritage-minded intellectuals couldn't (and still can't, if the recent Canadian plays about him are representative) deal with him except by selecting portions of his repertoire or his show for approval, and rejecting other parts. Some Canadian folklorists continue to view Messer not as the most important single individual in preserving and promoting the nation's old-time fiddle music in recent history but as a distant figure on radio, subordinate to "The most famous of the old-time fiddlers," Jean Carignon (Fowke 1988: 65). Carignon's well-deserved fame came through an acceptable network; he fell under the proprietorship of the Canadian folk music establishment, which had the pleasure of rescuing him from obscurity.

Don Messer's on-air persona—he never spoke, just smiled and played the fiddle—belied his importance. Through decades of records, broadcasts, and tours, all of them on a national level, he had established his skill as a fiddler who set new standards of technique, accurately maintained the old repertoire, and helped lesser-known younger fiddlers by performing their compositions and by having them appear as guests on his show. As such he was an important figure in the network of Canadian country music—establishing a dimension which still sets Canadian country music apart from American country music (Rosenberg 1994).

I considered Messer and the other fiddlers who related to him to be folk musicians who had entered the world of professional music. But that was *my* proprietary perspective, as one of a network of folklorists who take the tactic of arguing for country music as a product relevant to the strategic interests of our discipline. I had felt my interview with Ned Landry to be unsatisfactory because I didn't accept his interests in promoting his career in Nashville as being part of my concerns as a "researcher," even though I was willing to help promote him (or, as folklorists now say, "act as his advocate") within the confines of my own network. In that sense our meeting was a tactical struggle in which we both sought ways of using each other for different strategic goals. By the same token, I now believe that Art Marr was unwilling to speak with me because, having found his professional niche as the top local bandleader in the high-profile club, he had no need, tactically or strategically, for my proprietorship. I interpret his sending me to Landry as a tactic to get rid of me, based on his knowledge of Landry's strategic goals.

A few days after Marjorie Whitelaw's visit, when I began telling my informants in Brewster and elsewhere about having interviewed Landry, I discovered that their viewpoint differed from both mine and his. I expected responses which stressed the similarities and connections between well-known professionals like Landry and local public tradition performers like them. They acknowledged such links but regaled me with stories which denigrated him and others like him. Their experiences in the competitive profession of country music on the local level had made them suspicious of the professionals with whom they'd come into contact. Moreover, they had made the decision *not* to be professional musicians, and whether this was perceived negatively as an admission of defeat or positively as a pragmatic move that allowed them to maintain their artistic integrity, they viewed professionals as being different from themselves. They might praise a professional's music but tell stories about the person's stinginess, or drinking, or song stealing, or promiscuity. Or they might condemn the star for in some way bastardizing or betraying the music. So where I saw a continuum, they looked from the perspective of their own experiences and saw discontinuities.

What have I learned from all of this? Quite simply I think it is important to know that when you are doing field research, your motives and goals may not coincide with those of your informants, or of your fellow intellectuals. The earlier in your career you discover this, the better equipped you will be to understand someone whom you respect when they tell you that they do not see what you find significant in the people and things you are studying. In such situations both academic strategies and fieldwork tactics must be very carefully considered.

Note

Thanks to Colleen Lynch, James Moreira, and Peter Narváez.

References Cited

Arnstberg, Karl-Olov. 1987. "Research Models and Popular Models." *Ethnologia Scandinavica* 3–10.

Carpenter, Carole Henderson. 1979. *Many Voices: A Study of Folklore Activities in Canada and Their Role in Canadian Culture.* Ottawa: National Museums of Canada.

Doucette, Laurel. 1993. "Voices Not Our Own." *Canadian Folklore canadien* 15:119–37.

Fowke, Edith. 1988. *Canadian Folklore.* Don Mills, Ont.: Oxford University Press.

McKay, Ian. 1994. *The Quest of the Folk: Antimodernism and Cultural Selection in Twentieth-Century Nova Scotia.* Montreal: McGill-Queen's University Press.

Mathews, Robin, and James Steele, eds. 1969. *The Struggle for Canadian Universities: A Dossier.* Toronto: New Press.

Rosenberg, Neil V. 1976. *Country Music in the Maritimes: Two Studies.* St. John's: Memorial University of Newfoundland.

———. 1987. "Big Fish, Small Pond: Country Musicians and Their Markers." In *Media Sense: Folklore and Popular Culture,* ed. Martin Laba and Peter Narváez, pp. 149–66. Bowling Green: Popular Culture Press.

———. 1994. "Don Messer's Modern Canadian Fiddle Canon." *Canadian Folk Music Journal* 22:23–35.

———. 1995. "Picking Myself Apart: A Hoosier Memoir." *Journal of American Folklore* 108:277–86.

Sellick, Lester B. 1969. *Canada's Don Messer.* Kentville, N.S.: Kentville Publishing Company.

Stekert, Ellen J. 1987. "Autobiography of a Woman Folklorist." *Journal of American Folklore.* 100:579–85.

Wilgus, D. K. 1968. "The Hillbilly Movement." In *Our Living Traditions: An Introduction to American Folklore,* ed. Tristram P. Coffin, pp. 263–71. New York: Basic Books.

12

Oral and Written Tradition:
A Micro-View from Miramichi
Edward D. Ives

I had just arrived in Newcastle, New Brunswick, from a year's doctoral work in folklore at Indiana University. I had received a small grant to continue my study of local songs, especially those having to do with the lumberwoods, and even more especially those to be found along the Miramichi River, where that lumbering tradition had been heavily concentrated.[1] Even before we settled ourselves in our temporary home in Chatham Head, just across the river, Bobby and I and our three children went to have dinner with Louise Manny, chief among those who knew things about Miramichi. All through dinner I talked of what I hoped to accomplish that summer; then, as we were about to leave, Louise announced that *we* were driving down to Sackville Friday morning to attend a music teachers conference. "They've asked me to present some of our Miramichi singers," she said. "I want you to pick up Nick and Wilmot about eight, so they'll be ready to sing about ten. And get them there sober, please."

That was Louise's way. It never entered her head that I might have had different plans for Friday—and I did—any more than it would have occurred to her that Wilmot MacDonald and Nick Underhill might not have considered a trip to Sackville as something they wanted to take a day off from work for, but they were two of the best singers in her by now well established Miramichi Folksong Festivals, and that was all there was to it. Needless to say, Friday morning I was on the job, picking up Nick first in Northwest Bridge just north of town and then Wilmot at his home in Glenwood, twelve miles down the road to Sackville.

A few more words about Louise Manny before I continue my story. Back in the 1940s, she had been asked by Lord Beaverbrook to gather some of the old songs he remembered hearing in his youth (he was born in Newcastle, and he and Louise were old friends). She knew absolutely nothing about folksongs and had no idea how or where to start, but, knowing no better way, she simply let it be known via the local paper and movie hall that she was looking for old songs and would people who knew them please come to the local Legion hall, where they would be recorded. I can't think of a less likely way for someone to begin, but the response was gratifying and she soon had a sizable collection of songs for His Lordship, who acknowledged them and that was that.[2]

But now Louise herself was interested, and she began a fifteen-minute Sunday afternoon program over the local radio station on which she played her recordings of woodsmen and farmers singing the old come-all-ye's in the old unaccompanied way, and that program developed a loyal and devoted following all through the Miramichi area and even as far away as the west end of Prince Edward Island. Then in 1958, she organized the Miramichi Folksong Festival, and for three nights those same woodsmen and farmers got up on the stage of the local town hall and performed in the old way.

Louise died in 1970. What she accomplished was a brief folksong renaissance in Miramichi, not one for young urbanites with their guitars and dulcimers but for those local folk who still had the old tradition within them. Through her radio programs she called attention to it, and through the festivals she created an arena for its performance by singers like Wilmot MacDonald and Nick Underhill. As a by-product of this effort, Louise also became New Brunswick's recognized expert on folksongs. Hence when a regional teachers organization wanted a program on that subject for their annual convention, they called on her, and her writ ran so strong locally that no-one—not Wilmot, not Nick, and certainly not a young graduate student from away—would have considered even a token demurrer to anything she requested. As I said, Friday morning I was on the job, and the three of us were on our way to that convention.

The trip down was a bit formal. Nick and Wilmot knew each other, to be sure. Both were well-known festival singers; both had spent a good portion of their lives working in the woods and on the drives; and both had their family roots in the Gray Rapids, a community a few miles upriver near Blackville. But I doubt that they had ever spent this much time before in each other's company, and the conversation was largely a feeling around, a getting to know each other. I was alone in the front, and the two of them sat right behind me. Both men wanted something to drink, and I felt the ass every time I shot the car past a liquor store on the excuse I didn't have time to stop. They were getting a little annoyed with me, and I didn't blame them at all, but I promised that as soon as we got to Sackville I'd see that they got something before they had to sing. I was as good as my word too, stocking up enough Lamb's Navy Rum both to get them through their required singing and to make up for the aridity of the down-trip on the way home!

They did their job splendidly. Louise was delighted, and the teachers were properly educated, having heard some of the finest traditional singing to be heard anywhere. We were given lunch, thanked, and sent on our way home. The bottle went round, and, believe me, the fun began as those two timber beasts began swapping songs. How I wished I'd had a tape recorder with me! But I knew that had I had one nothing would have been quite the same. It never is. I contented myself with simply listening to one of the greatest afternoons of song it has ever been my privilege to enjoy.

Many of the songs they sang were familiar to me from the festivals, but many too I knew from my reading and my studies, and what interested me more than the songs themselves was the way they'd talk about them after they'd sung them. "Remember the way Fred MacMahon would sing that? . . . Frank O'Hara made that one, and the old woman never forgave him for it . . ." And so on—wonderful stuff for the young graduate student driver who had decided some time ago that context was just as important as text. At one point Wilmot sang "The Thrashing Machine" and "The Red Light Saloon," two off-color songs I'd never heard him do before. The rum was having its effect, I figured. Everyone was really relaxed. Then he sang another new one, about a young woman who rode off with a man who, when they came to a river, told her he was going to drown her just as he had drowned six other women. He then said she was to take off her clothes; she told him to look the other way, and, when he did, she threw him into the stream and rode back home alone. The song ended with a conversation between the woman and a parrot, the parrot asking why she was up so early and the woman telling the parrot to say nothing about it and she'd give it a golden cage "with doors of ivory."

As soon as Wilmot finished, Nick spoke up. "Wilmot," he said, "I heard Fred Jardine sing that on Renous back in 1927. He called it 'Pretty Polly.' I liked that song, but I never did learn it."

"I never cared much for it," said Wilmot. "Just up and down, that air. My mother used to set and sing that song for hours."

"Well, Wilmot, will you word that off for me sometimes, so's I can learn it?"

Wilmot said he would.

I stuck to my driving, but my mind was racing back over all I knew about that song, which was quite a bit. I recognized it, of course, as "Lady Isabel and the Elf Knight," number four in Francis James Child's great collection, *The English and Scottish Popular Ballads*.[3] I knew it was well known in Great Britain and—having read Holger Nygard's *The Ballad of Heer Halewijn* (1958) and Iivar Kemppinen's long study as well (1954)—I also knew it was known in various forms in almost every European language. I further recalled from Tristram Coffin's *The British Traditional Ballad in North America* that it was one of the so-called Child ballads most often found in American tradition, and I knew that versions of it had been collected in Newfoundland, Nova Scotia, and Maine (1964: 25–28). Therefore I was not surprised to hear Wilmot singing it, and, about two weeks later, while I was recording some songs and stories at his home, I got him to sing it over for me again.[4]

His singing of it this time was just about identical with his singing of it on the way home from Sackville, so far as I could tell, and when I asked him he repeated that he'd never cared for the song, that the air was "just up and down," adding that it was just a two-line air and he liked the four-line airs (what we'd call a double or come-all-ye stanza) better. I pretty well agreed with Wilmot, and as a scholar I felt that far too much fuss had been made over Child ballads anyway. I was more interested in the few stanzas he was able to sing me of a local song, "The Wedding at Kouchibouguac," and the wonderful background he was able to give me for one called "The

Home Brew Song" made up by an old friend of his, Frank O'Hara, from the Gray Rapids. As I was leaving, I asked if he'd had a chance to get "Doors of Ivory" to Nick yet. No, he hadn't, but a couple of weeks later when I was back again he said he had.

All that was in 1961. I didn't get back up to Newcastle again until just in time for the next year's festival. Meantime, Louise and Wilmot had had a serious falling-out, and as a result Wilmot boycotted the whole three days of the festival. Nick was there, though, and one of the songs he sang was "Pretty Polly."[5] It sounded very much like Wilmot's version—at least the words did, but the tune was clearly something else again. The only problem was that Nick's version seemed much longer than Wilmot's, but then, given Nick's extremely slow *parlando* style, any song would sound longer when he sang it, and I let it go at that for the time being. As I said earlier, I wasn't all that interested in the Child ballads.

Then in July of 1963 I went up and spent about a week with Wilmot, listening to his songs and stories and talking to him about life in the Miramichi lumberwoods. One evening as we were getting toward the end of a rather long session during which we had passed a couple of bottles back and forth between us several times and were both wonderfully relaxed and easy, I asked him to sing "Doors of Ivory" for me again. He did, singing it as beautifully as I'd ever heard it—as beautifully as *anyone* would *ever* hear it, I'm sure—slowly and with that marvelous pacing no-one could get better than Wilmot.[6]

The next afternoon I was over in Northwest Bridge with Nick Underhill, and I got him to repeat his version for me.[7] What he sang was identical with what he had sung at the festival the year before—the words clearly Wilmot's, the tune anything but Wilmot's. The two had nothing in common. That was obvious on the face of it, but it wasn't until some years later when I set about to make some careful comparisons between the two men's various singings that I saw that there were other differences, and equally interesting ones, as well.

Briefly, let's review what I had. First, there was the version Wilmot sang in the car on the way back from Sackville in June of 1961. I did not record that one, but I did record his singing of it a couple of weeks later, and my memory told me these two versions were, for all practical purposes, identical, both being eleven stanzas long. Next came Nick's singing at the 1962 festival, which I discovered not only seemed longer than Wilmot's but *was* longer by three stanzas. The addition came in the final scene. Here's the way Wilmot sang it:

> The parrot being high in the window
>> And this to the lady did say:
> "Oh lady, dear lady, come tell unto me
>> Why you're riding so long before day."
>
> "One turn, one turn, pretty Polly," she cried,
>> "One turn you done to me.
> Now your cage shall be made of the glittering gold
>> With doors of ivory."

And here is how Nick handled it:

> The parrot was out on the window,
>> And it to the lady did say,
> "Now lady, dear lady, come tell unto me
>> Why you're riding so long before day."
>
> "Hold your tongue, pretty Polly," said she,
>> "And tell no tales on me,
> And your cage may be made of the glittering gold
>> And doors of ivory."
>
> The old man arose in the morning,
>> And then to the parrot did say,
> "Pretty Polly, pretty Polly, come tell unto me
>> Why you're talking so long before day."
>
> "The cat was here on the window sill,
>> And she was staring at me.
> And that is the only reason I had
>> For talking so long before day."
>
> "One turn, one turn," m'lady replied,
>> "One good turn you done for me,
> Now your cage shall be made of the glittering gold
>> With doors of ivory."

Since Nick's resinging of it for me in 1963 is just about identical with his festival singing, we can safely speak of them both as representing Nick's version. Where, I wondered, had those three extra stanzas come from? Had Nick simply invented them? Very unlikely. First of all, that wasn't Nick's way. I had plenty of examples of Nick fixing up what seemed to him a faulty text or improving on his own version, but that amounted to changing a word or a phrase; in the present instance, for example, he changed Wilmot's having the girl return to "her own father's house" to having her return to "her father's abode." But I had never known him to make up whole stanzas. Besides these "new" stanzas were well-established ones in oral tradition, being found in hundreds of examples in well-known collections, even collections made in the Maritimes. Was it possible these were a memory from his having heard Fred Jardine singing it way back in 1927 and, as he worked to commit Wilmot's worded-off version to memory, these stanzas came back to him? That seemed quite possible, and I had pretty well decided that was how it was, until I came to transcribe Wilmot's wonderful 1963 singing. And there, by the Lord Harry, were those three extra stanzas!

The question now was where did *Wilmot* get them? In 1961 they weren't there, but in 1963 they were. Could he have learned them from Nick, who had them in his 1962 festival singing? That seemed both logically and chronologically sound but, as I mentioned earlier, Wilmot had boycotted the 1962 festival, and he and Nick never saw each other socially except at the festival. Could he have learned them from someone else's singing? That is possible; I have heard at least one other person from the general area sing that song with those stanzas in it. But I doubt that he cared enough about the song to take that kind of trouble over it. Could he, through repeated singing, simply have rerembered those stanzas? That is what I believe happened, and here's why.

To begin with, Wilmot claimed he never cared for that song. It was one of his mother's songs, one he heard her sing over and over again as she went about her chores. Obviously Wilmot had a quick ear for songs, and he probably committed some of her repertoire to memory without trying or even knowing that he had done so. "There are some songs you just can't forget," he told me one time, implying that it didn't matter whether you liked them or not, and certainly his mother's songs fell into that category. Women sang songs around the house, within the family; men sang songs on public occasions, at parties, and in the lumbercamps, and it would have been this public and hence men's tradition of songs that would have interested young Wilmot the most.[8] What inspired him to sing "Doors of Ivory" that day in the car there is no way of telling now. As I recall it was a kind of throwaway, but when he did sing it he found an interested audience. Nick liked it and wanted the words, and that young professor in the front seat got him to sing it again two weeks later. Shortly after that, he "worded it off," but I am sure he didn't write it out himself, since writing wasn't that easy for him. More likely he dictated it to his wife or one of the children, but however it was done, the process of committing it to writing meant going over it slowly and carefully, repeating phrases, pausing, thinking it over. Thus, after decades of lying dormant in the dark at the back of his mind, two singings followed by a dictating within the short space of a month could easily have been enough to have brought those stanzas back to him. It is quite possible that as he dictated he didn't even recall that he hadn't sung those stanzas before.[9]

Nick, then, received all fourteen stanzas from Wilmot. But what of the "new" tune? I questioned him about that in 1963 as follows:

> Ives: That was the tune that he [Fred Jardine] used, though—the one that you sang here?
> Nick: Yes, yes, that's right. And that's the air that Wilmot had for it.[10]

That was a poor way for me to ask, since my question implied the answer I was looking for, but, even so, it may well be that Nick *was* working with a memory of Jardine's tune. We should also remember that Nick had heard Wilmot sing that song exactly once—that time in my car—and he may have honestly believed that his singing *was* the same as Wilmot's. But in folksong tradition the words are the important thing, the tune being often no more than a vehicle to carry those words forward, and this was especially true for Nick, who moved tunes around from song to song quite easily. I one time pointed out to him that he sang two songs to the same tune, and he flatly denied it, even after I played them side by side for him.

It remains for me to critique my own fieldwork. In his 1984 presidential address to the American Folklore Society, Bruce Jackson pointed out that "scholarship based on fieldwork is based on scholarly artifacts, not on the facts themselves." He amplified that as follows: "Fieldwork collections, published or unpublished, reflect what individual collectors found, preserved, and selected, based on their own personal idiosyncrasies, the facts of the moment, and their ideas of what folklore was, what folklore information could be used for, and what recording technology was at hand. . . . No one collects everything that might be collected, and no one publishes every fact recorded and every observation made" (Jackson 1985: 131–32). He is quite right, and the present exercise is a case in point. What I have had to work with is not what was there but what I happened to record of what was there while I was looking for something else. As I mentioned earlier on, I wasn't especially interested in Child ballads. Besides, by the terms of the grant that was paying my way, I was supposed to be researching locally made songs, especially satirical ones made by well-known songmakers like Larry Gorman and Joe Smith. Still, I was going to be teaching a folksong course at Maine in the coming year, and since I knew it would certainly be incumbent upon me to devote a decent amount of time to these so-called aristocrats of the ballad world, I made a mental note on the way back from Sackville to make sure and record Wilmot's singing of this very well known exemplar. I recorded Nick's singing of it in the 1962 festival because Sandy Paton and I were recording the whole festival and there it was on the last night's program.

Then in 1963 I had a chance to put together an album of field recordings from Maine and the Maritimes, and since I wanted to include at least one Child ballad, since Wilmot's "Doors of Ivory" was the best singing of such a ballad I had ever heard, and since my 1961 recording of it had been badly miked, I asked him to record it again. While I was at it, almost as an afterthought, I decided to get Nick's version again. At no point in the whole process did I purpose a close study of this ballad; always I was up to something else. Aside from that shift in tunes—pretty obvious even at first hearing—I never really noticed the changes I have been speaking about until some years later when I brought the different versions together for a class presentation to demonstrate the interplay of oral and written traditions, and it wasn't until I began to put this paper together that I thought of all the wonderful questions I should have asked. The following is a fair example:

Was Wilmot conscious of the changes he had made? When he first sang the song, did he know he wasn't singing the whole of it but was making do? Unfortunately, even though I spent a lot of time with Wilmot in later years,

I never thought to ask, and now it is too late. As a corollary to that—and equally unanswerable—had I not already known from my studies what that final scene with the parrot was all about, would I have been puzzled by the ballad's close? Evidently as I heard what Wilmot sang, I also "heard" the missing stanzas, and it all made perfect sense. However, I've noticed my students are often puzzled at first hearing; then when they hear the second version they understand. Then there's that all-important "wording off." Who wrote it? What did it look like? Did Nick still have it, and could I have made a copy? Unfortunately again, by the time its existence assumed any importance for me, Nick was gone, his wife was gone, and whatever papers might have been left behind disappeared into the big night.

All very well. I can beat my breast in a thousand mea culpas, but the plain fact is that in folklore—as in other disciplines dependent on people-studying-people fieldwork, hindsight is a very cheap and common commodity, and such lapses as mine, lamentable as they seem to be, are an inevitable product of the way we go about our work. Often enough, we don't know what we should have been looking for or in what terms we should have been asking about it until long after it is too late to go back. Our fieldwork is the resultant of many vectors, only one of which is the controlled search for some specified thing, and our scholarly rigor should take all of them into account in any assessment of what we find. To put that another way, we must be as objective as possible about the probable subjectivity of our data. Yet, when we come to work up our field data, we should not be discouraged because it is not as clean or complete as we now see it should have been any more than we should fool ourselves that we are being truly objective when we gather it. We have to do the best we can with what's available. In the present instance, I believe my data—gathered along the way while I was either looking for something else or not really looking for anything in particular—can, for all its tentative nature, give us a look at how, in a new performance context created by scholars and promoters, a single song moved from one singer's passive to his active repertoire as it also was passed on by him to become part of another singer's active repertoire. But I have also tried to place that data in a second context: that of the collector's experience and shifting agendas—something I haven't seen done very often, and I thought it would be worth a try.

Finally, as Bruce Jackson suggested to me one day, it all goes to show that the facts—for whatever reason collected—know more than we do at the time, and, if they are properly saved and stored away, they may some day answer questions we never knew enough to ask. Of course, rather than providing answers, they may raise questions for future investigation. Either way, they provide us with more than we could ever know they had to offer. That is a comforting thought for an archivist.

Notes

A version of this paper was presented at a meeting of the Atlantic Association for Canadian Studies of Edinburgh, May 1988, and then published in *Acadiensis* (Ives 1988).

1   The results of this fieldwork are summarized in my book, *Larry Gorman: The Man Who Made the Songs* (Ives 1964), pp. 1–179.
2   For an easily available look at most of the Beaverbrook Collection, see Manny and Wilson 1968.
3   Francis James Child, *The English and Scottish Popular Ballads* (Boston: Houghton Mifflin, 1882–98), vol. 1, pp. 22–62.
4   Northeast Archives of Folklore and Oral History (South Stevens Hall, University of Maine, Orono, Maine), Accession 1.105. Hereafter all references to this archive will be abbreviated thus: NA 1.105. Manny and Wilson (1968: 202–3) give both tunes and a full text. See also Ives 1989: 72–76.
5   NA Ives 62.6.
6   NA Ives 1.125.
7   NA Ives 1.128.
8   For a full discussion of men's and women's traditions, see Ives 1978: 393–96.
9   As an interesting parallel, when Albert Lord had Yugoslavian epic singers dictate an epic they had previously sung, the dictated version was frequently longer than the sung version (Lord 1960: 128).
10 NA Ives 1.128.

References Cited

Coffin, Tristram P. 1964. *The British Traditional Ballad in North America*. Rev. ed. Philadelphia: American Folklore Society.

Ives, Edward D. 1964. *Larry Gorman: The Man Who Made the Songs*. Bloomington: Indiana University Press.

———. 1978. *Joe Scott: The Woodsman Songmaker*. Urbana: University of Illinois Press.

———. 1988. "Oral and Written Tradition: A Micro-View from Miramichi." *Acadiensis* 13 (Autumn):148–56.

———. 1989. *Folksongs of New Brunswick*. Fredericton, N.B.: Goose Lane.

Jackson, Bruce. 1985. "Things That from a Long Way Off Look like Flies." *Journal of American Folklore* 98:131–32.

Kemppinen, Iivar. 1954. *The Ballad of Lady Isabel and the False Knight*. Helsinki: Kirja-Mono Oy.

Lord, Albert. 1960. *The Singer of Tales*. Cambridge: Harvard University Press.

Manny, Louise, and James Reginald Wilson. 1968. *Songs of Miramichi*. Fredericton, N.B.: University Press.

Nygard, Holger Olof. 1958. *The Ballad of Heer Halewijn*. Helsinki: Folklore Fellows Communications 64:169.

13

Stumbling upon Lancashire Mill
Culture in New England
Anthony G. Barrand

In January 1989, I began learning the wooden shoe dance repertoire of "The Dancing Marleys" in a former mill town, Rockville, Connecticut. This essay is about my sudden discovery of the actual scope, meaning, and implications of the Marley project when I unexpectedly remembered a long-forgotten visit with an old concertina player, John Wright, a former mill worker and child of English immigrants, in New Bedford, Massachusetts, fifteen years earlier. I always liked Lewis Hyde's way of putting this kind of revelation in perspective: "The gift," he said, "only moves into the empty bowl" (Hyde 1979). When I met Mr. Wright, the bowl was full and I did not follow up on the gift as offered. Meeting the Marleys was entirely a different matter.

Wooden Shoe Dancing in a Connecticut Mill Town

A former student and now colleague, Rhett Krause, called me in September 1988. He thought I would be interested in the story his mother had just told him over the phone. She had been over at the house of their neighbor, a man called Dan Marley who had lived literally next door for almost thirty years. Dan and his wife were moving out to Arkansas partly for his health but also partly to be near their children. Mrs. Krause was helping them pack and Dan asked where Rhett was. "Oh, I think he's at some dance event," she replied, "that's usually where he is on the weekend."

"I was a dancer, you know," said Dan, "all my family were English clog dancers." This was the first Rhett's mother had heard of it. She called him at the first possible opportunity. He headed home right away and confronted old Mr. Marley.

"Why didn't you tell me you were a dancer?"

"You never asked."

Actually it turned out that Dan hadn't been taught to clog dance with the rest of the family because he "wouldn't dance only below the waist" and had a hard time with the very formal English stepping that his father, William Marley, drilled into four of his other children. So he, Dan, didn't really know the steps, but his sister, Ann, had taught "tap, clog, and everything else" to young children before retiring two years previously. Rhett told me that he had called Ann Marley and, yes, she knew the steps but she didn't dance any more. Did I want to come and visit her? "Of course," I said, "and I'll get her to dance."

In my experience, English clog dancers are as competitive a bunch of individuals as you could find. They see someone else dancing, they have to show they're better. Due to health problems, I hadn't done much clog dancing in over two years so I knew that if I took my clogs and did a few steps for her she wouldn't be able to resist letting me know where I stood.

Miss Marley agreed to meet with us on a Saturday morning shortly afterwards. Rockville is bleak, dominated by two big but run-down woolen mills and classically set up with the factory buildings fitted onto the craggy hillside interspersed with mill pools and dams and waterfalls. The house overlooks one of the mill pools and has one of those blind, steep driveways you hope you never have to negotiate in February or March after one of Connecticut's freezing rains. Rhett, my wife Margaret Dale Barrand, and I rang the bell at what seemed like the back door. A short but active seventy-year-old lady opened the door, which let us straight into a dance studio. Oak flooring covered the whole basement and there was a low stage area on one side of the room which housed a spinet piano, its back pointing out to the room so the player could see the dancers. Benches lined two walls. This was clearly the room where a lot of dance classes had happened.

Anna ("I answer to Ann, Anna, or Anna Mae") sat in a lecture-room type of chair in what seemed like the familiar spot for teaching sessions. There was a little of the sort of wary conversation which is rather like two fighters circling around each other before one makes a move. I, as the junior, then gave in to the pressure to put on my clogs. Margaret Dale played and I danced a few steps of waltz clog, reel, and hornpipe. Anna uttered a sound for which there is no successful spelling, though it is sometimes approximated as "tcch." "I can do better than that," she said, pulling out a dusty pair of tap shoes. She apologized for not having clogs. She has a pair which no longer fit but which she wore as a teenager. They are very like English clogs which have a one-piece wooden sole with a regular leather top which closes with laces or, on fancy ones, buckles.

"A lot of the steps don't sound good in taps, and I haven't danced in over two years." Nevertheless, she got up and snapped off several bars of steps in different rhythms, steps of exhibition quality, performed at breakneck speed. As with all excellent step dancers, all of the beats were very clear and distinct.

There were many signs that these were, as Anna claimed, "English" clog dance steps. For example, the "shuffle" or double beat with the sole of the clog is danced with a round movement involving a turn of the ankle as is common in Lancashire and Durham clog dancing, the beats being made side by side as the clog moves from outside to inside. This contrasts with the double beat made by a forward and back movement as is less common in England but found throughout tap dancing and Appalachian styles of "clogging."

Anna asked what tune Margaret Dale was playing. It was "The White Cockade," one of two tunes almost universally used by dancing masters in the north of England for the "Reel" steps in the "Buck and Wing" rhythm. Going over to her fiercely out-of-tune piano, Anna played a few bars of the tune which her father always used and which, he insisted, "had all the steps in it." Despite the ambiguous notes, it was instantly recognizable as "Soldier's Joy," the other and the best-loved of the tunes used by English dancers.

Further, the usual formal English clog dancing pattern was rigidly followed: in 4/4 tunes, both reel and hornpipe, six bars are danced repeating a one- or two-bar motif followed by a two-bar ending phrase which completes almost every step. What Anna called "the first step" of the Marley "Buck and Wing" is identical to the first full English clog dance step I and most dancers were taught, commonly called "First Lancs" or the "First Lancashire Step."

Anna danced the steps at a, to me, alarming speed that is rarely seen among clog dancers but that usually indicates an aesthetic based on stage performance, in this case, vaudeville. In sessions after this, when I could finally get a few steps up to something approximating this rate, Anna would exclaim, "Now, that's the Marley clog," or "Now you're dancing like the Marleys!"

Anna sat down. "The difference between your dancing and mine is that mine has class. It's smooth." She was right. Would she teach me the steps? She wasn't sure. Her brother, Jim Marley, who was the "real dancer," was taken into intensive care the previous day. There was clearly a sense that the steps were his by right to teach. "If he wasn't sick, Jim could really teach you." Anna tried to get me through the first step of the "Marley Clog," a dance done on a sixteen-inch-square pedestal to a dotted 4/4 or hornpipe rhythm much loved by English clog dancers. I was a determined but hopeless student. Even on this first step, the movements were complex and unusual. Anna gave up in short order.

We got a few more details about the Marleys before the end of that first meeting. Suddenly, though, as Anna talked about her family and the central role of clog dancing in it, a fieldwork project of massive scope opened up before my eyes, but I thought of it as only about clog dancing in its American and English forms and the implications that might have for a theory of where tap dancing came from.

We learned that the Marley family in Rockville included father, William, and mother, Margaret Donovan Marley. They had fourteen children in all, eight of whom survived to adulthood: three sons, Bill, Jim, and Dan, and five daughters, Marge, Kay, Matty, Anna, and Gert. William and Margaret were married in Taunton, Massachusetts. William Marley was born ca. 1870, in Taunton, and Margaret J. Donovan in East Windsor, Connecticut, both of Irish immigrant parents. All the children except Bill were born in Rockville.

It remains unknown where William learned to clog dance. Anna believes her father "taught himself." She doubts that he learned it from his father. When asked where he may have seen or learned the clog dancing she speculated that he may have seen it "on the circuits" (an apparent reference to touring vaudeville or minstrel troupes). She states definitely, however, that the dancing is English. William Marley danced as an amateur with

William ("Professor") Farley at community events in and around Taunton, billing themselves as "Farley and Marley." The Marleys know nothing else about Mr. Farley except that he later became a barber in Taunton. Reportedly they danced in skintight pants with "spangles." They also wore short vests and no hats. William was also an excellent baseball player and sometime after the birth of eldest son Bill (1899) and prior to the birth of son Jim (1901), he was recruited as a catcher by the Rockville baseball team. In order to get him they had to find him a job at a local mill. He moved, breaking his relationship with Mr. Farley who, we later discovered, danced on the Keith vaudeville circuit as part of the duo "Farley and Dugan" until he retired in 1923.

William did not dance for several years, being busy with work and family. When William saw his son Jim, at age fifteen, dancing in some sort of minstrel show in school he thought it was time to start teaching him clog dancing. They practiced for an hour every night after work and performed at local events. Father and son danced locally but never toured seriously due to family responsibilities. The oldest son, Bill, was a pilot and banjo player, a three-time Connecticut champion. Sisters Martha (Matty), Anna, and Gert performed clog together as schoolgirls. Anna recounts that the three girls were expected to come home from school during the lunch hour to practice. "Ten minutes to walk home, ten minutes to eat, thirty minutes of dancing, and ten more to walk back." This was before the dance studio was built in the basement, and Anna reports that her father had a clogging mat three feet wide by twenty feet long made of maple strips which he would roll out onto the living room floor on which they would practice.

In 1923 there was a family vaudeville troupe, "The Dancing Marleys," with the father, son, and daughters clog dancing, mother playing piano, and son Bill playing banjo. Brother Dan was often on tour with different family members working the curtains and occasionally playing mandolin. The men wore top hat and tails and danced holding the cane in front of them with both hands. The women always wore fancy dress. A Will Finley of Rockville wrote and arranged two tunes, "Marleys Clog" and "Dancing Marleys," both in the distinctive dotted hornpipe rhythm. William's and Gert's clogs survive from this period and are stamped with the manufacturer's name "Neely," who took out patents from a Chicago address.

William died in 1930 when Anna was about eleven. During the Great

Depression, Jim, eighteen years Anna's senior and seemingly the nurturing male figure in her life, lost his job and was very hard up. In 1936, he suggested to his sister Anna (then age seventeen) that they dance professionally. They "practiced up" and went to New York for a Thursday audition for the Major Bowes Amateur Hour. At the audition, they were told that "the Major" wanted them back that Sunday night for the national broadcast by radio live from New York City. They won the grand prize.

Anna remembers that Bill "Bojangles" Robinson was in the studio audience and while they were dancing he was yelling out enthusiastic encouragement and humorous comments. Later he came backstage to compliment them on their dancing. One of Anna's favorite stories is that when Robinson was starring in Hartford, Jim sent a messenger backstage to ask if Robinson remembered him. Ann quotes Robinson as saying "Jim Marley? Of course I remember him, he was the only one to give me competition."

Jim and Anna toured by bus with Major Bowes Unit #1 (the "All-Stars") from June to December in 1936, mostly on the West Coast and Texas. Jim Marley kept a detailed diary of the trip which indicates that they did four shows a day for all but six of the 178 days. They came home no better off financially than when they left and did not tour again professionally. Jim and Anna were invited by Major Bowes to dance at the Palladium in London but Jim could not go due to family commitments. Anna was asked to join the show alone but her family would not allow her to go unescorted.

After World War II, Anna taught dance school in Rockville. Jim Marley continued to dance occasionally at local "minstrel shows" by himself, with Anna playing, and, occasionally, with his daughter, Eleanor Marley Lessig, until her marriage in 1948. At our first meeting, Anna produced a cassette tape recording of Jim and Eleanor dancing the Buck and Wing, the Waltz Clog, and the Pedestal Clog with Anna playing piano. The recording is poor but the clarity of the clog sounds in the stepping and the raw speed of the dancing is dramatic. The audience clearly is also familiar with the Marley clogging for they interrupt particular moments in the sequences with applause in the way that crowds do when they see something they know and like.

Jim Marley died a few weeks after our visit, shortly after Thanksgiving of 1988. In January 1989, I called Anna and arranged to visit her again. When we arrived, she told us that she and her sisters, Marge and Kay, with whom she lived, had discussed teaching me the steps. They had decided that the Marley style of clog dancing would be lost if someone didn't learn the steps. She laid down the rules:

"If I'm going to teach you, though, you're going to have to learn it right. I'll teach you one step at a time and you don't get another one until you can do that one. That's the way my father taught us. He'd make us dance the steps over and over, sometimes turning his back or going in the next room and he'd yell if it didn't sound right."

I readily agreed. Anna's approach to teaching is just like that of my mother, my school rugby coach, my favorite history teacher, and every "Dancing Master" I had observed working with English Morris dance teams or who had been described by other fieldworkers. Often known as the "Generalissimo," they declared there was a right way to do things and you did it that way or not at all.

I have gone back almost once a week since then and Anna's niece, Eleanor, a spry woman just a few years younger than Anna, began coming "just to dance." Anna refers to my visits as "lessons." Her goal is clearly not to have the steps documented but performed. It is not enough for me to know how the step goes but it is necessary to dance it in a performance sequence and, ultimately, at something close to Marley tempo. Anna knew I would be performing at festivals and dance camps in the summer of 1989 and during April and May pushed extra hard to get the Buck and Wing into shape. At some point in June, I danced it well enough one morning that she announced with some satisfaction, "OK, now it's yours. You should dance it at these competitions this summer." Actually, they were festivals and dance camps at which I was to perform and teach, but to Anna any public situation where one clog dances is a show and a competition.

Anna, indeed, is so much the performer first that she has no compunctions about inventing steps, borrowing steps, and adjusting sequences to make a good show. At one point in the spring, my wife and I were working together on the Marley waltz clog sequence. Anna had refused to teach me the waltz steps unless the two of us did it since it "is supposed to be done by two people dancing shoulder to shoulder." She couldn't quite remember the sequence she had danced with Jim and we only had seven steps. I asked if there was a step in which the dancers slap their clogs with their hands. She thought about it a minute and taught us a sequence which she put in as a "brake" at the end of the second step. The next week, when Eleanor watched us dance the waltz clog, she asked about the slap step, which she had never seen. Anna confessed to making it up based on a slap sequence in another routine. "Borrowing" ideas from other step dancers is also an essential part of the art and was especially so when dancers with different styles met in the competitive professional atmosphere of vaudeville. The Marley Buck and Wing has a step they call the "Robinson Roll" which Anna says Jim adapted after seeing the legendary Bojangles dance.

Anna's willingness to experiment is usually tempered by Eleanor's desire to have her father's routines performed again exactly as he did them. On one occasion when Eleanor had not been present, Anna had shown me a "front crossover" step in which the toe of one clog kicks the heel of the other as the feet are uncrossed. It was very similar to an English step which in Lancashire and Durham is often called "kicks" and which I danced for Anna. She liked it and strongly suggested that I dance it instead of the second of three repeats of the Marley crossover movement. When Eleanor saw it, she commented that it was not what her father had danced but that it was all right as long as I could still dance it the other way.

Eleanor's role in the process of learning the Marley clog steps has been particularly instructive. She is a very good dancer in her own right and picked up the steps from her father without being formally taught as Anna was. Most significantly, she represents the most active member of a whole family of clog dancers. She mentioned at some point that she comes to our lessons because she loves to dance and because she never had lessons from her aunt and good friend, Anna, like the other members of the family. "The other members of the family?" There are, I discovered, eight other "nieces" who as recently as 1983 performed the Buck and Wing and another Marley routine Anna calls "The Irish Jig," a character dance for eight performers to the tune of "The Irish Washerwoman." Anna gave me a program from a performance given on April 30, 1983, called "Ann Marley's Pupils Salute Vernon." While she was teaching, Anna gave such concerts at the end of a teaching session of several weeks. The penultimate piece, item number 40 on the program, is listed as "BUCK AND WING SPECIAL—Nieces and Great Nieces of Ann Marley."

Anna has a photograph of another performance which she thinks was also in that year, 1983, which shows her with eight Marley women in pants with green suspenders, wearing green derbies, a costume for "The Irish Jig." The group includes an age range from mid-sixties to a ten-year-old, Theresa. The Marley clog may be dormant but it has clearly played a major role in establishing the identity of an extended family over at least four generations. In May of 1990, Anna mentioned that her great niece, Theresa, who was graduating from high school, was going to be dancing a set of Buck and Wing steps on a pedestal as a "party-piece" which each senior was required to do for the rest of the class. Theresa does not seem to have any pretensions about being a clog dancer but when presenting herself as a Marley to her class in this important situation, a sort of rite of passage, she asked her great-aunt to help her work up the major family inheritance.

The Marleys are unusual in several ways. It is, first of all, uncommon among emigrant families with at least three generations of Americans to have so many family members participate in any folkloric activity that is demonstrably a survival from the nineteenth century. Second, it is not easy to find New England families who have maintained step dancing of any kind over several generations, even among Irish- and Franco-Americans. But I had not even heard of one individual in North America who had kept up any form of the dancing in clogs which was a very active part of social and competitive life in northern England into the 1950s.

The Marleys represent what has since been found to be several survivals of wooden shoe or clog dancing in North America in this century. This should not be confused with what in parts of the South is called "clogging." Among the most important differences are that Southern "cloggers" dance freestyle rather than in formal patterns and the basic body carriage involves a lowering of the center of weight, giving a "flatfoot" effect, in contrast with English and Irish dancers who elevate the torso and perform on the ball of the foot with occasional heel-beats. Nor can it be identified with the dances known as "clogs" which were popular among physical education instructors in American schools in the 1920s and 1930s.

Clog Dancing on the American Stage

I had known that dancing in wooden-soled shoes had been an important part of the vaudeville stage in the late nineteenth century as it had been on the English music hall stage. Indeed, there were performances of the "Lancashire Clog Hornpipe" in Boston in the 1840s and 1850s. I had assumed, though, that this had existed just at the professional level along with the dozens and perhaps hundreds of other "character" dances which pervaded vaudeville.

It was not surprising to me that one would find clog dancing in this professional context, with so many music hall and vaudeville performers crossing back and forth between English and American stages. I assumed that English dancers must have toured on vaudeville where their clog dance steps would have been seen and used, as Stearns and Stearns (1968) suggested, to cross-fertilize the style of step dancing we know as "tap," which became dominant on the American stage.

The influence seems to have been in both directions, though. For example, in his classic *American Vaudeville: Its Life and Times,* Douglas Gilbert wrote:

> Possibly clog did not originate in America, but America made it its own, and our performers were unbeatable. A clog dancer named Queen electrified the English music halls when he went abroad for a tour in the eighties. They found his triples, rolls, and nerve steps uncanny, refused to believe he accomplished them unaided by tricks, and caused him no end of embarrassment by demanding to see his shoes. Queen stopped all that by making his entrance in slippers and passing around his shoes for the audience to examine, as proof that he used no clappers or other Yankee gadgets. When the shoes were returned he put them on in full view of the audience and went into his act. (1940: 24)

When I went back to check, I was disappointed to find that Gilbert gives no other details about the dancing, except for the following crucial piece of information:

> An interesting phase of the eighties varieties was the contests among performers. There were all kinds of matches between clog dancers, jig dancers, harmonica players, bone soloists, pantomimists—who competed usually for silver cups. A winner aided his booking time.
>
> Most popular and most numerous were the clog-dancing

contests: Lancashire clog, American clog, hornpipe clog, trick clog, pedestal clog, and statue clog. Dancing was judged according to time, style, and execution, and separate judges checked each feature. It was the habit of some judges to go beneath the stage and listen to the beat. Sand jig dancing was judged in the same manner. (24)

I read it again: "Clog-dancing contests" and "it was the habit of some judges to go beneath the stage and listen to the beat." That could have been written about almost anywhere in northern England at the same time but particularly about Lancashire, what may have been the most competitive region of the whole country.

Then it came together.

This, I now saw, was a project about the largely unexplored folkloric impact of dancing on the vaudeville stage on American life around the turn of the century. More significantly, it was about Lancashire immigrants and an aspect of mill culture in New England before 1930.

Lancashire Mill Culture in Eastern Massachusetts

My story had really started, I suddenly realized, in New Bedford, Massachusetts, more than fifteen years earlier. In the fall of 1973, I had created, directed, and performed in a show called "An Evening at the English Music Hall" in collaboration with several British and American singers and musicians. It was an attempt to replicate what I loved about the great era of working-class entertainment in England during the late Victorian and Edwardian times. This led me to New Bedford, home of cast member Maggi Peirce, a magnificent Scots-Irish balladeer and storyteller and the organizer of a successful church-sponsored coffee house. It was a natural place to gather the cast for a dress rehearsal in front of an audience before we tackled a huge crowd in the 1200-seat 1870s opera and theater palace of the Troy Music Hall in Troy, New York.

An unexpected bonus was that the crowd included a substantial contingent of the local British Society, many of who, it turned out, were descendants of English or Irish people from Lancashire who had emigrated to the United States between about 1890 and 1930 to work in the local mills.

These mills had suffered after that point because labor was cheaper in the South, but many of the families had stayed on. I received many books of music hall sheet music from Mrs. Nellie Clegg, a small, cheery weaver who had emigrated as a girl and was thrilled to hear the old music hall songs she had played before arthritis took the pleasures of the piano away from her. My singing partner, John Roberts, an Englishman from Worcestershire, was, at the time, just learning to play both the so-called English and Anglo-German concertinas. Mrs. Clegg mentioned that she knew a Mr. John Wright, a Lancashire immigrant like herself, who used to play the concertina.

We tracked down Mr. Wright's daughter, who arranged for us to visit him in the nursing home. He had two concertinas, both in poor shape. I was able to fix up one with enough air and enough wheezy notes to get a tune going. Not having picked the instrument up in twenty years or so, Mr. Wright was nevertheless able to play a few bars of tunes which, he said to our surprise, were part of the repertoire of the "New Bedford Concertina Band" formed in 1913 by his father. These included "Over the Waves" and other popular marches of the period. From the family of another former band member, Mr. Arthur Skinner, we were able to get a photograph of the group, which played in the New Bedford area from 1913 until 1915.

Bands performing march music were common in Lancashire and other parts of the industrial north of England at the time. Most made use of brass instruments but concertina bands were not unusual. The bands were almost always attached to and sometimes sponsored by a mill or a mine. From the sketchy information we were able to obtain, it seemed as if the New Bedford Concertina Band had also consisted primarily of workers, fifteen of them in the 1913 photograph, from the same mill.

Prior to this, I had not known that the eastern Massachusetts mills had been worked by immigrant weavers from Lancashire. The discovery of a mill culture in New Bedford which was robust enough to support something as specialized as a concertina band was a surprise. At the time, I did nothing more with the material. Mr. Skinner had been in intensive care when we obtained the picture from his family and died within a matter of weeks, and Mrs. Clegg and Mr. Wright were gone shortly afterwards. I got the impression locally that the vitality had gone from this mill culture by the 1930s, when the mills moved into the southern states to find cheaper labor and New Bedford went rapidly downhill after the whaling industry collapsed.

Since the remaining work seemed to be primarily that of checking imprints, I had put it off as something which could be done anytime.

For some reason it had never occurred to me that there might be other aspects of the culture that was so common in Lancashire to be found in New Bedford. It was the reference to clog dancing competitions that linked Mr. Wright with the Marleys. In Lancashire, working-class people compete over anything and everything, from the size of marrows to racing pigeons to clog dancing. The mills and the neighborhoods around the mill also supported sports teams.

The clues then seemed endless. William Marley moved from Taunton, a mill town near New Bedford, to Rockville, another mill town, to play for the local baseball team after he had been guaranteed a job at Regan's Mill. Local sports teams were commonly tied to Lancashire mills. The Marleys insist that their dancing is English and Anna, after I asked directly, remembered that her father used to call it Lancashire clog. First danced in the Boston area in the early 1840s, the "Lancashire Clog Hornpipe" was a familiar sight on Massachusetts stages throughout the nineteenth century. Farley and Marley had first teamed up in Taunton. Could they have learned their clog dancing locally within a clog dancing environment established or, at least, nurtured by Lancashire immigrants? Dance competitions would have fed quite naturally into the demand for new acts on the thriving vaudeville circuits which, as happened in the 1930s for Jim and Anna Marley, used local competitive situations as auditions for two- and three-week circuits of a troupe.

If this was right, the Marleys may not be unique. There must have been other clog dancing families in the Taunton, Brockton, and New Bedford areas; perhaps there were even Farleys who still knew the dancing. Dr. Krause put a classified ad in the local Taunton paper asking if anyone knew anything about a Bill Farley who was a clog dancer and a barber. Several letters came in response, one from a Phil Farley who was old Bill Farley's nephew. No, he had never heard of William Marley, but as a boy and young man he had clog danced on stage with his uncle and a local man, George S. Silver (or Silva), and a boy known as "Little Dickie Belcher." Yes, there used to be regular clog dancing competitions in the area. No, he couldn't really remember the steps because he hadn't danced since World War II when, as a sergeant in the Marines, he had had his leg shot up charging a machine gun nest at Okinawa.

When Dr. Krause and I visited Phil and his wife, Alice, they pulled out a hunk of plywood for me to dance several of the Marley steps I had learned. Phil thought they looked familiar but wasn't sure until I danced one particularly difficult waltz clog step. He suddenly exclaimed that he could hear his uncle yelling at him about doing that step right. From his description of their stage act, it is not hard to get the impression that Marley and Farley each re-created their original duo act after Marley left for Rockville. In addition to his act with George Silver and his nephew, Phil remembered that Bill Farley had danced with a Mr. William Dugan, and he knew of another local clog dancer named McGunigle.

I found it interesting that at least some Irish-Americans were dancing English clog styles when the local references clearly indicate that Irish jigs and reels were part of the local lore. A reasonable hypothesis was that the Marleys and many other Irish immigrants to that area were from among the Lancashire-Irish, a large population that evolved and maintained a unique style of clog dancing in the Lancashire mill towns which could still be seen in the 1950s.

Phil Farley's memories of the clog dancing in eastern Massachusetts prior to World War II have been confirmed in conversations with Dick Belcher, billed in 1936 at age twelve as the "New England Wooden Shoe Champion" and now a retired superintendent of schools. Further leads have been culled from a treasure trove of newspaper clippings of the minstrel shows and other Brockton area performances between 1925 and 1942 kept by Dick's mother, Dorrice Belcher. The scope of the project to understand and document the impact of Lancashire immigrant culture seemingly expands daily. However, while there are many memories and accounts of the occasions when dancing happened, there is small likelihood of any more of the kind of details about the dancing itself which survives with the Marleys of Rockville.

References Cited

Gilbert, Douglas. 1940. *American Vaudeville: Its Life and Times.* New York: McGraw-Hill.

Hyde, Lewis. 1979. *The Gift.* New York: Vintage Books. Reprint, 1983.

Stearns, Marshall Winslow, and Jean Stears. 1979. *Jazz Dance: The Story of American Vernacular Dance.* New York: Schirmer.

14

How I Learned What a Crock Was
Howard S. Becker

In the fall of 1955, I moved to Kansas City to begin fieldwork at the University of Kansas Medical School, as the first fieldworker in a project led by Everett Hughes, part of a team that eventually also included Blanche Geer and Anselm Strauss.[1] We were going to study medical students and medical education but, to be truthful, I had very little idea of what I was going to do beyond "hanging around with the students," going to classes, and whatever else presented itself.

I had even less idea what the problem was that we were going to investigate. There was a field of sociology called "socialization," and Robert Merton and his students had been studying the socialization of medical students to the role of doctor. My dissertation, a study of schoolteachers' careers, could have been said to be in the "sociology of education," but that didn't prepare me to study medical students. As far as I had gone in conceptualizing my problem was to say to myself that these kids came in at one end and four years later came out at the other end, and something certainly must have happened to them in between.

In any event, I was more concerned with our family's move from Urbana (what a relief to get out of there!) to Kansas City (which I hoped, and it turned out to be true, would provide a better place to practice my other trade of piano playing), and with getting to know my way around the what seemed to me enormous buildings that were the University of Kansas Medical Center.

I knew next to nothing about the organization of medical education, and consoled myself about my ignorance with the "wisdom" that told me that therefore I would have no prejudices either. How scientific! I didn't even know, and had to be told, that the first two years of the four-year medical course were mostly academic, while during the last two "clinical" years students actually worked on hospital wards, attending to patients.

Fortunately, the dean of the school took me in hand and decided that I should begin my investigations with a group of third-year students in the Department of Internal Medicine. There were two third-year student groups, superintended by different faculty members, and he took care that I ended up with the one run by the "benign" doctor. I learned soon enough that the other was one of those legendary terrors who cowed students, house staff, and most of his patients with his temper.

I didn't know what internal medicine was but learned quickly enough that it had to do with everything that wasn't surgery or pediatrics or obstetrics or any of a lot of other named specialties. I soon learned too that the people who practiced internal medicine considered themselves, and were considered by others, to be the intellectuals of the medical business, as opposed to the surgeons, who were thought to be money-grubbing brutes, or the psychiatrists, who were thought to be crazy themselves.

With no problem to orient myself to, no theoretically defined puzzle I was trying to solve, I concentrated on finding out what the hell was going on, who all these people were, what they were doing, what they were talking about, finding my way around, and, most of all, getting to know the six students with whom I was going to spend the next six weeks. I was a Jewish smart aleck from the University of Chicago and they were several varieties of small town and larger city Kansans and Missourians, but we got on well from the start. They were interested in what I was doing and curious about my work and job ("How much do they pay you to do this?" they wanted to know). They thought it was nice that I got paid to study them, and did not doubt that they were worth the trouble.

None of us were sure what I was "allowed" to do or which things they did were "private," while others were OK for me to follow along on. Clearly I could go to class with them, or make rounds of the patients with them and the attending physician. But the first time one of the students got up and said, "Well, I have to go examine a patient now," I could see that I had to take matters into my own hands and set the right precedent.

Neither the dean nor anyone else had said I could watch while students examined patients. On the other hand, no one had said I couldn't do that. My presence during a physical examination might have been construed as a violation of patient privacy except that it would be a joke to raise that matter in a medical school, where such intimate procedures as rectal and vaginal exams were often carried out before a sizable audience. The student, being new at examining patients, wasn't too eager to have me watch him fumble. But if I let the situation get defined as "The sociologist can't watch us examine patients" I'd be cut off from one of the major things students did. So I said, with a confidence I didn't feel, "OK. I'll come with you." He must have thought I knew something he didn't, and didn't argue the point.

Making rounds worked like this. The physician whose group I was working with had a "service," a number of beds occupied by his patients. A resident or two and an intern worked on the service, and six students were assigned to it. Every patient was assigned to a student, who was responsible for doing a physical exam, taking a history, ordering diagnostic tests, making a diagnosis, and planning a course of treatment. Mind you, all that work was done again by an intern, a resident, and the physician.

Every morning the whole group assembled and walked around to see all the patients on the service; that was making rounds. At each bed, the physician talked to the patient, asked the house staff about any developments since yesterday, and then made that patient the occasion for an informal quiz of the student to whom he or she had been assigned. The quiz could be about anything, and students were nervous about what might come up.

During my first week in the school, while I followed the students and others through the ritual of making rounds, I made my discovery. It wasn't the "Ah-ha" that researchers often report. Rather, it was a piece of detective work that took me, and several of the students, most of the next week. Its ramifications occupied me and my colleagues for the duration of the project.

One morning, as we made rounds, we saw a very talkative patient, who had multiple complaints to tell the doctor about, all sorts of aches, pains, and unusual events. I could see that no one was taking her very seriously and, on the way out, one of the students said, "Boy, she's really a crock!" I understood this, in part, as shorthand for "crock of shit." It was obviously invidious. But what was he talking about? What was wrong with her having all those complaints? Wasn't that interesting? (By the way, this first patient was in fact a woman and the non-crock that followed a man, which exactly suited the medical stereotypes which said that crocks were overwhelmingly women.)

As I've already said, my discovery of what the word "crock" meant was not a lightning bolt of intuition. On the contrary, it was guided by sociological theorizing every step of the way. Like this. When I heard Chet call the patient a crock, I engaged in a quick but deep theoretical analysis. I had a piece of theory ready to put to work here. To put it most pretentiously: When members of one status category make invidious distinctions among the members of another status category with whom they regularly deal, the distinction will reflect the interests of the members of the first category in the relationship. More specifically, perhaps less forbiddingly, the invidious distinctions students made between classes of patients would show what interests they were trying to maximize in that relationship, what they hoped to get out of it.

So, when Chet called the patient a crock, I made this theoretical analysis in a flash and then came up with a profoundly theoretical question: "What's a crock?" He looked at me as if to say that any damn fool would know that. So I said, "Seriously, when you called her a crock, what did you mean?" He looked a little confused. He had known what he meant when he said it, but wasn't sure he could explain it. After fumbling for a while, he said it referred to someone with psychosomatic illness. That let him off the hook for the moment by partially satisfying my curiosity, though I still wanted to know what interest of his as a student was violated by a patient with psychosomatic illness.

But, as a good scientist, I wanted to check my finding out further, so I held my tongue. The next patient we saw, as it turned out, had a gastric ulcer, and the attending physician made him the occasion for a short lecture on psychosomatic illness, with ulcer the example at hand. It was quite interesting and, when we left the room, I tried out my new knowledge and said to Chet, "Crock, huh?" He looked at me as though I were a fool, and said, "No, he's not a crock." I said, "Why not? He has psychosomatic disease, doesn't he? Didn't you just tell me that's what a crock is? Didn't we just spend ten minutes discussing it?" He looked more confused than before and another student, eavesdropping on our discussion, undertook to clear it up: "No, he's not a crock. He really has an ulcer."

I don't remember all the details of what followed. What I do remember is that I got all the students interested in the question and, between us, with me asking a lot of questions, and applying the results to succeeding cases, we ended up defining a crock as a patient who had multiple complaints but no discernible physical pathology. That definition was robust, and held up under many further tests.

But my problem was only half solved. I still had to find out why students thought crocks were bad. What interest of theirs was compromised by a patient with many complaints and no pathology? When I asked them, students said that you couldn't learn anything from crocks that would be useful in your future medical practice. That told me that what students wanted to maximize in school, not surprisingly, was the chance to learn things that would be useful when they entered practice. But, if that was true, then it seemed contradictory to devalue crocks, because there were many such patients. In fact, the attending physicians liked to point out that most of the patients a physician saw in an ordinary practice would be like that. So a crock ought to provide excellent training for practice.

When I pursued that paradox, students told me that you might have a lot of patients like that later on, but you couldn't learn anything from seeing them here in school. Not what they wanted to learn, anyway. Which was what? They explained that all their teachers ever said about what to do with crocks was that you should talk to them, that talking made crocks feel better. The students felt they had learned that with the first one. Succeeding crocks did not add to their knowledge of crockdom, its differential diagnosis, or its treatment. A crock presented no medical puzzles to be solved.

What they wanted to learn, students said, was a certain kind of knowledge which could not be learned from books. They studied their books dutifully, preparing for the quizzes that punctuated rounds and other such events, but believed that the most important knowledge they would acquire in school was not in those books. What was most worth learning was what my colleagues and I eventually summarized as "clinical experience," the sights, sounds, and smells of disease in a living person: what a heart murmur really sounded like when you had your stethoscope against a patient's chest as opposed to its sound on a recording, how patients whose hearts sounded that way looked and talked about how they felt, what a diabetic or a person who had just suffered a heart attack looked like.

You could only learn those things from people who had real physical pathologies. You learn nothing about cardiac disease from a patient who is sure he's having heart attacks every day but has no murmurs to listen to, no unusual EKG findings, no heart disease. So crocks disappointed students by having no pathology you could observe firsthand. That showed me an important and characteristic feature of contemporary medical practice: the preference for personal experience over scientific publications as a source of the wisdom you used in guiding your practice. We eventually called this the "clinical experience" perspective and found its traces everywhere. Perhaps most importantly, even faculty who themselves published scientific papers would say, in response to a student question about something reported in a medical journal, "I know that's what people have found but I've tried that procedure and it didn't work for me, so I don't care what the journals say."

Crocks had other irritating characteristics, which students eventually explained under my barrage of questions. Students, perpetually overworked, always had new patients to work up, classes to go to, books and articles to read, notes to record in patient charts. Examining patients always took time, but examining crocks took forever. Crocks had dozens of symptoms to describe and were sure that every detail was important. They wanted to describe their many previous illnesses in similar detail. Many of them had been able to persuade physicians (who, the students thought, should have been less pliable) to perform multiple surgeries which they also wanted to describe fully. (I remember a patient who had had so many abdominal surgeries that her navel had been completely obliterated. She made a deep impression on all of us.)

So crocks took much more of your time than other patients and gave you much less of anything you wanted for your trouble. That showed me another important feature of medical school life: everything was a trade-off of time, the scarcest commodity for a student or house officer, for other valuable things. We found the traces of that proposition everywhere too. For instance, students often traded patients with each other. Why? Well, if I've had three patients with myocardial infarcts (as I learned, with the students, to call a heart attack) and you've had three patients with diabetes, it's obviously mutually advantageous for us to trade, so that neither of us wastes our time learning the same facts three times while missing another equally useful set of facts altogether.

Students disliked crocks, I eventually learned, for still a third reason. Like their teachers, students hoped to perform medical miracles, and heal the sick, if not actually raise the dead. They knew that wasn't easy to do, and that they wouldn't always be successful, but one of the real payoffs of medical practice for them was to "do something" and watch a sick person get well. But you can't perform a medical miracle on someone who was never sick in the first place. Since crocks, in the student view, weren't "really sick," they were useless as the raw material of medical miracles.

We eventually called this attitude the "medical responsibility" perspective and saw its traces everywhere too. Perhaps its most bizarre outcropping was the idea that you weren't fully operating as a doctor unless what you did could, if done wrong, kill people. This was enshrined in a putdown of the specialty of dermatology we heard several times: "You can't kill anybody and you can't cure anybody." A more accurate rendition of the general principle involved would have been "You can't cure anyone *unless* you can kill them."

Learning what a crock was thus was a matter of carefully unraveling the multiple meanings built into that simple word, rather than the Big Ah-Ha the editors of this volume may have had in mind. This little ah-ha may have a lesson for us when we experience the Big Ah-Ha. Intuitions are great but they don't do much for us unless we follow them up with the detailed work that shows us what they really mean, what they can really account for.

Notes

This essay previously appeared in *Journal of Contemporary Ethnography* 22, no. 1 (April 1993): 28–35. Copyright Sage Publications, Inc. Used by permission.

1   The study was reported in full in Becker et al. 1961. A one-paragraph description of the discovery of the meaning of "crock" appears in Becker 1958.

References Cited

Becker, Howard S. 1958. "Problems of Inference and Proof in Participant Observation." *American Sociological Review* 23:658.

Becker, Howard S., Blanche Geer, Anselm L. Strauss, and Everett C. Hughes. 1961. *Boys in White: Student Culture in Medical School.* Chicago: University of Chicago Press.

15

Who's Gypsy Here?
Reflections at a *Rom* Burial
Carol Silverman

Monday, March 27, 1978. The phone rang at 9:30 A.M. and it was Debbie.

"Hey Carol, can you be over here in ten minutes? We're going to the cemetery to bury Skipa."

"I'll be right over!"

I jumped into my clothes, grabbed my camera and tape recorder, and ran three blocks down Flatbush Avenue to the apartment with the "Reader and Adviser" sign where Debbie lived with her mother and father. After two years of fieldwork among *Machwava* and *Kalderash Roma* (Gypsies),[1] I was about to attend my first burial. I was excited at the opportunity to observe the relationship between the living and the deceased at a burial. Little did I realize that the cemetery would be the site of an angry confrontation between mourning *Roma* and actors impersonating *Roma* from the film *King of the Gypsies.* This confrontation would shock me into some realities concerning popular representations of *Roma* and also raise issues of reflexivity and performance, theirs as well as mine.

Running to the *ofisa* (fortune-telling parlor), I remembered my anticipation at attending Skipa's funeral the previous Saturday. While dressing up for the funeral, Docha, Sherry, and Peaches (the teenage cousins in the extended family with which I was working) talked about the available boys who might be there. They were anxious to attend any social gathering where they would meet other *Roma,* hear the latest news, and make connections. Even elderly Neta, whom we called Mami (grandmother), was excited about going to the funeral even though she rarely went out. She put on her best *romano suto* (*Rom* clothing), a silk blouse and skirt with matching scarf.

Driving to the funeral home from Brooklyn to lower Manhattan and then uptown on Third Ave., Mila (Peaches's mother, Neta's daughter) pointed out all the *ofisi*, explaining who was related to whom and who had the nicest furnishings and best reputations. I realized I was getting a private tour of *Rom* New York. They could recognize *Roma* from blocks away, and I, too, was developing the skills.

A row of Cadillacs[2] from various states were lined up in front of the Walter B. Cooke Funeral Home on 85th St. and Third Ave., for *Roma* believe that family and friends should show respect for a dead (or sick) person who led an honorable life. The dead continue to affect the living in important ways, both good and bad, depending on how one treats them. Respect for the spirits of the dead (*mule*), then, is necessary if one wishes to avoid illness and bad luck. The six-week period following death is most crucial, for the spirit wanders during this time.[3]

Skipa, whose *gazhe* (non-Gypsy) name[4] was Steve Nicholas, was a very well respected *Rom* in his mid-forties. People said he had "everything to live for—children, family, money." He was survived by his wife Helen and numerous children, some his own, some adopted from the larger kindred and some adopted from *gazhe*. The close family was very much afflicted. They were dressed in black and they would not change their clothes, wash, or shave for three days.

The other *Roma*, by contrast, socialized quite normally, joking, laughing, and catching up on news about relatives and friends. At the funeral home, there were three rooms in which to congregate, one for men only, one for women only, and one for the coffin. The entrance hall was filled with people milling around, especially segregated groups of teenage boys and girls eyeing each other. Like other social gatherings, funerals require sexual segregation due to the *Rom* taboo system and the accompanying rules of interaction.[5]

The coffin was open, set on a raised platform, and surrounded by flower arrangements in the shape of cards (aces, kings, etc.). White with gold trim on the outside, it was lined in white silky velvet with a quilted pattern. I was a little taken aback at the sight of the embalmed body, for at the Jewish funerals I had attended, the coffin was closed. Skipa was dressed in an expensive suit, shirt, shoes, tie, gold tie clip, and many gold rings. His hat was placed next to his head and nearby was a photograph of him and his wife. His hands were folded, with a rosary entwined in his fingers, and on his chest lay a huge pile of money. I estimated that the bills, mostly ones, fives, and tens, totaled a few hundred dollars.

"People give this money to pay his way to heaven. Like Mami gives some and says, 'Give it to Papo [grandfather] up there.' Some people take out some of the money before they close the coffin, if they really need it, but most leave it in. A lot of wealth gets buried with *Roma*. If anyone robbed *Rom* graves they'd get rich!" explained Mila.

People came up to the coffin to talk to the body, to touch it, to relate to it, and to put in some money. There was no sense of awkwardness or revulsion, even babies fingered the corpse. Close family members spent the longest time at the coffin. Relatives and friends told stories about other funerals: Sherry told of the drowning of two *Rom* boys, Mami remembered Papo's funeral at the same home, and Debbie told of her sister's funeral last year. The viewing of the body was the occasion to reflect on those who died recently.

I asked Mila if she thought I could take a few pictures, and she said I should ask the close family. I mustered my courage and walked over to Helen, the widow, and Patsy, a daughter-in-law whom I knew, and ventured, "Patsy, do you think it's OK if I take a picture?"

"*Kon san* [who are you]?" queried Helen.

Before I could answer, Patsy said, "She's a *rakli* [non-*Rom* girl] but she knows all the *Roma*."

"I came with Neta and Mila—I used to tutor for some of the people[6]— I'm interested in *Rom* customs," I blurted out.

"Sure honey, you can take a picture, but why?" asked Helen.

"I want to show *Rom* traditions . . ."

"That's nice, honey. Don't you take the live people?"

"Sure, I've got pictures of weddings, *pakivi* [feasts of respect], *slavi* [saints' days]."

"*Dzhanes tut Romanes* [Do you know how to speak Romani]?"

"*Dzhanaw zalagitsa* [I know a little]."

"Do you want to marry a *Rom?*"

"No."

"Why?"

"I'm Jewish. You know, my parents would be upset."[7]

"Sure, I understand. You know, of all the people, the Jewish are most like the Gypsies, even with the funeral. Yesterday when I was buying the coffin, I told the man I couldn't hand him the money—it was *nay mishto* [shameful].[8] He was Jewish and said they do it like that too."

"Yeah, and also not shaving for three days."

"Take the pictures, but do me a favor—don't show them to anyone."

"OK—you mean not to Americans?"

"No, don't show them to the people—*Roma.*"

"OK fine, you're the boss. Would you like a copy?"

"No, I want to remember him the way he used to be."

This conversation underscored the ambiguous position I occupied with the *Rom* community. Among the three or four extended families in Flatbush I felt like somewhat of an insider, having gained access to guarded realms such as fortune-telling, and having lived and traveled with them on a daily basis. Yet in the larger *Rom* network I was constantly reminded of my outsider status, and I had to prove myself over and over again, repeating the process I went through in the early stages of fieldwork.

Due to centuries of persecution and discrimination,[9] *Roma* tend to be wary of outsiders, especially curious outsiders like me. When my first tutoring sessions grew into long afternoons of helping around the house, Mami took me aside and said, "Don't ask so many questions. The kids don't like you asking all the time—They get suspicious when you want to know about everything." Mami's advice should have earned her an honorary instructorship in Fieldwork Methodology, for it elicited patience and sensitivity from an overzealous fieldworker.

At first it was difficult to find a balance between the roles of paid employee (tutor) and ethnographer. I felt that if I allowed myself to tutor for free I would be regarded as gullible; on the other hand, if I insisted on receiving a "fair" wage I would risk alienating the family. This dilemma was solved by the advent of the father's heart attack and hospitalization. In the resulting crisis the family was thrown closer together, including me. Tutoring was suspended as more pressing duties took precedence, such as baby-sitting and supplying food for an increasing number of guests. As relatives and friends arrived to be near the sick man, I met them as a member of the household. Henceforth, services such as chaperoning, shopping, and helping with the fortune-telling mail were performed by me with no monetary considerations.

The attitude of the teenage children toward me gradually began to change: they began to show an interest in me, to question me, and to ask me to spend more time with them. At first the girls' biggest interest was my appearance, which they thought was pitiful.

"You dress corny, your earrings are odd, you got to get some nice clothes. Come on, let me fix you up, tweeze your eyebrows, cut your hair, put make-up on you. The main thing is to catch the boys. They'll be running after you. It's about time, Carol, you're twenty-five years old!" said Docha.

An afternoon's activity would sometimes consist of "fixing me up," during which the girls tried to remake me into an available girl, *Rom* style.[10] I was given advice about numerous aspects of female behavior such as fortune-telling, singing, dancing, cooking, cleaning, dream interpretation, sexual segregation, and taboos. *Machwaya* and *Kalderash Roma* have an elaborate taboo system which defines *gazhe* as potentially polluting and regulates social interaction with them. For example, at first I was served food on the "dirty dishes," those reserved for outsiders, but after a few months of daily contact I was warned not to eat from the same dishes lest I become ill.

The negotiation of my status was behind me, or so I thought, when I received that telephone call from Debbie to go to Skipa's burial. But at the cemetery new questions arose about my role, and, indeed, about all non-Gypsy/Gypsy relationships.

Evergreen Cemetery is located in Hillside, New Jersey, near Elizabeth, about thirty minutes from Manhattan. Driving into the "Gypsy section," Debbie and I noticed a movie set and crowds of people, but we had important business to accomplish before exploring. Debbie's sister Lola, who was only thirty-four years old, had died of cancer the previous November, and as we approached her grave, Bessie (their mother) broke into a sustained wail, "*Loli, Loli, Loli dzhela* [Lola has gone]!"

Bessie and her husband Milano placed Lola's favorite foods (Devil Dogs, Chunkies, cherry soda, beer) on her grave and invited her to partake.[11] "*Te avel angla tute* [may this be before you]. Here, for a hangover," said Milano as he poured libations on the ground. Later he explained, "At the grave site, you would take soft drinks or wine and you say, *te avel angla tute*. In other words, you're giving her drink, and you pour it on her grave or on her stone. In a way you're asking God to place this before them so they won't thirst." Pouring libations for the dead was a frequent practice among *Machwaya* and *Kalderash,* and I had observed it on many other occasions such as *slavi* [saint's day celebrations] and *Patradzhi* (Easter).

Since we had some time until Skipa's burial, Debbie took me around to the numerous *Rom* graves and told me stories of various tragedies and family histories. The gravestones were, for the most part, quite large and elaborate, carved with personal touches such as the name of the favorite song of the deceased. Some had insets with photographs of the deceased.[12] A spread of food and drink was visible on many, just like Lola's.

Then Debbie and I remembered the movie set and walked toward it, past dressing-room vans and past New Jersey housewives and teenagers hoping for a glimpse of a movie star. Sure enough, it was the set for *The King of the Gypsies,* a Paramount film based on Peter Maas's best-selling novel, directed by Frank Pierson and starring Shelly Winters, Susan Sarandon, and Sterling Hayden. The book, supposedly a true story, depicted the struggle for power between a father and son of the Bimbo *vitsa* [kin group] of Massachusetts. It was written in exposé style[13] and contained gross misrepresentations of Gypsy violence and swindling and many inaccuracies about *Rom* culture. Gypsies, in general, have very low rates of reported violence and crime, yet the popular stereotypes of them as lawless thieves abound in film, literature, and art.[14]

The *Roma* I knew had all heard of or read the book and were convinced that Steve (the son) had dictated an exaggerated story to Maas just to make money. They had no particular love for the Bimbos, calling them "the bad seed," but they especially resented Steve's greed, lies, and lack of family respect. I wondered if there were any Bimbos on the movie set.

"*Joj Devla* [oh, God], are those people supposed to be Gypsies? They don't look anything like us. God help me, I'm the real thing!" said Debbie excitedly when she got a glimpse of the actors on the set.

The actors' faces seemed wrong. While there was a general correctness in dress, such as skirts below the knee,[15] the actors looked hokey; they looked like they were wearing costumes instead of clothes. *All* the young women and girls were wearing head scarves, instead of just the married women,[16] and everyone, instead of just the close kin, was wearing black for the burial scene. The huge flower arrangements were fairly accurate, and some displayed the same designs as Skipa's! I started to feel a if I were in a Fellini movie, and wondered what Debbie thought about these impersonators of her culture.

"Who's Gypsy here?" she asked an official-looking type with a clipboard, "Aren't there any Gypsies in the movie?"

Steve (the son) and his sister were pointed out to us on the set and the sister approached us. Speaking *Romanes,*[17] she explained that Steve was the "legal adviser," meaning he could give advice but that the directors didn't have to follow it.

"So what's the use? He sold the book to them and has no more rights. Now, some Bimbos are suing him for a couple of million dollars because he wrote about them and didn't give them any money. I hope it's a flop! It shows a lot of bad things about *Roma,* and it has two sexy scenes."

"Oh no, now I can't see it[18]—if my parents find out, they'll kill me!" interrupted Debbie.

The sister explained that there was a scene which she told them to cut because it wasn't true: "*Roma* don't walk around naked in front of each other."[19]

In the meantime, about twenty feet from us, the teenagers and other groupies surrounded Steve.

"Can we have your autograph?" they chorused.

"Are you really a Gypsy, like in the book? I'll be your body guard!" screamed one.

Debbie listened incredulously and then turned to the sister, "Why don't you come down to the funeral?"

The sister declined the invitation, saying she was wearing pants[20] and also that she had to keep an eye on her daughter, the only real Gypsy in the film. She said Steve would be in big trouble if he were to go down there with the other *Roma.* She also told us about another feature film being produced with real *Roma,* focusing on a ten-year-old boy.[21]

Sensing that it was getting late, Debbie and I said good-bye and returned to Skipa's burial. Suddenly we were back in the midst of grief. Debbie seemed to have less trouble than I switching frames, and I realized that on a regular basis *Roma* have to deal with inaccurate stereotypes of themselves. They crop up everywhere in western culture, on television, in films, and in children's books.

While we were at the movie set two Rolls Royces and ten Cadillacs had arrived at Skipa's burial plot, and it was very crowded. As the coffin was being removed from the hearse by the young male kin, the women began to wail loudly. An Eastern Orthodox priest sang in Old Church Slavonic[22] and the coffin was placed above the freshly dug grave. *Roma* crowded in, with the close family in the first row and relatives (separated by gender) behind. The atmosphere was so emotional that I dared not ask anyone if I could take photographs, so I let my camera hang limply around my neck.

Suddenly Skipa's sister noticed that some of the actors from *The King of the Gypsies* had come over to watch the burial, and that a few were trying to take pictures.

"Stop, stop, stop everything! Who are those people? Get out of here. You have no right to be here! Get them away—confiscate their film!" she shouted. And a few male relatives chased the actors away and took their film.

I stared dumbfounded at my camera and quickly shoved it into my purse, not wanting to be identified with the intruders. But deep down inside I wondered if I was just another kind of intruder, collecting bits of culture and arranging them for public consumption. Surely my motives were more lofty than the actors', who were curious to see the real thing that they were dramatizing; surely my motives were more lofty than those of the producers of *The King of the Gypsies*, who wanted to make money by capitalizing on stereotypes of Gypsies as exotic and dangerous, all untrue. I saw myself as an educator, breaking down stereotypes and presenting real people and a real culture. And yet perhaps my work, too, was guilty of overgeneralization and exoticism[23] or was just plain misguided. Did the *Roma* really want me there or were they only tolerating me? What right did I have to be there?

All these thoughts went through my head as the burial resumed and the actors retreated to the movie set. I saw myself adrift among a series of overlapping frames.[24] First there was the movie frame, where sex, violence, and exoticism were the pillars, where profit was the measure of success, and where actors tried to convince us they were Gypsies through realistic performances. Then there was the *Rom* frame which required certain performances for in-group events, such as funerals, and other performances for *gazhe* interaction, such as fortune-telling.[25] Where did I fit in among the frames? I was certainly not a Gypsy, nor did I pretend to be so, yet it was precisely my convincing performance as a Gypsy which gave me access to their culture. The more I learned about appropriate *Rom* behavior, the better I could myself act like a Gypsy. I knew that one of the prime reasons the *Roma* accepted me was because I accepted them as people and accepted their cultural norms as my own when I was with them. Yet I had another life separate from them. Was I an actor or an ethnographer, or some of both? In analyzing the performances of *Roma*, shouldn't I be analyzing mine too?[26]

These questions occupied me as the coffin was lowered, and continue to occupy me today, after years of fieldwork among other groups of *Roma*. As people poured wine and beer on top of the coffin and threw in coins and flowers, I wondered if my ethnographic stance was being buried with Skipa. As for the *Roma*, some went home to eat with the grief-stricken family while others went to watch the filming of the burial scene, cracking jokes all the while. As for me, Bessie and Milano dropped me off in Chinatown where I sat down in a restaurant and wrote down everything I could remember.

Notes

1   *Machwaya* and *Kalderash* are the two most numerous groups of Romanes-speaking Gypsies (or *Roma* as they designate themselves) in the United States. Arriving from Eastern Europe mainly during the second wave of immigration, 1880–1920, they currently number over 1,000,000 in the United States. Historical and cultural overviews have been published by Gropper 1975, Sutherland 1986a, Hancock 1974 and 1979, and Silverman 1982, 1988, and 1991. *Roma* are originally from northwest India.

2   Cars are important status symbols among *Machwaya* and *Kalderash*. Moreover, many *Rom* men are in the used car business.

3   Beliefs concerning the dead, including *pomani* [memorial feasts], are a central part of *Rom* religion (Salo and Salo 1977: 162–74; Silverman 1979: 133–45; Sutherland 1992: 37–38).

4   Among themselves *Roma* are usually known by kin designation (Silverman 1979: 270–71).

5   The taboo or *marime* system is an important element in defining group identity (Sutherland 1977 and 1986b; and Silverman 1981).

6   My identity among *Roma* was originally tied to my role as private tutor, one of the few roles which allow a non-*Rom* access to the home life of *Roma*. This role gradually faded, although it remained a symbolic one (Silverman 1979: 19–33).

7   The question of my marrying a *Rom* arose often and was the subject of much laughter as well as serious talk. Most *Roma* couldn't comprehend why a twenty-five-year-old wasn't married already. On many occasions I was offered specific men. If the discussion was in fun I would answer that I was too old for the boy (most of those offered were seventeen to eighteen years old, the typical age for marrying) and that I wanted to shop around some more, or that I would wait longer since my brideprice seemed to be increasing! If the discussion was serious, I honestly said I didn't think I would ever marry a *Rom*.

8   Considering money when dealing with the dead is viewed as disrespectful to the *mule* [spirits of the dead] and therefore dangerous. Thus funerals and *pomani* are opulent and expensive. In a related case, a family refused to sue for malpractice even though it was clear a doctor had caused a woman's death. Collecting money because of someone's death was *nay mishto*. Consequently, *Roma* rarely buy life insurance.

9   *Roma* have endured persecution, slavery, and genocide for centuries, including slavery in Romania and near extinction during the Holocaust (Hancock 1987a; Tyrnauer 1989; Kenrick and Puxon 1972; Crowe 1994; Crowe and Kolsti 1991). East European *Roma* are currently experiencing a new wave of anti-Gypsy violence and scapegoating (Silverman 1995; Barany 1994)

10   The age difference didn't matter to them. If I was unmarried, I was automatically in their social group, even if I was ten years older. For the parent generation, however, my age and education gave me more status and responsibility and thus I was frequently asked to chaperone for the girls to make sure they didn't engage in inappropriate behavior (Silverman 1979: 63–65, 85–90).

11   Sometimes a cassette machine playing the dead person's favorite songs is left on a grave.

12   Cultural geographer David Nemeth (1981) describes Gypsy cemeteries in detail.

13   Maas became famous for *Serpico*, an exposé of corruption in the New York police force.

14   Hancock (1976, 1981, 1987b, and 1988) perceptively analyzes stereotypes.

15   According to the *marime* system, the lower half of a woman's body is polluting, thus skirts below the knee are required in public (Silverman 1981 and 1991; Sutherland 1977).

16   A head covering of some sort is required in public of *Kalderash* and *Machwaya* women after marriage.

17   *Romanes* functions as an in-group language among *Roma* and immediately establishes someone as an insider, privileged to certain treatment.

18   Movies and television programs with sexual content are considered inappropriate for unmarried girls. In general, references to sex are taboo in public.

19   *Roma* are usually very shy about revealing their bodies, even among people of the same sex.

20   Pants are considered inappropriate attire for women in public because they reveal the outlines of the lower body; see note 15 above.

21   She was referring to *Angelo My Love,* which was produced in collaboration with *Roma* and which gives quite a good portrayal of them.

22   Skipa's family engaged an Eastern Orthodox priest for the funeral and burial. Some *Rom* families have little to do with institutional Christianity, except for baptism and burial.

23   Most of the scholarly literature on American Gypsies, including mine, is about Romani-speaking groups in the Vlax dialect group. This group is not only the most documented, it is also the least assimilated and least educated, and thus the most potentially exotic. Recently, educated *Roma* from other groups such as Ian Hancock and William Duna have pointed to the lack of both scholarly and media attention to their groups. The tendency to overgeneralize about all Gypsies from the Vlax dialect group is an ever-present problem, even in my own work. See Hancock 1981, Sutherland 1986a, and Silverman 1982 and 1988.

24   I use the word "frame" in the sense of Goffman 1974.

25   I used Goffman's concept of "impression management" to analyze the various performances of *Roma* in Silverman 1982. Also see Andersen 1987.

26   The reflexive stance is now quite established in anthropology and folklore. See the recent forum in the *Journal of American Folklore* 108, issue 429 (1995). Pioneering works such as Ruby 1982 and other treatments—such as Dwyer 1982, Rabinow 1977, Stoller and Olkes 1986, and Geertz 1988—make the fieldwork situation part of the analysis.

References Cited

Andersen, Ruth. 1987. "A Subtle Craft in Several Worlds: Performance and Participation in Romani Fortune-Telling." Ph.D. dissertation, University of Pennsylvania, Department of Folklore and Folklife.

Barany, Zoltan. 1994. "Living on the Edge: East European Roma in Postcommunist Politics and Societies." *Slavic Review* 52, no. 2:321–44.

Crowe, David. 1994. *A History of the Gypsies of Eastern Europe and Russia.* New York: St. Martin's Press.

Crowe, David, and John Kolsti, eds. 1991. *The Gypsies of Eastern Europe.* Armonk, N.Y.: M. E. Sharpe.

Dwyer, Kevin. 1982. *Moroccan Dialogues: Anthropology in Question.* Baltimore: Johns Hopkins University Press.

Geertz, Clifford. 1973. *The Interpretation of Cultures: Selected Essays by Clifford Geertz.* New York: Basic Books.

———. 1988. *Works and Lives: The Anthropologist as Author.* Stanford: Stanford University Press.

Goffman, Erving. 1974. *Frame Analysis: An Essay on the Organization of Experience.* New York: Harper & Row.

Gropper, Rena. 1975. *Gypsies in the City: Culture, Patterns, and Survival.* Princeton: Darwin Press.

Hancock, Ian. 1974. "Gypsies in Texas." *Roma* 1, no. 1:36–47.

———. 1976. "Romance vs. Realism: Popular Notions of the Gypsy." *Roma* 2, no. 1:7–23.

———. 1979. "Gypsies." In *The Harvard Encyclopedia of American Ethnic Groups,* ed. S. Thernstrom, pp. 440–45. Cambridge: Harvard University Press.

———. 1981. "Talking Back." *Roma* 6, no. 1:13–20.

———. 1987a. *The Pariah Syndrome: An Account of Gypsy Slavery and Persecution.* Ann Arbor, Mich.: Karoma.

———. 1987b. "The Origin and Function of the Gypsy Image in Children's Literature." *The Lion and the Unicorn: A Critical Journal of Children's Literature* 11, no. 1:142–45.

———. 1988. "Gypsies in Our Libraries." *Collection Building* 8, no. 4:31–36.

Kenrick, Donald, and Grattan Puxon. 1972. *The Destiny of Europe's Gypsies.* New York: Basic Books.

Nemeth, David. 1981. "Gypsy Taskmaster, Gentile Slaves." In *The American Kalderash: Gypsies in the New World,* ed. Matt T. Salo, pp. 29–41. Hacketstown, N.J.: Gypsy Lore Society.

Rabinow, Paul. 1977. *Reflections on Fieldwork in Morocco.* Berkeley: University of California Press.

Ruby, Jay, ed. 1982. *A Crack in the Mirror: Reflexive Perspectives in Anthropology.* Philadelphia: University of Pennsylvania Press.

Salo, Matt, and Sheila M. G. Salo, eds. 1977: *The Kalderash of Eastern Canada.* Ottawa: National Museums of Man.

Silverman, Carol. 1979. "Expressive Behavior as Adaptive Strategy among American Gypsies." Ph.D. dissertation, University of Pennsylvania, Department of Folklore and Folklife.

———. 1981. "Pollution and Power: Gypsy Women in America." In *The American Kalderash: Gypsies in the New World,* ed. Matt T. Salo, pp. 55–70. Hacketstown, N.J.: Gypsy Lore Society.

———. 1982. "Everyday Drama: Impression Management of Urban Gypsies." *Urban Anthropology* 11, nos. 2–3:377–98.

———. 1988. "Negotiating Gypsiness: Strategy in Context." *Journal of American Folklore* 101:261–75.

————. 1991. "Strategies of Ethnic Adaptation: The Case of Gypsies in the United States." In *Creative Ethnicity*, ed. Stephen Stern and John Allan Cicala, pp. 107–21. Logan: Utah State University Press.

————. 1995. "Persecution and Politicization: Roma (Gypsies) of Eastern Europe." *Cultural Survival* 19, no. 2:43–49.

Stoller, Paul, and Cheryl Olkes. 1986. *In Sorcery's Shadow: A Memoir of Apprenticeship among the Songhay of Niger.* Chicago: University of Chicago Press.

Sutherland, Anne. 1977. "The Body as Social Symbol among the Rom." In *The Anthropology of the Body*, ed. John Blacking, pp. 375–90. New York: Academic Press.

————. 1986a. *Gypsies: The Hidden Americans.* Prospect Heights: Waveland.

————. 1986b. "Gypsy Women, Gypsy Men: Cultural Paradoxes and Economic Resources." In *Papers from the Sixth and Seventh Annual Meetings*, Gypsy Lore Society North American Chapter, ed. Joanne Grumet, pp. 104–13. New York: Gypsy Lore Society, North American Chapter.

————. 1992. "Health and Illness among the Rom of California." *Journal of the Gypsy Lore Society* 2, no. 1:19–59.

Tyrnauer, Gabrielle. 1989. *Gypsies and the Holocaust: A Bibliography and Introductory Essay.* Montreal: Interuniversity Centre for European Studies.

16

The Perfect Informant
Bruce Jackson

Je t'apporte l'enfant d'une nuit d'Idumée!
(I bring you the child of an Idumean night!)
Stéphane Mallarmé, "Don du poème"

The conversations that form the substance of this article are based on my notes, some of which are more detailed than others. I sometimes don't know until later what's really important, so my field notes may provide sketchy information on what mattered most and a great deal of detail about what turned out to have been of marginal significance. As you'll learn shortly, what I thought was going on in this series of encounters wasn't what was going on at all, and what I was focusing on as subject was only evidence of the real subject, like the ionized track in a Wilson cloud chamber telling you where a radioactive particle just was. I don't think I re-created the gist of any of these conversations, but you should take them the way you would if we were walking around the block and I were telling you a personal experience story rather than the way you might if you were in a jury box and I were a witness testifying under oath. If I *were* testifying under oath and if the cross-examiner asked, "Are those the exact words, Mr. Jackson?" I would respond, "Maybe, maybe not, but that's what we said."

Stewart's Call

My friend Stewart[1] called one fine autumn day a few years ago. "Are you still working on that book about oral histories from the Vietnam War?" I told him that I'd left the project for a while to do other things and that I'd never gotten back to it. "Well," Stewart said, "I've got someone who wants to meet you. When you meet him, you may find yourself back in it again."

Not likely, I told him, not likely at all. For one thing, Diane Christian and I were deep in the editing of a film, a job that would consume most of our nonteaching time for the next several months. And there were other projects and commitments: obligations were stacked up like planes at O'Hare. There were other reasons, but I didn't tell Stewart what they were.

I'd begun the research for the oral history book in 1976. I thought it would be useful to record how veterans were remembering the war and what they had to say about coming home. I'd done enough personal narrative research to know that reality is rewritten constantly by memory and that the further you are from the event the further you are from any accurate redaction of it. The stories would change over time, as is the way of stories in active tradition, so it would be good to have some baseline narratives. The project really should have begun five or six years earlier, but back then I was too deep in antiwar activities to have thought of or been able to do anything like this.

The politics of which-side-are-you-on were pretty much over by 1976. Former war-resisters were beginning to learn that the vets weren't the guys who had kept the war going all those pointless years, and the vets had already tired of defending a war that made sense in no terms other than sunk costs. It was hard to write off the antiwar movement as subversive and the vets as a group of right-wing militaristic thugs because Ron Kovic and people like him were blowing those stereotypes away. I thought we'd be at least as long coming to terms with the emotional residue of that war as we would the economic burdens it imposed on us and our children. So the interviews were both feasible and reasonable.

The interviews were mostly free-form, but there were a small group of questions I asked nearly every time, each of which produced long and involved answers. One was, "What did you do in Vietnam?" Most men would answer, "What do you mean by *do?*" to which I'd shrug or say, "I don't know. Whatever you think it means." And then they'd take some meaning of *do* and hang a bunch of narratives on it. Another question was "What happened when you came home?" To which several said, "What happened in what regard?" to which I'd also shrug or say "I don't know," and that would occasion another narrative or string of narratives.

Lydia Fish, a friend at a nearby university, was teaching a class called "The Vietnam Experience." She asked me to talk to her students, nearly all of whom were Vietnam vets, about the antiwar movement at home. She said I would find the visit interesting because I wouldn't have to prepare a formal talk and the class had a pattern of a lot of vigorous give and take. She was an old pal so I said okay, expecting a lot of flak.

But the flak didn't come. Maybe it was that the war was by then long enough in the past or because I was a vet from another time or because some of the men in the class knew me from when I ran for Congress in 1968 as an antiwar candidate. In the course of the discussion, one of them said something like, "In World War II and in Korea, people went over as a unit and stayed together as a unit and came back as a unit. And the going and coming took a long time. With us, we went alone, stayed a year, and came home alone."

"If you made it through the year," someone else said.

A third man said, "You got to understand the feeling you get when you're in the Nam one day and the next day you're in San Francisco airport getting spat on by an old lady or a hippie."

"That happened to *you?*"

"A buddy of mine."

This anecdote had turned up more frequently than any other in my interviews. The first few times I heard it I had marveled at the rudeness of the old lady and the stupidity of the hippie. I mean, you have to be crazy to spit on a guy just out of the jungle. I'd ask, "What did you do when that happened?" and invariably I got a vague answer. I began pushing: "A hippie spat on *you?*" and the answers were like those that came up in Lydia's class: "Well, not me, exactly. A good buddy of mine. It happened to him."

So I asked Lydia's students: "How many people in this room had a buddy that was spat upon by an old lady or a hippie or something like that?"

Maybe a third of the hands went up.

"How many people in this room were spat upon themselves?"

No hands went up.

"Don't you think that's odd—that one out of three people in this room has a pal that happened to but it didn't happen to anybody here. I mean, if you guys are at all representative, and I'm sure you are, then it happened to a large percentage of men coming home through San Francisco. So how come it didn't happen to any of you?"

"It happened to some guys we know," someone said.

"Yeah," someone else said.

"What's your *point?*" someone else said.

I told them that my point was that stories weren't just facts, they were also strategies, that when people told them to one another when they were hanging out it was okay to just listen and come back with your own, but when we talked about them in a classroom situation we ought to be looking behind the narration for the reasons a particular story has a particular power. While I was talking to them I understood for the first time what the story was really about: in addition to the personal experience narratives that each man used to manage his own past, there were also a group of shared narratives that were taken on as if they were personal experiences. The lie was that it happened to the teller; the truth too hard to articulate was that the stories were a way of containing a desperate need.

After the class, a bunch of them invited me to join them at the campus bar. We closed the place, drinking beer and telling stories. Later, I interviewed some men from the class. They were similar to the other interviews I'd done.

I started wondering if some kinds of narratives in my interviews were as common as they seemed or if something I was doing was eliciting those kinds of narratives rather than others. That is, I wondered if I was finding real patterns or if I was finding what I wanted to find. So I prepared a list of what had developed as my basic outline questions and asked several friends in various parts of the country to do a few interviews using those questions as starting points. Some were done by men, some by women; some were done by Vietnam vets, some by people who had never been on a military base; some were done by people who thought the war an evil America had imposed on the world, some were done by people who thought the war had been a noble enterprise. Though they were different in detail, the contours of these interviews were similar to mine, so I thought I was on the right track.

I was heading toward an easy book that would probably sell very well, but it just didn't feel right. I was uncomfortable because it seemed that I had an opportunistic relationship with the narratives: I was gathering fascinating material without much real effort or engagement or danger. I'm no Puritan; I don't think good things have to be painful to be deserved—but this wasn't close to painful. It was fieldwork on autopilot.

Then Diane and I got to know a couple whose only son had been killed by his own artillery fire the week he'd been due to come home. The father wanted us to do a book about what happened. We told him that a book already existed, *Friendly Fire,* and it was a very good book. "This is different," the father said. "What's different is it happened to you," I told him. "Just read the letters," he said. I did. I read all the letters the boy wrote his parents and his girlfriend. Some were interesting, some were poignant in light of what happened, and most were the kind of letters a kid far from home writes the people who are grounding him in the world. They reminded me of letters I had written home when I'd been in the marines twenty-five years earlier. I told the man I couldn't do his book for him.

And I realized I couldn't do mine either: I just hadn't earned it. I abandoned the project. I didn't even transcribe most of the tapes.

That's how I reconstruct it now, but my motives maybe weren't all that pure at the time. A good deal of material about Vietnam vets had begun to appear about then, and perhaps I thought that by the time I got through with all I had to do, the subject would be used up, stale, old news. Even my working title had appeared as the title of a successful Jane Fonda movie, *Coming Home.* The Vietnam War experience had become trendy: racist fantasy films by Chuck Norris were making megabucks around the world (the U.S. government couldn't get the POWs out or even convince itself that there *were* POWS; Norris did both) and the Vietnam War was on network TV as sentimental background for programs like *Magnum, P.I.* and *Simon and Simon.*

That's why the tapes were packed in boxes. Someday, maybe, I'd get back to them. Or they'd have some archival value. Someday. But not now, not me now.

Jim Bennett

That's where things were when my friend Stewart called. "It's a student," Stewart said, "he's read your books and he wants to meet you. He was in Special Forces in Vietnam, then he came back to the States for OCS and he came across your stuff while he was in OCS in Texas. Then he went back to Vietnam in Special Forces as an officer. He made captain, was discharged with disability; he's got several major decorations. Now he's a student here getting a degree and he's helping me on my research project. He's a terrific guy. And he told me that one of the reasons he came here was he hoped to meet you."

I'm no more capable of resisting a line like that than you. "Oh," I said, "in that case, set something up."

"Don't have to," he said. "He's coming to the screening of *Death Row* at the college Friday." *Death Row* was a film Diane and I had made several years earlier about men waiting to be executed in Texas.

Stewart found us in the lobby after the screening. With him was a thin, wiry man in his thirties. He introduced himself: "Hi, I'm Jim Bennett and I've been wanting to meet you for a long time. When I was in the special army program at University of Texas one of the teachers assigned us *A Thief's Primer* and I thought it was a fantastic book. You really got into that guy's world. I'd like to do something like that someday with some of the people I know." He said that when Stewart had assigned the book earlier in the term he'd been delighted at the coincidence, and then when he'd learned that Stewart was a friend of mine he'd asked him to arrange an introduction. He'd been through a great deal, he said, and he hoped to be able to write about it someday. He wondered if—he knew I was a very busy man and I shouldn't be at all embarrassed if I had to say no—if I'd be willing to talk to him some time about doing fieldwork, about interviewing, about going from fieldwork to printed documents.

"I was working on some Vietnam vet interviews," I said, "but it wasn't right. Maybe you can do the book I bailed out of."

"Maybe," he said, "and that's what I'd like to talk to you about. How about it?"

This was a perfect delight: what better way to get myself off the hook maintained by those unutilized interviews than to pass it on to someone with far more right to the material than I?

Over the next month we met three or four times. Jim came to dinner and we talked deep into the night. Mostly it was war stories. Some of the stories were like stories I'd heard in my interviews, some were entirely new to me, and some reminded me of stories I'd heard from old salts who'd been in Korea a little too long. We got deep really fast because, I think, it was like the conversation was already in progress when we joined it for the first time.

Jim telephoned early one morning. "How'd you like to meet General

Westmoreland?" There was, he said, a luncheon with the general before his talk at the state college later in the week. About thirty people would be going and he had reserved tickets for us.

I'd just read Westmoreland's autobiography, *A Soldier Reports,* and I thought him a pompous and self-deceiving fool, more so than I'd thought when I'd seen him interviewed over the years. He was still blaming civilians back home for the failure of the American war in Vietnam he directed. He hadn't understood then why he was losing and he couldn't admit now why he had lost. His only triumph was in a slander suit against CBS. During the years of his command our troop commitment expanded geometrically, frequently on the basis of promises by him that if he were sent only this or that many more young bodies he'd take care of the commies in no time.

"You still there?" Jim said.

I told him I had been thinking about something. I said some vile things about Westmoreland.

"If you feel that strongly," Jim said, "then you certainly should come. See what you're so angry at."

Couldn't argue that, so I said we'd meet him down at the Waterfront Hilton. We did. Westmoreland, dressed in a conservative blue suit, was a good deal smaller than I'd expected. Most of the army publicity photos of him must have been taken from fairly low angles. He talked briefly about the grand mission they'd all been part of over there and said how much he respected and thanked them every one and how much he missed the boys who didn't make it back. There was great applause and communal feelings. The rest of the luncheon was pleasant enough, though it reminded me of the scene in *Night of the Generals* when the homicidal Nazi played by Peter O'Toole is to address the surviving former members of his SS battalion.

Jim got close to Westmoreland and introduced himself. He reminded the general of the time Westmoreland had come to a line outfit to visit the troops and Jim had been there. "I was just a lieutenant then," Jim said. He told the general what his nickname had been. Westmoreland brightened, said he remembered, shook Jim's hand enthusiastically. Jim introduced us. Westmoreland shook our hands enthusiastically. Then he moved on, shaking other hands, happy with people who understood him. "Great guy," Jim said, "and he's got a great memory. He remembers everybody." Later he told us that everyone in 'Nam had a nickname. "That made it easier for every-one else when someone got killed, and it made it easier coming home be-cause it was easier separating yourself from what you did over there. At least for some guys. It was good for me that way."

Jim called to say he had something that would interest me. "You use a Nikon, right?"

"Leica mostly. But I have Nikons."

"Well, I'm asking about the Nikons. I got a nightscope that fits on a Nikon lens. You can take pictures in matchlight from a thousand feet. You can read lips in starlight. The CIA developed it. You can fit it on a movie camera too. Fantastic. We used them in 'Nam for nighttime sniping. But you can use it for anything. Look around at the other cars in the drive-in, for instance."

"I don't go to drive-ins."

"With this lens, it might be interesting going to drive-ins."

He had two of them, he said, and he'd let me have one for as long as I wished.

Jim knew, as did anyone who spent much time around my house, that I loved gadgets that did things. I have no interest in gadgets for their own sake, but anything that is functional, no matter how complex, I'm delight-ed to try until I decide if it will be useful or silly. I told him that I'd seen a *60 Minutes* segment the previous week in which they had used just that sort of device for some terrific nighttime shots of malefactors. "Oh yeah," he said, "I think I caught that show."

He didn't have the scope when he came over for dinner a few days lat-er. He'd meant to bring it, he said, but he'd forgotten it because he'd decid-ed to tell me about a project he'd been thinking about for some time but had thus far hesitated to mention.

"Go ahead," I said. "What is it?"

"No," he said, "I don't want to impose."

"Don't be silly," I said.

"Well, it's about your project about guys coming home."

"My ex-project."

"I know. You told me. But I think you ought to do it. But not as a book. Do it as a movie. There's lots of guys I can introduce you to, some of them living in the bush, some of them who wouldn't ever talk to anyone else, and you can do a film about what it was like for them coming back then and what it's like for them now. Not just guys: there's some nurses you ought to meet. See, for a lot of us, it's not over. It won't ever be over. And people don't know that. These are *interesting* guys. Interesting to me, anyway. But we'd have to travel to where some of them are and you probably don't have time for that."

The more reasons he gave for difficulty, the more interested I became. By the end of that visit I was making notes about possible funding sources. We'd interview and follow with our camera men and women in New York, Texas, Montana, California, and New Mexico. Some of them had jobs and families; some lived like jungle rats. The location work would take months and editing would be a monstrous job but, we all agreed, it would be worth it.

The matter of credits came up. Jim said he didn't care about credits, he just wanted to do the job. Diane and I said he had to be either director or producer. His contacts, after all, would make the film possible, and his expertise on the post-Vietnam experience would provide the perspective. I think we wound up with Diane and me as producers, and Jim as director. We would apply for the grants jointly, with the three of us as project directors, him the expert on war and us the experts on documentary film.

The next time he came over we talked about funding possibilities for the film. He again didn't have the scope with him. I didn't say anything about it, though I was lusting for the thing, because I didn't want Jim to think that I was interested in him only for what he could give me, like information and nifty devices. That is, I didn't want him to know what was pretty much the truth: without the war information and without the devices, we didn't have much to talk about and we sure wouldn't have been pals. (Every fieldwork relationship has that measure of using one another to it, I think, and the important thing is making sure that it's at least reasonably bilateral.) We talked about the film. Diane had talked to someone at NEH to see if there was a possibility it might fit one of their funding programs. Jim said he thought we could get money from some corporations that had highly placed vets in management, like Federal Express. "I can get the names and addresses of those people," Jim said. "No problem at all."

We made preliminary budget notes. Film, processing, travel, equipment. Salaries, one of which was for him for a year. I asked how much he wanted. He said a number, I no longer remember what it was, but I do remember that it was far too low. I doubled it. "Oh," he said, "do you really think that's a reasonable amount?"

"Sure," I said.

"Well," he said, "all right then. I guess it's okay."

After he left, Diane said, "I don't think he was satisfied with the salary we put him in there for." I reminded her that it was double what he'd put himself in for. "Yes," she said, "but I had a feeling he was just being modest or something, that he knew perfectly well he was asking for too little, that he expected us to kick it up. And I don't think we went as far as he wanted."

"Maybe you're right. I'll increase it another 50 percent. How's that?"

"Fine with me," she said. "But you should check with Jim."

I did. I called him the next day, said Diane and I had been going over the budget and we'd decided his salary was still too low for someone of his expertise and experience, especially given his centrality to the project. "So we'll boost it another 50 percent."

"Fifty percent more on what I proposed or on what you proposed?"

"On what we proposed."

"Good," he said, "that *is* okay."

He had been trained, he said, in the whole panoply of infantry weapons, but he had specialized in those that were silent, especially the crossbow. He was known everywhere among the Green Berets, he said, as the expert with the crossbow. He was also, he said, an expert in the use of nitroglycerine. I'd never heard of military people using nitro. When I'd been in the marines we'd had plastique and I'd received a little training in its use. I knew that there were stronger versions of plastique around during Vietnam. "Why nitro?" I asked him. "Why not plastique?"

"Because plastique has to be made in a factory and you need to fuse it somehow. Nitro, if you don't have it, you can make it. They taught us how to make it. Just like with the crossbow: they taught us how to make that too. So if you're caught out somewhere, you're not defenseless. You can do 'em anywhere," he said.

One time he'd been on an assassination mission with his crossbow and after the kill he'd been separated from the others in his unit and then wounded. He holed up in enemy territory for several days until he could make his way back. His wound infected. He treated the infection using a folk remedy he'd learned from a Buddhist monk: he got maggots from a dead animal and put them into his wound. He had no anesthetic. "Maggots are nature's way of keeping the world clean," he said with terrific equanimity. Diane asked if it didn't hurt terribly. Jim shrugged. The shrug said, these are the kinds of things men like us endure.

He told us in great detail about the respect everyone had for the monks. "You could be in a terrific firefight," he said, "and a line of those saffron monks would come out of the bush and walk across the clearing and go into the bush on the other side. The whole time they were there, all the firing stopped. Nobody said anything. It was just what everybody did. And then when they were gone, the firing started up again like nothing had happened."

"Why did the Communists stop shooting?" Diane asked.

"Because the monks were holy men. Doesn't have anything to do with communism or anything else."

Jim told us he was involved in the CIA's Phoenix Project—assassination of village officials with supposed VC connections. "Not just the officials," Jim said. "Their wives and children and goats and chickens. Everything died." He didn't like talking about that phase of his experience, he said. Maybe another time. He told us that since he was attached to the CIA for that part of his tour, his work was so secret that false military records were made as cover and for deniability later. Even his DD214, his official discharge document, covered up his real assignments. "You look at it," he said, "and you wouldn't know I was in 'Nam or that I was wounded twice or anything. The only way you can see my real records is if you got top secret clearance, and even that might not do it." It was the secret nature of his assignments during his second tour in Vietnam, he said, that was the cause of his problems with the Veterans Administration. He had been trying to get disability payments for the lung disorder resulting from the time he'd been doused with Agent Orange when he'd been on recon. "Those pilots couldn't have known we were that far north," he said, so his gripe wasn't with them. The pilots were just doing their job, and a dangerous one it was; his gripe was with the VA, which wouldn't give him disability. They disallowed his claims because their version of his records didn't show him in Vietnam at all; they just showed him in Germany, which was his cover story. He said he was trying to get the people who control such things to declassify his records so he could get what was coming to him. He said it was really rotten that after all that had happened to him, he had to fight so hard to get his benefits.

Jim fell off a roof. I visited him in the hospital a few times. He told me war stories, talked about his job as a sheriff's deputy, told me again about how he had come across one of my books while he'd been in the special officer's training program at University of Texas. He said his lung problems and improper healing of some old wounds weren't making getting over the fall any easier. Then we talked more about the project.

Jim got out of the hospital and I visited him at home. Several of the guys from the local vets' organization were there. They told stories about people at school, not much about the war. One of the guys said, "Say, Jim, you through with my medals? My wife, she's after me to get them back."

"Oh, sure," Jim said.

Someone else said, "If you're doing that, I'd like my CIB, if you're done with it."

"No problem," Jim said. He got out of the chair with obvious difficulty and limped into the bedroom. He came out with several framed medals. I couldn't see them all, but I made out a Silver Star, Bronze Star, Purple Heart. And he held an unmounted Combat Infantryman's Badge.

The guy with the medals left and the others went into the kitchen for more beer. While they were gone, I asked Jim, "How come you had their medals?"

"Oh, mine got lost in one of those moves and Alice [his girlfriend] and some other people wanted to see what they looked like."

One of those moves. I had no idea what moves he was talking about, but it seemed a minor point so I didn't pursue it.

I looked around to see if I could spot the nightscopes, but they weren't anywhere in sight. This didn't seem an appropriate time to ask for one of them and Jim never raised the issue.

Bud Johns, a friend in San Francisco, called to say hello, and that was the night things with Bennett began to unravel. Bud told us what was going on with him and we told him what was going on with us. One of those conversations you have with distant pals once or twice a year to keep the lines open so when you do manage a visit there isn't an inordinate amount of catching up to do. We told him about Jim.

"He sounds fantastic," Bud said.

"He is," I said.

"So why do you believe him?"

"What do you mean? Why shouldn't we believe him?"

"I don't know," But said, "but you might at least give it some thought, and it doesn't sound like you've done that yet."

While Diane chatted with Bud I began going over what I'd said to him thus far. I'd told him at least a half-dozen terrific Jim Bennett stories. There weren't many people about whom I could repeat so many stories so easily—and that's what Bud responded to and it's what I now, for the first time, began thinking about critically. Everything he told us was so spectacular. So many great stories. And there he was, just waiting to meet *me*. I had been so pleased that he'd been waiting to meet me that I never considered the silliness of a desire: *why* should a guy between combat tours going through OCS in Texas want to meet a professor in Buffalo? Sure, it was a possibility, but it wasn't likely. Just as each of those other stories was a possibility, but in contiguity they weren't likely.

Before joining Levi Strauss, Bud had been a newspaper reporter for many years. When Diane put me back on the phone I told him that he'd probably ruined my evening and that I thought his old journalistic cynicism was coming out. "Maybe," he said, "but I wouldn't call it cynicism. Caution is what I'd call it. I always preferred finding out a story was wrong before it got printed than afterwards." He gave me an avuncular lecturette on checking the facts, especially the ones that are so good they're almost too good to be true. I asked if that were more newsman's savvy. "No," he said, "I got that from a Dashiell Hammett story."

I hung up the phone and said to Diane, "Bud's a cynical bastard."

"I know," she said.

"I think he may be right."

"I know," she said.

We began going over the coincidences in Jim's various stories and also the things that didn't get delivered, like the nightscope, which I was now convinced had never existed, and the records that couldn't be found or were so secret they couldn't be shown. I said that I thought it weird that someone's military records were so secret that he'd have difficulty getting medical attention from the VA.

"It's worse than weird," Diane said.

It was the nitro, and the Langvei story, that brought him down.

Jim told about the time his Special Forces camp in Langvei had been overrun by tanks and fried with napalm. The Americans hadn't known the VC *had* tanks or napalm, he said, so they weren't ready for either. Nearly everyone was killed. The survivors barely made it to the marine base at Khe Sanh, which at that time was in the middle of its major assault of the war.

Something was vaguely familiar about the story and I said so. "Sure," Jim said, "anyone who was in Special Forces knows about it." I wasn't in Special Forces so Jim's explanation didn't satisfy. Later, I recounted the conversation to Lydia Fish. Lydia said, "It's not just Special Forces vets who know the story. Anyone who's read Michael Herr's *Dispatches* knows it. Herr tells it really well."[2]

A Special Forces vet heard Jim tell the story several times, and after a while something in the narration didn't ring right to him. He called the Special Forces Association in Washington. "The guy there said only a dozen guys came out of that battle and he knew the names of every one of them and Jim Bennett wasn't one of the names." That wasn't all: SFA had no listing for anyone named Jim Bennett ever having served in Special Forces at any rank. Someone else asked a colonel pal now based in the Pentagon to look into the matter of Bennett's service. The colonel checked the names of all men above the rank of warrant officer who had served in Southeast Asia; he found no record of anyone named Jim Bennett. What if Bennett had been doing top secret work, our friend asked the colonel, would his records be hidden from you now? This, the colonel said, is the one place the records would not be hidden. "This is where we do the hiding."

I wasn't there for the nitro fiasco, but Stewart was. Jim was going on about his nitro expertise and some guy he didn't know, who was sitting on the edge of the group and apparently hardly paying attention at all, looked at the ground and said in a flat voice, "You're full of shit, Bennett."

"What are you talking about, man?"

"I said you're full of shit. There wasn't any nitro in 'Nam."

"Damn right there was. And lots of it too."

"No. No, there wasn't. There wasn't any at all. Nitro is unstable over 85° and in 'Nam it didn't hardly ever go *under* 85°. You take nitro off ice and it blows up. No way you could take it into the bush 'less you took a truckload of ice too. So that's why you're full of shit. I don't think you ever were in 'Nam."

Later, Stewart told me that some of the men in the veteran's group had figured Jim for a phony several months before it all unraveled and that one had seen some official records that said Jim had spent his entire overseas time in Germany and that he'd left the military under a cloud. He asked one of the group's leaders why they didn't say anything. "He was doing such a good job calling campus attention to veteran's problems," the vet said, "that we thought we'd wait a while."

Not long ago I ran into a vet who had been in my classes some years ago, a fellow who was still around the fringes of the university trying to get a degree. He was less crazy than when I'd known him, but he was still a spooky guy. I asked him if he had known Bennett. "Sure," he said. I asked if he'd known that Bennett was a phony, "Sure," he said. He'd been a Green Beret himself and he'd been at one or two of the places Jim said he'd been, so he knew Jim was making it up.

"Why didn't you ever blow the whistle on him?"

"Wasn't doing me any harm. And he told such great stories. I loved listening to him tell those goddamned stories. I mean, I was *there* and I couldn't tell stories like that guy."

Substitute Lives

I've told you about a project that didn't happen, about how my own desire for a project with meaning let me ignore meaningful facts already in my field of view, how it took the intuitive remark of a transcontinental pal in the course of a casual telephone call to start turning on the daylight.

I'd felt like a fool, but at least I'd learned something: it's not enough just to think about how you can execute your project; you've also got to think about your investment in the project and evaluate how that investment may be ordering the way you're looking at the things of this world. Faustus went all the way, but we're making deals with our devils too. I don't know if we ever really win, but I do know that if we're not aware of the compromises, the negotiations, of the battle to achieve some vision that goes beyond our own interests, we're sure to lose. Or betray.

I was still running on emotion. I was still thinking about it all in terms of myself, how I'd been deceived because I'd been complicit in the enacted narrative. It wasn't until I sat down to write this essay that the second realization hit, and it too was about a failed inquiry. The first resulted from Jim's scam and my willingness to be complicit in it; the second resulted from my willingness to let it end there.

Because the end of that project that didn't happen was really and already the middle of another one that did, an inquiry for which I already had a good deal of data: not the story of the heroes, but the others, those who are so desperate to acquire the reality of another they gather up and process more folklore than any folklorist ever could or would. Had Jim's stories been only true, I would have been involved in a project of obvious interest; had I been cool or smart or objective enough to look at the story Jim and I were both enacting, I would have been led to something that dealt not with stories told but with the telling of stories, a study not in texts but in the profound feelings that make texts necessary and useful.

Jim, by the way, wasn't unique. Since that misadventure, I've heard of numerous men who went to extraordinary lengths to convince people they had seen combat in Vietnam, and who were astonishingly successful at their deceptions. There was, for example, Jeffrey "Mad Dog" Beck, a broker with Drexel Burnam Lambert,

> decorated for heroism as a special forces platoon leader in Vietnam, rumored to have worked for the Central Intelligence Agency. No one, friends say, can make fighting in the steaming jungles of Southeast Asia come alive as can Mr. Beck, who has held many a Manhattan dinner party in thrall with his wartime tales. He likes to pull up his left shirtsleeve, point to a scar on his wrist and explain how it was shattered by a bullet from an AK-47 rifle during fighting in the Ia Drang Valley; only a bulky Seiko watch, Mr. Beck says grimly, saved his hand. For calling in napalm strikes on his own patrols and other exploits, he tells rapt listeners, he earned a Silver Star, two Bronze Stars and four Purple Hearts. [Burrough 1990: A1]

Beck became involved with Michael Douglas, who planned a movie based on Beck's life. He became friends with and consultant to director Oliver Stone. "The only problem," Burrough writes, "is that the banker's stories are almost all lies. A reporter's investigation into the star deal-maker's career reveals that much of Mr. Beck's 'past' has been created from whole cloth, the product, friends and business associates say, of the banker's active fantasy life." Burrough's "army records and his first wife's family confirm that he never served in the special forces, never fought in Vietnam, never, in fact, came closer to combat than the Army reserves." Like Jim Bennett, Beck claimed the discrepancies between his stories and his official records resulted from his having been an intelligence agent (Burrough 1990: A1).

In the summer of 1989, a Salt Lake City man named Robert Fife committed suicide at the age of forty-six and left behind a 449-page manuscript that detailed his experiences as a POW in Vietnam. He had been seeing a therapist who had been treating him for posttraumatic stress syndrome related to his time as a prisoner of war. Twenty years earlier, his wife's

> sneakers seemed to drive [him] berserk. He told her that his captors wore sneakers when they came to his cage to beat him and urinate on him and that the enemy soldier he strangled to escape was wearing sneakers.
>
> Robert Fife had a certificate, purportedly from the U.S.S. Ranger Committee, listing medals he said he burnt to protest bad treatment of Vietnam veterans. They included the Navy Cross.
>
> The certificate, which appeared to have been signed by Adm. Thomas H. Moorer, retired Chief of Naval Operations, said Lieut. (j.g.) Robert J. Fife, who had flown 130 missions over enemy territory, was "one of only four naval aviators to escape from enemy prison camps."

After his suicide, Fife's wife attempted to have his name included on Utah's Vietnam War memorial. Shortly before it was engraved, she learned that it was all a sham: Fife had been in the military for only eight months after his September 1965 enlistment. He had been given a medical discharge because a childhood injury to bones in his right foot had never healed properly, and the only decoration he received was the Defense Service Award, which had been given to everyone in uniform ("Dead 'War Hero' Unmasked" 1989).

A con man I once knew told me that "It takes two people to run a con. Somebody like me and somebody who wants it to happen. I'm the realist; he's the dreamer." Jim Bennett, Jeffrey Beck, Robert J. Fife, and others like them, may have been dreamers when it came to their careers in Vietnam, but when it came to managing most of the people with whom they came into contact, they were the realists. They created the pasts they preferred to their own, and they got a number of highly educated people acting in terms of their creations.

I think one reason I wasn't critical earlier of Jim's stories and self-critical of my own motives in listening to them was that Jim fit perfectly the kind of narrator I wanted to hear at that time. His stories were rich in detail and visual in imagination; as he talked, I knew his stories would work well on a printed page. The political content of his stories let me be involved in a rapprochement I don't think I sought but which I welcomed when it appeared: we could do something about the vileness of the Vietnam War without at the same time disparaging the sacrifice of the people who, for whatever reason, suffered there. It gave me a chance to do something with or at least partially grounded in all those earlier interviews, that uncompleted, unresolved inquiry occupying boxes of tapes, piles of transcription folders. And probably, at a deeper and more personal level, the conversations and rapport with Jim (whose military years were almost exactly halfway between the present and my own military years) provided a middle-aged professor a secondhand but nonetheless welcome connection to his own distant and romanticized youth.

If I had designed the perfect informant for this project, the informant I would have designed would have been Jim. Jim sensed my need and he gave me what I wanted. He was able to do that because, for reasons very much his own, he already had cast and directed himself in the role he had long readied himself to play. In addition to all the other mistakes I made in our discussions about the project was who was going to occupy what role: Jim was director all right. He was also producer and one of the principal actors. I was another actor, and also part of the audience.

But why did he bother? What were his reasons for this elaborate deception?

I don't think you can ever fully know someone else's motives; you only know for sure what they do. Jim was a terrific collector and processor of stories. He listened to people, he read, and then he began to tell. If he had a way of telling the story in the third person, he would have been Homeric, or at least a novelist; because he had no venue for such narrative he was instead pathologic. His need wasn't to find a good story in someone else's life, rather it was to find a good story for his own, and since his own experience didn't provide that, he set about expropriating the narratives of other people. Instead of becoming a successful social scientist or reporter he became a fraud. He was brilliant at creating venues in which he could recite his stories. He was self-creative, not self-destructive, as evidenced by the protective devices he tried to set up, such as the story about his secret records and his avoidance of being tape-recorded. My friend Stewart, who had become deeply involved with Jim in a long-term research project, provided one kind of listener and offered one set of opportunities; I provided another. Working with the two of us, Jim accumulated power of a kind: he was a central coordinator of Stewart's research project and he was going to be director of our film. He became a bigshot in one of the local veterans' organizations. The stories got some of the war heroes he fervently wished he had been to accept him as one of their own; they also got academics who controlled or influenced resources to steer resources his way. None of that would have happened on the basis of having been an enlisted man doing menial work in Europe.

But what a curious narrative he devised! Jim designed a minefield, then shredded his map and stomped straight across to the other side. I think he *knew* he had to blow up, that he'd be caught, and that he'd be propelled into the real world and branded as a phony, a liar, a sicko. He was dealing with gullible but not stupid people: the arithmetic was inevitable. Jim wasn't stupid either; it took real intelligence to absorb and retell all those extended narratives, to manipulate so many of us in so complex a scenario.

Here's my guess on Jim's real payoff: once he got found out, Jim Bennett became what he wanted to be more than anything else—a Vietnam war casualty. It didn't happen to him in Southeast Asia, but it came out of that war anyway. He created a wound that really was his own, a scar the authenticity of which none of us can or would deny. His Vietnam story was a lie, but the pathology revealed and the shame created by that lie are real. Jim Bennett may not be one of the honorably wounded, but he's one of the wounded nonetheless, and probably for him that's as close as he could get. Once he was exposed, there was no longer any dissonance between his imaginary and his real worlds, between his private and public selves, so he could, perhaps for the first time, relax perfectly.

For most of us, there is murky area at the edge of experience that can be used to tune our narratives and enhance our understanding of real-life moments. It's the place where it's okay to talk about getting spat on in the San Francisco airport by the hippie, where it's efficient to collapse what happened to you one year with what happened another, where it's comfortable to be cooler or smarter or more alert than anyone outside of movies and memory ever is. Jim Bennett went to the far side of that area, to a place where the narratives became a substitute for real life rather than a way of understanding it. Jim Bennett ran into a no-man's-land of the imagination and couldn't come back until we caught him there. When it happened, I thought we were finding him out; now, six years later, I think we were a rescue party.

That's what I think. I don't know what Jim thought, because after things fell apart we never talked again. Neither of us thought we had anything more to say to the other, and that was another error. We had lots more to talk about.

That describes Jim Bennett and maybe it describes Robert J. Fife and others like them; but it still doesn't explain them. Many, perhaps most, of us would like to have fair claim to pasts more glorious or romantic or heroic or interesting than the ones we happen to have accumulated. But we don't create a history and try to occupy the present that history would have warranted.

Like hell we don't. We all, each and every one of us, continually re-create ourselves. Accidents of fate or whims of the moment in the distant past become, with the fulfillment of the present, meaningful, and we see those accidents and whims in structures that, if they ever existed at all, were totally transparent to us at the time. We understand human affairs in terms of narrative, and the narrative of our lives is protean, forever subject to new depths or breadths of understanding, new configurations and alignments of parts that previously seemed carved in stone. I think that is the real reason our personal experience stories, the stories we tell about ourselves over and over again, change over time: as our sense of contexts changes so changes our sense of what mattered, what was big and what was little, which words were essential and which words were air.

I told you that this affair taught me how important it is to look at one's own motives, reasons, passions, needs. I'm not sure you can always do this sort of thing alone. I'm certain I could have learned a good deal listening to Jim Bennett—in that conversation we didn't get to have—talking about what he thought I was getting out of our relationship, what strings he was playing and how he knew the harmony. He knows things I don't.

Another thing I learned from thinking about the inquiry I missed because of my anger about the inquiry that wasn't there was this: just because you get burned doesn't mean you've got to shut down. Fire teaches.

And the third thing I learned was said exquisitely by Stéphane Mallarmé more than a century ago in the fourteen lines of "Don du poème." At the first breaking of dawn the poet brings to his wife the poem he created in agony in the long night. He tells her that only by the grace of her nurturance can the poem, the "child of the Idumean night," take breath, live.

No story exists out there by itself. The story takes life from two of us: the teller and the listener, writer and reader, actor and watcher, each a necessary participant in the creation of the space in which the utterance takes life, in which all our utterances take life. So this is the good part: all our stories are coauthored and as long as we keep telling them we're never really alone.

Notes

An earlier version of this essay appeared in *Journal of American Folklore* 103 (1990): 400–416.

1   Stewart isn't his real name; he preferred not to be identified here. The name "Jim Bennett" is also a pseudonym.
2   See Herr 1977: 111–14. Herr situates the Langvei story within his larger description of the Khe Sanh battle (91–178).

References Cited

Burrough, Bryan. 1990. "Self-Made Man: Top Deal Maker Leaves a Trail of Deception in Wall Street Rise." *Wall Street Journal,* Jan. 22: A1, A6.
"Dead 'War Hero' Unmasked: A Life of Lies to Hide Failures." 1989. *New York Times.* 10 October.
Herr, Michael. 1977. *Dispatches.* New York: Knopf.

Contributors

ANTHONY G. BARRAND is Associate University Professor and Associate Professor of Anthropology at Boston University. He is the author of *Six Fools and a Dancer: The Timeless Way of the Morris* (1991), editor of numerous publications on traditional music and dance, and producer of a 12-volume set of videotapes, *Ceremonial Dance in England* (Country Dance and Song Society of America, 1979).

HOWARD S. BECKER is Professor of Sociology and Music, University of Washington. His most recent books are *What Is a Case?* (co-edited with Charles Ragin[1992]) and *Essays on Literature and Society* by Antonio Candido (1995), which he translated and introduced.

MICHAEL BUONANNO teaches English and anthropology at Manatee Community College, Bradenton, Florida. His articles on Italian and Italian American folklore have been published in *New York Folklore* and *Journal of American Folklore.* He is currently working with narratives of the Seneca Nation.

CAROL BURKE is a Associate Dean, College of Arts and Sciences, Johns Hopkins University, and Associate Professor in the Writing Seminars Department. She is the author of *Vision Narratives of Women in Prison* (1992). *Plain Talk* (1983) is a collection based on her fieldwork in north central Indiana.

EDWARD D. IVES is Professor of Folklore in the Department of Anthropology, and Director of the Maine Folklife Center and the Northeast Archives of Folklore and Oral History at the University of Maine (Orono). He is the author of several books, including *The Tape-Recorded Interview* (1980, rev. 1995), *Joe Scott, the Woodsman Songmaker* (1978), and *George Magoon and the Down-East Game War: History, Folklore, and the Law* (1988).

BRUCE JACKSON is SUNY Distinguished Professor and Director of the Center for Studies in American Culture, State University of New York at Buffalo. He has been editor of the *Journal of American Folklore*, president of the American Folklore Society, and chairman of the Board of Trustees of the American Folklife Center in the Library of Congress. The most recent of his twenty-two books are *Fieldwork* (1987) and *Disorderly Conduct* (1992).

NANCY KALOW's documentary, *Sadobabies*, was produced with May Petersen in 1988. It has been used as an educational and fundraising tool for starting up an advocacy organization for runaway youth, The Sanctuary, in Northern California. *Sadobabies* received a Gold Hugo Award from the Chicago Film Festival, first place in the American Film Institute's Visions video competition, and honors from the San Francisco, Atlanta, and Berlin Film festivals. A sequel, *The Losers Club*, was screened during the "Southern Circuit" tour in 1993. Ms. Kalow is a folklorist and filmmaker in Durham, North Carolina.

LYNWOOD MONTELL has been engaged in folklore and oral history fieldwork since 1958. Much of his research activities have been concentrated in the Upper Cumberland region of Kentucky and Tennessee. From that work has come a number of books, including *The Saga of Coe Ridge: A Study in Oral History* (1970), *Ghosts along the Cumberland: Death Lore in the Kentucky Foothills* (1975), *"Don't Go up Kettle Creek": Verbal Legacy of the Upper Cumberland* (1983), *Killings: Folk Justice in the Upper South* (1986), *Singing the Glory Down: Amateur Gospel Music in South Central Kentucky, 1900–1990* (1991), and *Upper Cumberland Country* (1993). He has taught at Western Kentucky University since 1969, where he founded and directed the Folk Studies Program until 1984 and again from 1992 to 1994.

ALESSANDRO PORTELLI teaches American literature at the University of Rome "La Sapienza." His work in oral history includes an oral history of the town of Terni, *Biografia di una città: Storia, memoria e immaginario* (1986), and a collection of essays, *The Death of Luigi Trastulli and Other Stories: Form and Meaning in Oral History* (1991). His most recent book, *The Text and the Voice: Writing, Speaking, and Democracy in American Literature* (1994), is an interpretation of the meanings of orality in American literature. He has recently collaborated with a student collective on an oral history of the students of the University of Rome, *L'aeroplano e le stelle. Storia orale di una realtà studentesca prima e dopo la Pantera* (1995).

DWIGHT F. REYNOLDS teaches Arabic language and literature at University of California, Santa Barbara. He has conducted research on several genres of Arab classical and folk music, as well as the oral epic-singing tradition described here. His dissertation won the Malcolm H. Kerr prize for outstanding dissertation in the humanities from the Middle East Studies Association in 1991 and his book on the Sîrat Banî Hilâl epic, *Heroic Poets, Poetic Heroes: The Ethnography of Performance in an Arabic Oral Epic Tradition*, was published in 1995. Other articles on Arabic epic have appeared in *Oral Tradition, Pacific Review of Ethnomusicology*, and *Harvard English Studies*.

DAN ROSE teaches anthropology at the University of Pennsylvania, where he is professor of landscape architecture and of anthropology. With Paul Stoller he edits the Series in Contemporary Ethnography published by the University of Pennsylvania Press. His books include the narrative ethnographies *Patterns of American Culture* (1989) and *Black American Street Life* (1987); and he has made and exhibited a number of artist books. In addition to ethnography he has written allegories of ethnographic inquiry and contributed articles in the area of literature and anthropology. Fieldwork conducted in America has taken him from the underclass to the upper class, from hustling on the street to foxhunting; he is currently engaged in a five-year research project among the senior executives in the office of the president of State Farm Insurance Company.

NEIL V. ROSENBERG is Professor of Folklore at Memorial University of Newfoundland. A folklorist and ethnomusicologist with strong interests in history and popular culture, he is the author of *Bluegrass: A History* (1985) and editor of *Transforming Tradition* (1993). He has conducted fieldwork in Indiana, New Brunswick, Nova Scotia, Prince Edward Island, and Newfoundland. Articles based on his Maritimes fieldwork have appeared in a number of publications, including *Journal of Canadian Studies, Journal of the Canadian Oral History Association, Bulletin of the Folklore Studies Association of Canada,* and *Folklore Studies in Honour of Herbert Halpert* (1980).

CAROL SILVERMAN is Associate Professor of Anthropology and Folklore at the University of Oregon. She has done fieldwork with *Roma* in the United States, Bulgaria, and Macedonia, and is currently doing a comparative study of Macedonian *Roma* in Skopje and New York City. The relationship of ideology to culture is a major focus of her work, which explores the arts, gender, and ritual. She has also published articles on politics and folklore of Eastern Europe.

CANDACE SLATER is Professor of Spanish and Portuguese at the University of California, Berkeley. The books associated with the moments described in her essay are *Stories on a String: The Brazilian "Literature de Cordel"* (1982, and with a new preface by the author, 1989), *Trail of Miracles: Stories from a Pilgrimage in Northeast Brazil* (1986), *City Steeple, City Streets: Saints' Tales from Granada and a Changing Spain* (1990), and *Dance of the Dolphin: Transformation and Disenchantment in the Amazonian Imagination* (1994).

ELLEN J. STEKERT teaches folklore at the University of Minnesota, where she is Professor of English and American Studies. She has had extensive experience collecting folklore in the United States, notably in Detroit, the southern Appalachians, New York State, Michigan, and Minnesota. She is a former president of the American Folklore Society, former Minnesota State Folklorist, and has taught fieldwork method and techniques at universities since 1963.

BARRE TOELKEN has taught at Washington State University, the Universities of Utah and Oregon, and currently heads the Folklore Program and directs the American Studies Graduate Program at Utah State University. He has had two Fulbright professorships (Freiburg, Tübingen), and in 1971 was the recipient of the E. Harris Harbison Award for Gifted Teaching (Danforth Foundation). He has been a president of the American Folklore Society, editor of the *Journal of American Folklore,* and chairman of the Board of Trustees of the American Folklife Center in the Library of Congress. He is a member of the AFS Fellows. From 1976 to 1979 he chaired the Folk Arts Panel at the National Endowment for the Arts.